The Body Reader
Social Aspects of the Human Body

The Body Reader
Social Aspects of the Human Body

Pantheon Books, New York

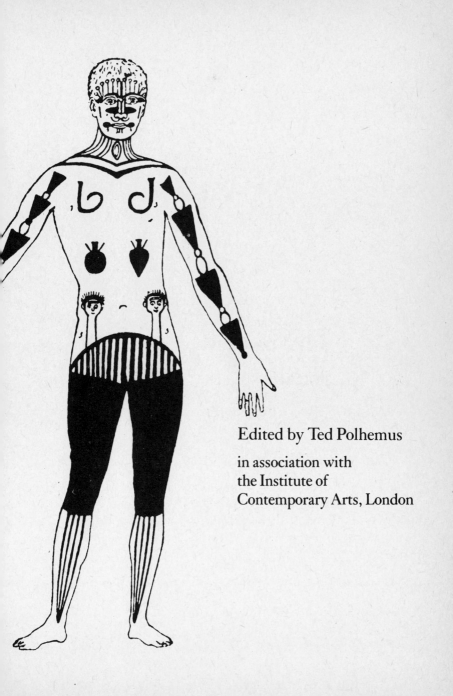

Edited by Ted Polhemus

in association with
the Institute of
Contemporary Arts, London

All rights reserved under International and Pan-American Copyright Conventions. Published in the United States by Pantheon Books, a division of Random House, Inc., New York. Originally published in Great Britain as *Social Aspects of the Human Body* by Penguin Books, Ltd., London.

Library of Congress Cataloging in Publication Data

The Body Reader.

Bibliography: pp. 308-24
Includes index.
   1. Mind and body. 2. Nonverbal communication.
I. Polhemus, Ted.
BF161.B57   152.3'84   77-5195
ISBN 0-394-48792-3
ISBN 0-394-73319-3 pbk.

Manufactured in the United States of America

FIRST AMERICAN EDITION

For Ken Kensinger and John Szwed –
who introduced me to anthropology
(but remained friends nevertheless)

Contents

Part II Special Problems and Perspectives

Preface

The centenary, in 1972, of the publication of Charles Darwin's *The Expression of the Emotions in Man and Animals* was celebrated by the appearance of R. A. Hinde's edited collection *Non-Verbal Communication* (Cambridge University Press, London, 1972) which by and large continues the tradition established by Darwin – arguing that bodily expression is cross-culturally universal and transmitted from generation to generation by biological inheritance. Hinde is broad-minded enough to include sociologically inclined contributors such as the anthropologist Edmund Leach, but the discussion never quite gets free of Darwin's shadow which hides the roots and the development of another approach which would have focused on the social aspects of the human body.

If one goes back to the work of two French sociologists of the Durkheimian *Année Sociologique* tradition, the threads of development of this sociological study of the human body become visible. Robert Hertz in 1909 and Marcel Mauss in 1935 initiated an approach to the study of the body which increasingly warrants our attention, but which has remained quite separate from the Darwinian tradition. Hertz and Mauss and others who have (often without being aware of it) followed in their footsteps have emphasized the relationship of the physical body and the 'social body' of society. This approach seeks to integrate our understanding of the physical and the social levels of experience so that what we know about one contributes to our understanding of the other.

Except in the writings of anthropologists such as Mary Douglas, this Durkheimian-based approach to the study of the human body has been largely ignored. However, it is increasingly difficult to go on ignoring the social aspects of the body as we have come to appreciate that the social level of experience may occupy a central role in human and other animal modes of existence. Durkheim and his students (including Hertz and Mauss) were witness to the emergence of Freudian psychology with its implication that a purely physical understanding of the body and of behaviour is not sufficient in that psychosomatic phenomena cannot be adequately explained. The Durkheimians, however, saw this paradigm shift as only a first stage of transition: it was important to incorporate the psychological approach within the framework of sociology so as to emphasize the stamp of socio-cultural context upon the idiosyncrasies of the psychological.

The philosopher Roger Poole has commented that Hinde's *Non-Verbal Communication* reveals the sorry fact that those who have examined the human body and human behaviour through Darwin's Victorian spectacles have made little progress in one hundred years of research. (See Jonathan Benthall and Ted Polhemus, eds., *The Body as a Medium of Expression*, Allen Lane; Dutton, New York, 1975, p. 74.) And indeed it would seem that Darwin and his followers' pre-phenomenological and at the same time pre-sociological view of human behaviour has been caught up in an academic time-warp. As Ray Birdwhistell (who initially set out in Darwin's footsteps) has suggested, Darwin's lack of understanding of the social life of human and non-human primates prohibited him from adequately answering many of the questions which he himself raised (*Kinesics and Context*, Allen Lane The Penguin Press, 1971, pp. 37–8). Most of the contributors to Hinde's volume have chosen to remain isolated from the significant breakthroughs in the social sciences and they remain with Darwin in an age which is pre-Durkheimian. But if we begin from the assumption that man is a *social* animal, evolution, communication and the human body can be understood with a new dimension of insight.

Since Hertz and Mauss, social scientists in France, England and the United States have conducted research based on the assumption that the behaviour and expressivity of man's physical form need to be appreciated within the context of the social reality of human life. This present volume attempts to bring together as many as possible of the multiple threads of this argument, and to overcome as much as possible the differences of opinion within this area of research, which Gordon Hewes has labelled 'the Maussian programme'.

The student now has a summary of the Darwinian–universalist tradition in Hinde's *Non-Verbal Communication*, a focus of the psychological literature dealing with the human body in Fisher's and Cleveland's *Body Image and Personality* (Van Nostrand, Princeton, N.J., 1958) and a *résumé* of the phenomenological–philosophical literature on the subject in Zaner's *The Problem of Embodiment* (Martinus Nijhoff, The Hague, 1971). Sociologically inclined research has produced Hertz's 'The pre-eminence of the right hand' (in Robert Hertz, *Death and the Right Hand*, trans. R. and C. Needham, Cohen & West, 1960), Mauss's 'The techniques of the body' (trans. Ben Brewster, *Economy and Society*, 2, 1 (February 1973), 70–88), Birdwhistell's *Kinesics and Context*, Hall's *The Silent Language* (Fawcett Publications, Greenwich, Conn., 1959), Lomax's *Folk Song Style and Culture* (American Association for the Advancement of Science, Washington D.C., 1968, publication No. 88) and Douglas's

Natural Symbols: Explorations in Cosmology (Penguin Books, Harmondsworth, 1973). However, a comprehensive co-ordination of these and other important works is not available and has, with the recent proliferation of material, become increasingly necessary.

For the dual subjects of dress and adornment, a comprehensive survey of the literature is available in Roach and Eicher's *Dress, Adornment and the Social Order* (Wiley, New York, 1965, Chichester, 1970). But here, I feel, the subject-matter is not broad enough to resolve the problem. Although I have in the present volume presented material which pertains to dress and adornment, I feel that to study what is put *on* the body prior to studying *the body itself* is to put the cart before the horse. In this volume I have chosen to keep the subject – the human body *and* its 'aids' of clothing and adornment – as broad as possible and instead to edit out works which are readily available elsewhere or which do not emphasize to my satisfaction a sociological approach. Thus, *Social Aspects of the Human Body* is not really about the human body and its adornment – it is about the role of the body and adornment in social interaction and the role of the body as a concrete symbol of that social interaction.

My own personal interest in this subject came firstly from exposure to Ray Birdwhistell's and Erving Goffman's research while I was an undergraduate student of anthropology at Temple University, Philadelphia. Secondly, this interest has been nourished by studying under Mary Douglas at University College, London, where I have, for the last three years, been engaged in writing a thesis entitled 'Body Sets and Body Systems: Towards a Social Anthropology of the Human Body'. I was able to introduce this research to a wider audience thanks to an invitation from Jonathan Benthall to co-organize with him, and to lecture in, a programme at the Institute of Contemporary Arts on the theme of 'The Body as a Medium of Expression'. While engaged in assembling the bibliography for my lecture ('Social Bodies') in this programme, I realized that many of the works which I had found to be invaluable in my research were practically inaccessible to the public at large as well as to most students. This then was the practical point of origin of the present volume.

In assembling *Social Aspects of the Human Body* I have been lucky to find willing contributors who have in some cases assisted with the editing and revision of their texts. As a student and as the editor of this volume I wish to thank these authors for their contributions to this field of research; I hope that I have been true to their ideas in my introductions here and in other writings.

This project was also greatly aided by academic colleagues who sent me reprints and bibliographies and who have, in some cases, also helped by criticizing the organization and presentation of the material in this volume. In particular I would like to thank Mary Douglas, Kenneth Kensinger, James Ury, John Szwed, Peter Ucko, Cecil Helman, Dr E. Stonehill, Nicolas Godian, Phil Burnheim, Adam Kuper, Mike Nicod and Jonathan Benthall for academic assistance (while, of course, acknowledging that full responsibility must lie with me alone).

Several libraries have been indispensable in this project: the library of the Royal Anthropological Institute, Senate House library (The University of London) and the medical sciences and anthropology library of University College.

Secretarial and organizational assistance has been given by Linda Lloyd Jones of the ICA and by my indispensable assistant Lynn Procter. I should also like to thank many of the other members (and ex-members) of the ICA staff for their assistance and encouragement.

Most important, however, is that acknowledgement should also be given to my family (including Mrs Ruth Tickner) and to Marcel Duchamp, Marilyn Monroe and Charles Atlas who have provided continued inspiration pertinent to the subject at hand.

Ted Polhemus

Acknowledgements

For permission to use copyright material from the works mentioned the editor is indebted to the following:

Addison-Wesley Publishing Co. Inc. for C. Kluckhohn, 'Culture and behavior', *Handbook of Social Psychology*, vol. II, 1954, ed. G. Lindzey

American Anthropological Association for Edward T. Hall, 'A system for the notation of proxemic behaviour', *American Anthropologist*, vol. 65(n.s.), no. 5, 1963; G. W. Hewes, 'World distribution of certain postural habits', *American Anthropologist*, vol. 57, no. 2, 1955; S. Postal, 'Body image and identity: A comparison of Kwakiutl and Hopi', *American Anthropologist*, vol. 67, pp. 455–60, 462, 1965; Horace M. Miner, 'Body ritual among the Nacirema', *American Anthropologist*, vol. 58, no. 1956

Anthropos for Simon D. Messing, 'The non-verbal language of the Ethiopian toga', *Anthropos*, 55, 1960

Beacon Press and Jonathan Cape Ltd for fig. 115, from Ray L. Birdwhistell, 'Kinesics and communication', *Explorations in Communication*, ed. M. McLuhan and E. Carpenter

E. J. Brill, Leiden, for H. Th. Fisher, 'The clothes of the naked Nuer', *International Archives of Ethnography*, vol. 50, 1964

Cambridge University Press for fig. 38, from R. Baden-Powell, *Scouting for Boys* (Arthur Pearson), reproduced in *Nonverbal Communications*, ed. R. A. Hinde; I. Eibl-Eibesfeldt, 'Similarities and differences between cultures in expressive movements', from Hinde, ed., ibid.

Jonathan Cape Ltd and Farrar, Straus & Giroux Inc. for Roland Barthes, 'The garment system', *Elements of Semiology*, trans. A. Lavers and C. Smith

Leonard Cohen, Bolt & Watson Ltd and Viking Press Inc. for Leonard Cohen, *Beautiful Losers*

Dr E. J. Dingwall for figs. 56 and 64, from *Artificial Cranial Deformation*

Doubleday & Co. Inc. and Granada Publishing Ltd for figs. 5 and 101, from Bernard Rudofsky, *The Unfashionable Human Body*

Gerald Duckworth & Co. Ltd and University of Toronto Press for fig. 113, from James C. Faris, *Nuba Personal Art*

Duke University Press for W. LaBarre, 'The cultural basis of emotions and gestures', *Journal of Personality*, vol. 16, 1947

Encounter Ltd for Ali A. Mazrui, 'The robes of rebellion: Sex, dress and politics in Africa', *Encounter*, vol. XXXIV, no. 2, 1970

Helmut Goedeckemeyer for fig. 107 by Kaethe Kollwitz

Graphische Sammlungen Albertina, Vienna, Frau Gertrude Peschka-Schiele and Dr Alfred Zaufal for fig. 3, Egon Schiele, 'Nude female back'

S. Karger AG for fig. 1, from A. H. Crisp, 'Anorexia Nervosa, "feeding disorder", "nervous malnutrition" or "weight phobia"?', *World Review of Nutrition and Dietetics*, vol. 12, Basel, 1970

Macmillan Publishing Co. Inc. for S. Fisher, 'Body image', and Ray L.

Birdwhistell, 'Kinesics', both in *International Encyclopedia of the Social Sciences*, ed. David L. Sills

Macmillan Publishing Co. Inc. and Routledge & Kegan Paul Ltd for Robert Hertz, 'The pre-eminence of the right-hand: A study in religious polarity', *Death and the Right Hand*, trans. Rodney and Claudia Needham

Robert Maxwell & Co. Ltd for M. Douglas, 'Do dogs laugh? A cross-cultural approach to body symbolism', *Journal of Psychosomatic Research*, 15, 1971

M.I.T. Press for fig. 51, from Wathen-Dunn, ed., *Models for the Perception of Speech and Visual Form*

Mouton Publishers for P. Bogatyrev, 'Costume as a sign', *The Functions of Folk Costume in Moravian Slovakia*; David Efron, *Gesture, Race and Culture*; R. Firth, 'Postures and gestures of respect', *Échanges et Communications*

New York Academy of Sciences for figs. 20, 23–30, from G. Bateson and M. Mead, *Balinese Character: A Photographic Analysis*

Pitt-Rivers Museum, Oxford, for figs. 53a–c, 102, 103, from E. E. Evans-Pritchard, *The Nuer*, Oxford University Press

G. P. Putnam's Sons for M. Mead and F. C. Macgregor, *Growth and Culture: A Photographic Study of Balinese Childhood*

Mary Quant Cosmetics Ltd for fig. 54, from Overnighter Kit leaflet

Routledge & Kegan Paul Ltd for Marcel Mauss, 'The techniques of the body', *Economy and Society*, trans. Ben Brewster

Royal Anthropological Institute for C. R. Hallpike, 'Social hair', *Man*, 4, 1969

Editions du Seuil for J. Kristeva, 'Gesture: Practice or communication?', trans. J. Benthall, *Semioticé: Recherches pour une sémanalyse*

S.P.A.D.E.M. for fig. 2, A. Renoir, 'Nue au soleil' (© by S.P.A.D.E.M., Paris, 1974)

The Toucan Press for fig. 52, 'The City Tonsor *c.*1770', from John Woodforde, *The Strange Story of False Hair*, Routledge & Kegan Paul Ltd

University of Birmingham, Centre for Contemporary Cultural Studies, for Trevor Millum, 'A bibliography of non-verbal communication', *Working Papers in Cultural Studies*, 1971

University of California Press for figs. 105, 106, from Jane Richardson and A. L. Kroeber, 'Three centuries of women's dress fashions', *Anthropological Records*, vol. 5, no. 2, 1940; reprinted by permission of the Regents of the University of California

University of Chicago Press for Charles Darwin, *The Expression of the Emotions in Man and Animals*

Stuyvesant van Veen for figs. 108–11, from D. Efron, *Gesture, Race and Culture*

A.P. Watt & Son for Robert Graves, 'The naked and the nude', *Poems Selected by Himself*, Penguin, 1972

All attempts have been made to trace the copyright holders of the following, but without success: A. Dembo and J. Imbelloni, *Deformaciones Intencionales del Cuerpo Humano de Carácter Etnico* (figs. 55, 57–63, 65–100; D. Amaury Talbot, *Woman's Mysteries of a Primitive People* (fig. 4); William Tenn, The liberation of Earth'

Prologue

'How Joe's body brought him fame instead of shame'

An excerpt from Leonard Cohen, *Beautiful Losers*,
Panther Books, 1972, pp. 74–8

I will explain how F. got his extraordinary body. Once again I will
explain it to myself. HOW JOE'S BODY BROUGHT HIM
FAME INSTEAD OF *SHAME*: headline on the back of an
American comic which we both read one afternoon when we were
thirteen. We were sitting on some trunks in an unused solarium on
the third floor of the orphanage, a glass-roofed room dark as any
other because of the soot deposited by a badly placed chimney – we
often hid there. JOE'S BODY was the concern of an ad for a
muscle-building course. His triumph is traced in seven cartoon
panels. Can I recall?

1. Joe is skeletal. His legs are piteous sticks. His red bathing-suit is
the baggy boxer type. His voluptuous girl-friend is with him. Her
thighs are thicker than his. The calm sea beyond contrasts with Joe's
ordeal. A man with a grand physique is humiliating him. We cannot
see the torturer's face, but the girl informs Joe that the man is a well-
known local nuisance.

2. A tiny sail has appeared on the horizon. We see the bully's face.
We appreciate his beery chest. The girl-friend has drawn up her
knees and is wondering why she ever dated this no-assed weakling.
Joe has been pulled to his feet by the bully and now must sustain a
further insult.

3. The sail is gone. Some minuscule figures play ball at the edge of
the sea. Seagulls appear. An anguished Joe stands beside the girl he is
losing. She has put on her white sunhat and has turned her tits from
him. She answers him over her right shoulder. Her body is massive
and maternal, low-breasted. Somehow we have an impression of
stretched muscles in her abdomen.

JOE: The big bully! I'll get even some day.

HER: Oh, don't let it *bother* you, little boy!

4. Joe's room, or the remains of it. A cracked picture hangs askew
on the green wall. A broken lamp is in motion. He is kicking a chair
over. He wears a blue blazer, tie, white ducks. He clenches his fist, a
clawlike articulation from a wrist thin as a bird leg. The girl-friend

lies in some panel of the imagination snuggling in the bully's armpit, winking out a thousand shameful anecdotes about Joe's body.

JOE: Darn it! I'm sick and tired of being a scarecrow! Charles Axis says he can give me a REAL body. All right! I'll gamble a stamp and get his FREE book.

5. LATER. Could this be Joe? He flexes a whole map of jigsaw muscles before his dresser mirror.

JOE: Boy! It didn't take Axis long to do this for me! What MUSCLES! That bully won't shove me around again!

Is this the same red bathing-suit?

6. The beach. The girl has come back. She is having a good time. Her body is relaxed and hips have appeared. Her left hand is raised in a gesture of surprised delight as her vision of Joe undergoes a radical transformation. Joe has just thrown a punch which lands in an electrical blaze on the bully's chin, knocking him off balance, knitting his eyebrows with amazed pain. Beyond we have the same white strand, the same calm sea.

JOE: What! You here again? Here's something I owe you!

7. The girl touches Joe's memorable biceps with her right hand. Her left shoulder and left arm are obscured by Joe's massive chest but we know that she has shoved it down the back of his tight red bathing-suit and is working with his testicles.

HER: Oh, Joe! You ARE a real man after all!

AN ATTRACTIVE GIRL SITTING ON THE SAND NEARBY: GOSH! What a build!

THE ENVIOUS MAN BESIDE HER: He's already famous for it!

Joe stands there in silence, thumbs hooked in the front of his bathing-suit, looking at his girl, who leans lasciviously against him. Four thick black words appear in the sky and they radiate spears of light. None of the characters in the panel seems aware of the celestial manifestation exploding in terrific silence above the old marine land-scape. HERO OF THE BEACH is the sky's announcement.

F. studied the ad for a long time. I wanted to get on with what we had come for, the scuffling, the dusty caresses, the comparison of hair, the beauty of facing a friend and binding two cocks in my hand, one familiar and hungry, one warm and strange, the flash along the whole length. But F.'s eyes were wet, his lips trembling as he whispered:

'Those words are always in the sky. Sometimes you can see them, like a daytime moon.'

The afternoon darkened over the soot-layered glass roof. I waited silently for F.'s mood to change and I suppose I fell asleep, for I started at the sound of scissors.

'What are you clipping out there, F.?'

'Charles Axis thing.'

'You going to send away?'

'Bet your fucking life.'

'But it's for thin guys. We're fat.'

'Shut your fucking face.'

'We're fat, F.'

'Smack! Wham! Pow!'

'Fat.'

'Socko! Sok! Bash!'

'Fat fat fat fat fat fat fat!'

I lit a stolen match and we both huddled over the comic which had fallen to the floor. At the right-hand side of the ad there is an actual photo of the man who holds the title The World's Most Flawlessly Formed Man. Oh! I remember! In a flawless bathing-suit he stands on the clip-away coupon.

'But look at him, F., the guy's got no hair.'

'But *I* have hair. *I* have hair.'

His hands are fists, his smile is Florida, he does not look serious, he doesn't really care about us, maybe he is even a little fat.

'Just inspect this photo, F. The guy is soft in the gut.'

'He's fat, all right.'

'But –'

'He's fat. He understands the fat. Use your eyes! Look at his face. Now look at Plastic Man's face. Charles Axis wants to be our uncle. He is one of us slobs who dwells pages behind Plastic Man. But can't you see that he has made his peace with Plastic Man? With Blue Beetle? With Captain Marvel? Can't you see that he believes in the super-world?'

'F., I don't like it when your eyes get shiny like that.'

'The Fat! The Fat! He's one of us! Charles Axis is on our side! He's with us against Blue Beetle and Ibis and Wonder Woman!'

'F., you're talking funny again.'

'Charles Axis has an address in New York, look, 405 West 34th Street, New York 1! Don't you think he knows about Krypton? Don't you see him suffering on the outer limits of the Bat Cave? Has anyone ever lived so close to fantastic imaginary muscles?'

'F.!'

'Charles Axis is all compassion. He's our sacrifice! He calls the thin but he means both the fat and the thin; he calls the thin because it is worse to be fat than thin; he calls the thin so that the fat can hear and come and not be named!'

'Get away from that window!'

'Charles! Charles! Charlie! I'm coming, I'm coming to be with you at the sad edge of the spirit world!'

'F.! Uppercut! Sok! Thud!'

'Puff!*#‡! Sob! Thank you, my friend, I guess you kinda saved my life.'

That was the last time I ever equalled F. in a physical contest. He gave Charles Axis fifteen minutes a day in the privacy of his room. Fat fell away or turned to muscle, he increased his chest measurement, he was not ashamed to strip for sports. Once on the beach a huge man in a very white bathing suit kicked sand in his face as we sat sunbathing on a small towel. F. merely smiled. The huge man stood there, hands on hips, then he performed a little hop and jump, like a soccer kick-off, and kicked sand in his face once again.

'Hey!' I cried: 'Quit kicking sand in our faces!' 'F.,' I whispered: 'That man is the worst nuisance on the beach.'

The bully ignored me completely. He seized F.'s thick hard wrist in his own massive fist and yanked F. to a standing position.

'Listen here,' he snarled, 'I'd smash your face . . . only you're so skinny you might dry up and blow away.'

'Why did you let him shove you around?'

F. sat down meekly as the man strode away.

'That was Charles Axis.'

'But that man is the worst nuisance on the beach.'

PART I

The 'Physio-psycho-sociological' Study of Body Behaviour

Introduction

In an essay entitled 'The techniques of the body' Marcel Mauss (a student of the sociologist Émile Durkheim) proposed a three-pronged 'physio-psycho-sociological' study of the human body. Physiological approaches to and models of the body are commonplace and, to us, easily understandable. Psychological approaches are more novel, but we have come to accept the reality of psychosomatic illness and other phenomena of this type. The presence of the word 'sociological' in Mauss's phrase, however, might take us by surprise: few would consult a sociologist if their bodies were not functioning properly.

The present volume attempts to present and integrate studies of bodily expression and behaviour which recognize and proceed from the assumption that the human body does not exist and is not understandable apart from 'the social construction of reality'. Our bodies and our perception of them constitute an important part of our socio-cultural heritage. They are not simply objects which we inherit at birth, but are socialized (enculturated) throughout life and this process of collectively sanctioned bodily modification may serve as an important instrument for our socialization (enculturation) in a more general sense. That is, in learning to have a body, we also begin to learn about our 'social body' – our society.

To appreciate that the human body has social aspects, however, is not to deny the reality of its electro-mechanical-chemical physicality and its psychological individuality. It was, after all, Mauss's suggestion that the techniques of the body can and should be approached from a triple perspective – appreciating not only that the body possesses all three of these dimensions but more importantly that there is in the medium of the human body a unique inter-relationship of the physical, the social and the individual. As Berger and Luckmann have pointed out (*The Social Construction of Reality*, Allen Lane, The Penguin Press, 1967; Penguin Books, Harmondsworth, 1971), the physical object of the human body has a special role as a common ground of overlap between collective–social and individual–psychological levels of experience. It is ill-considered to argue in support of *either* a physiological *or* a psychological *or* a sociological approach, as the following example may help to demonstrate.

Anorexia nervosa is a dietary disease which has recently become quite common, especially amongst female adolescents in the urban

West. Principal symptoms of this disease include the rejection of food, cessation of menstrual periods, extreme and dangerous forms of dieting and an obsessive fear of being overweight which frequently involves an apparent distortion of the patient's image of his or her body such that extremely emaciated persons say that they believe themselves to be obese. The physical aspects of the problem are

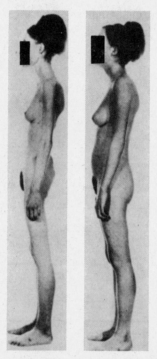

1. Anorexia nervosa in an adolescent female. The picture on the right is of the same patient immediately following treatment and was taken three months after the picture on the left.

obvious: records can be kept of weight, height, etc. Treatment of persons suffering from this disease and most general research have concentrated on the physical and psychological roots of the problem: clinical experience with patients has shown that they consistently exhibit particular psychopathological problems.

Although not everyone in the urban West suffers from anorexia, a social dimension of the problem can also be suggested. While it was once fashionable to be as plump and 'well-endowed' as ladies in

2. Renoir: 'Nue au soleil'.

paintings by Titian and Renoir, we have seen a shift towards an ideal of thinness as exemplified in the art of Klimt and Schiele and in fashion models such as Twiggy and Veruschka. This change in socially accepted style has been so complete that it is necessary to pause and remind ourselves that in other societies and historical periods girls who looked like Twiggy would have had to resign themselves either to camouflage or to staying at home. In parts of West Africa for example, men who could afford to do so traditionally sent

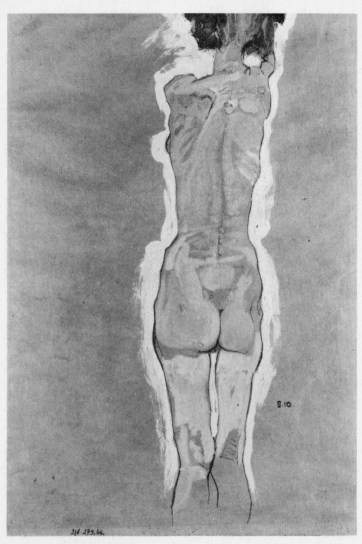

3. Schiele: 'Nude female back'.

their daughters to 'fatting-houses' where they were kept in seclusion, fed on fatty foods and allowed no physical exertion, so that after a year or more they would emerge pale and plump to the point of dangerous obesity. (See D. Amaury Talbot, *Woman's Mysteries of a*

Primitive People: the Ibibios of southern Nigeria, Cassell, 1915, or D. Amaury Talbot, *In the Shadow of the Bush*, Heinemann, 1912.) The anthropologist would not expect to find anorexia nervosa to be prevalent in these socio-cultural situations to the extent that it is currently epidemic in London, New York and Paris. Upon reflection,

4. Fatting-house women. From Talbot, *Woman's Mysteries of a Primitive People*, Cassell, 1915. See also Figure 80, p. 163.

it is obvious that anorexia nervosa and the like need to be appreciated from sociological as well as from psychological and physiological perspectives.

If physicians and psychiatrists have been amiss in overlooking the social aspects of the body, social and cultural anthropologists have been equally guilty of failing to integrate their own data and models with those of their non-sociologically inclined colleagues. Mauss's argument was not that a purely sociological approach should come to dominate the study of the human body. Despite his strong sociological bias in other works, he advocates a more ecumenical posture:

> What emerges very clearly . . . is the fact that we are everywhere faced with physio-psycho-sociological assemblages of series of actions. These actions are more or less habitual and more or less ancient in the life of the individual and the history of the society. ['The techniques of the body', trans. Ben Brewster, *Economy and Society*, 2, 1 (February 1973), 85.]
>
> It is the triple viewpoint, that of the 'total man', that is needed. [ibid., p.73.]

Anthropologists, however, have often ignored Mauss's ideas and have concentrated their research upon doing battle with physiologically and psychologically oriented students. It is true that it was (and still is) important to substantiate with ethnographic data those theories which deal with the social aspects of the human body, and Part I of this volume is largely devoted to this material. But it is also true that the fruits of Mauss's proposal for a tri-dimensional and unified programme of research have yet to be harvested.

If there has been a lack of interdisciplinary research between the social and the non-social sciences there has also been a scarcity of interdisciplinary co-ordination of research *within* the social sciences. And within individual social science disciplines this has also been unfortunately true. For example, there has been a communication breakdown (or black-out) between French, English and American students of the anthropology of the body. Mary Douglas has shown the English anthropologist the significance of Mauss's essay 'The techniques of the body', but American students of the subject (with the lone exception of Gordon Hewes) do not seem aware of Mauss's essay (or of Douglas's work for that matter). Likewise, it is only very recently that French and English students have given serious attention to the works of American researchers such as Birdwhistell, Hall, Hewes and Lomax. (See Julia Kristeva's essay in Chapter 9 of this volume, p. 264.) It would have been relatively easy to organize the present 'reader' according to these geographical categories – the key texts lend themselves to (if not force themselves into) such a classification. But this would not have aided, and might have indeed hindered, the development of a unified anthropology of the human body.

There is (as I have pointed out elsewhere) a definite value in an anthropological or socio-historical study of anthropology itself. (See my essay 'Social bodies' in J. Benthall and T. Polhemus, eds., *The Body as a Medium of Expression*, Allen Lane, London; Dutton, New York, 1975.) It is interesting, for example, that American students of the subject have concerned themselves largely with demonstrating the cross-cultural variability of body behaviour and with devising complicated notational systems for recording this variability. Their models have often been borrowed from linguistics and from studies of communication in general. Their goal has frequently been to simply overturn the universalist and biologically inclined arguments of Darwin and other ethologists. It is also interesting that British anthropologists have concentrated their attention upon the subject of body symbolism with special concern for the symbolic capacities of bodily waste products such as faeces, tears, fingernail clippings and hair. French studies began as an extension of the Durkheimian paradigm of the collective nature of human existence and have now turned to semiotic and phenomenological models. But although these observations may be historically significant they are not immediately helpful in bringing us towards a unified anthropology of the body.

The diversity of sociological, semiotic, linguistic and phenomenological approaches can serve to prepare a solid foundation for an anthropology of the body only if the inter-relationship between these various approaches is made explicit. As it happens, the human body is a subject *par excellence* for exploring the inter-relationship of these various disciplines. Firstly, because each individual discipline possesses a vast literature on the common subject and, secondly, because the medium of the human body is itself unusual in its multiplicity of aspects and capacities. For example, where phenomenology has emphasized the individualistic (sometimes depressingly isolationist) aspects of human existence and whereas sociology has tended to emphasize the collectivity of human life, the medium of the human body – in its unique capacity as a focal point for the integration of extremely individual and at the same time extremely collective levels of experience – can serve as a vehicle for furthering our understanding of how subjective and objective, individual and collective experiences are integrated in everyday reality. This can, in turn, provide a platform from which the relationship of the separate disciplines of phenomenology and sociology can be explored – as Berger and Luckmann (op. cit.) and Schutz (*Collected Papers*, vol. I, Martinus Nijhoff, The Hague, 1970) have shown.

But if there has been some movement towards integrating these separate disciplines, the co-ordination of research within anthropology itself has been frustrated in the last decade by a rapid proliferation of specialized sub-disciplines with little concern for their theoretical and methodological integration. For example, Ray Birdwhistell has established an anthropological sub-discipline of kinesics for the study of 'body-motion communication' and Edward Hall has established a sub-discipline of proxemics for the study of 'how man unconsciously structures microspace'. Both of these occupy a central role in our present concern, but their relationship to each other and to the anthropology of the body as a whole remains largely undefined. The problem is especially evident at a methodological level – any ethnographic fieldworker who would attempt to use both Birdwhistell's and Hall's separate systems of body behaviour notation would find much redundancy in the results of their combined application. But to rely only on one of these notational systems would not resolve the problem since it is obvious that much important material would not be adequately covered.

The lack of co-ordination between the social and non-social sciences, within the social sciences and finally between various anthropological sub-disciplines has, I believe, occurred at least in part because of a continual failure to delineate and define the subject of inquiry. Everyday body movement, gesture, posture, dance, bodily spacing, 'the techniques of the body' and facial expression have all been explored as individual mini-subjects – the generic classification of which has not been made explicit. This is perhaps because of the presumed obviousness of the subject as a whole – the subject of *the human body*. But can we really assume that the limits and boundaries of the human body itself are obvious? Does 'the body' end with the skin or should we include hair, nails and other epidermal body products within the bounds of the subject? What of bodily waste materials such as faeces, tears, sweat, urine and hair and nail clippings? Surely, the decorative body arts such as tattooing, scarification, cranial modification and body painting should also be considered if the medium of the human body is to be the definitional basis of the subject of inquiry. It has been shown that it is insignificant (if not inaccurate) to sharply differentiate between bodily decoration and adornment, on the one hand, and the clothing of the body, on the other hand. (See H. Th. Fischer's essay, 'The clothes of the naked Nuer', in Chapter 6 of this volume, p. 180.) So, it would appear that we are faced with a subject – 'the human body' – which resists precise cross-cultural definition.

An obvious answer to this problem is, of course, to permit the informant to supply his own, native definition of 'the body'. For each specific society, the ethnographer should investigate the natively assumed limits of ideal *body sets* (composed of the human body medium and its various aids of clothing, adornment, etc.). After information about the limits of body sets and the definition of 'the body' in various societies has been collated, we can then (and only then) move towards a cross-culturally valid definition of the subject of 'the body'. Because of ethnographic reports of clothing and adornment in societies such as the Nuer, which would in the Western mind be classified as 'naked', and because of the omnipresence of some bodily adornment and decoration in all societies of which we are aware, it seems unlikely that any peoples limit their own definition of 'the body' (and limit the boundaries of body sets) so as to include *only* the human body medium. There would seem to be no truly 'naked savages' and no anthropology of 'the body' can ignore this fact. But it also appears that to focus too much attention on body aids such as clothing would be to miss the point of our inquiry. The human body medium must occupy a central role in the anthropology of the body and in anthropology in general because of its unique position as a common ground between, and a crucial means of relating, individual and collective levels of experience. And as Schutz (op. cit.) has suggested: 'The place which my body occupies within the World, my actual Here, is the starting point from which I take my bearing in space.' It is ironic that the physical sciences cannot study the human body without regard for its social and cultural dimensions and that the social sciences cannot study social experience without regard for the underlying physicality of social behaviour.

A. The Physical and the Social Aspects of the Body

1. Is Bodily Expression Learnt or Inherited?

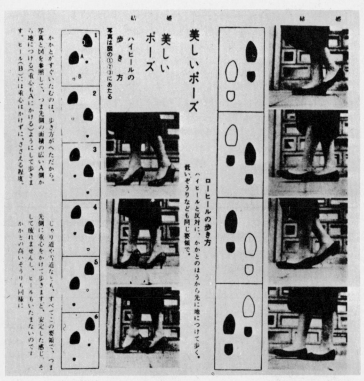

5. 'More than a hundred years after Western dress was introduced to Japan, part of it still baffles the wearer. A page from a modern etiquette book illustrates how women learn to walk in Western shoes. For some of them lifting their feet is more difficult than learning a new dance step is to us.' From Bernard Rudofsky, *The Unfashionable Human Body*, Hart-Davis, 1972.

The question of whether bodily expression is biologically determined via inheritance or socio-culturally determined via learning processes was first raised and 'tested' by Charles Darwin in 1872 in The Expression of the Emotions in Man and Animals. *Although allowing for a few exceptions, Darwin (as might be expected) presented the classic argument that bodily expression is inherited rather than learnt, a biological rather than a sociological phenomenon.*

Charles Darwin:

The Expression of the Emotions in Man and Animals (excerpt)

First published in 1872; republished in 1965, ed. Francis Darwin, University of Chicago Press, Phoenix Books, Chicago, Ill. and London, pp. 350–52.

That the chief expressive actions, exhibited by man and by the lower animals, are now innate or inherited – that is, have not been learnt by the individual – is admitted by everyone. So little has learning or imitation to do with several of them that they are from the earliest days and throughout life quite beyond our control; for instance, the relaxation of the arteries of the skin in blushing, and the increased action of the heart in anger. We may see children, only two or three years old, and even those born blind, blushing from shame; and the naked scalp of a very young infant reddens from passion. Infants scream from pain directly after birth, and all their features then assume the same form as during subsequent years. These facts alone suffice to show that many of our most important expressions have not been learnt; but it is remarkable that some, which are certainly innate, require practice in the individual, before they are performed in a full and perfect manner; for instance, weeping and laughing. The inheritance of most of our expressive actions explains the fact that those born blind display them, as I hear from the Rev. R. H. Blair, equally well with those gifted with eyesight. We can thus also understand the fact that the young and the old of widely different races, both with man and animals, express the same state of mind by the same movements.

We are so familiar with the fact of young and old animals displaying their feelings in the same manner, that we hardly perceive how remarkable it is that a young puppy should wag its tail when pleased, depress its ears and uncover its canine teeth when pretending to be savage, just like an old dog; or that a kitten should arch its little back and erect its hair when frightened and angry, like an old cat. When, however, we turn to less common gestures in ourselves, which we are accustomed to look at as artificial or conventional – such as shrugging the shoulders, as a sign of impotence, or the raising the arms with open hands and extended fingers, as a sign of wonder – we feel perhaps too much surprise at finding that they are innate. That these and some other gestures are inherited, we may infer from their being performed by very young children, by those born blind, and by the most widely distinct races of man. We should also bear in mind that new and highly peculiar tricks, in association with certain states of the mind, are known to have arisen in certain individuals, and to have been afterwards transmitted to their offspring, in some cases, for more than one generation.

Certain other gestures, which seem to us so natural that we might easily imagine that they were innate, apparently have been learnt like the words of a language. This seems to be the case with the joining of the uplifted hands, and the turning up of the eyes, in prayer. So it is with kissing as a mark of affection; but this is innate, in so far as it depends on the pleasure derived from contact with a beloved person. The evidence with respect to the inheritance of nodding and shaking the head, as signs of affirmation and negation, is doubtful; for they are not universal, yet seem too general to have been independently acquired by all the individuals of so many races.

We will now consider how far the will and consciousness have come into play in the development of the various movements of expression. As far as we can judge, only a few expressive movements, such as those just referred to, are learnt by each individual; that is were consciously and voluntarily performed during the early years of life for some definite object, or in imitation of others, and then became habitual. The far greater number of the movements of expression, and all the more important ones, are, as we have seen, innate or inherited; and such cannot be said to depend on the will of the individual.

The problem of the relationship of the physical and the social aspects of the human body was, for all intents and purposes, resolved by Robert Hertz in 1909. In 'The pre-eminence of the right hand' Hertz considered the question of whether a tendency towards right-handedness is biologically or socially determined, and he concluded that right-

handedness is a result of both physical and cultural factors. For Hertz, the human body constituted a subject that anthropologists and physiologists could approach symbiotically: there was no question of either biology or sociology.

Robert Hertz:
'The pre-eminence of the right hand: A study in religious polarity' (excerpts)

From Robert Hertz, *Death and the Right Hand*, trans. Rodney and Claudia Needham, Cohen & West, 1960, pp. 91, 93, 98, 111, 112–13.

There is no need to deny the existence of organic tendencies towards asymmetry; but apart from some exceptional cases the vague disposition to right-handedness, which seems to be spread throughout the human species, would not be enough to bring about the absolute preponderance of the right hand if this were not reinforced and fixed by influences extraneous to the organism.

Organic asymmetry in man is at once a fact and an ideal. Anatomy accounts for the fact to the extent that it results from the structure of the organism; but however strong a determinant one may suppose it to be, it is incapable of explaining the origin of the ideal or the reason for its existence.

How could man's body, the microcosm, escape the law of polarity which governs everything? Society and the whole universe have a side which is sacred, noble and precious, and another which is profane and common: a male side, strong and active, and another, female, weak and passive; or, in two words, a right side and a left side – and yet the human organism alone should be symmetrical? A moment's reflection shows us that that is an impossibility. Such an exception would not only be an inexplicable anomaly, it would ruin the entire economy of the spiritual world. For man is at the centre of creation: it is for him to manipulate and direct for the better the formidable forces which bring life and death.

If organic asymmetry had not existed, it would have had to be invented.

... The slight physiological advantages possessed by the right hand are merely the occasion of a qualitative differentiation of which the cause lies beyond the individual, in the constitution of the collective consciousness. An almost insignificant bodily asymmetry is enough to turn in one direction and the other contrary representations which are already completely formed. Thereafter, thanks to the plasticity of the organism, social constraint adds to the opposed members and incorporates in them those qualities of strength and weakness, dexterity and clumsiness [*gaucherie* = literally 'leftness'], which in the adult appear to spring spontaneously from nature.

What disputes there were formerly between the partisans of innate distinction and those of experience! And what a fine clash of dialectical arguments! The application of experimental and sociological method to human problems puts an end to this conflict of dogmatic and contradictory assertions. Those who believe in the innate capacity to differentiate have won their victory: the intellectual and moral representations of right and left are true categories, anterior to all individual experience, since they are linked to the very structure of social thought. But the advocates of experience were right too, for there is no question here of immutable instincts or of absolute metaphysical data. These categories are transcendent only in relation to the individual: placed in their original setting, the collective consciousness, they appear as facts of nature, subject to change and dependent on complex conditions.

Hertz's conclusions on the compatibility of physical and social explanations of the behaviour of the human body might have been seen by his contemporaries as an answer to the questions which Charles Darwin had raised just a few years before in his book The Expression of the Emotions in Man and Animals. *But unfortunately Robert Hertz's essay on handedness (1909) was not addressed to Darwin's argument and there is no indication that Hertz was even aware of Darwin's book. If he had addressed himself to students of animal behaviour and if anyone had bothered to consider the significance of the relationship of the two works one to the other, and if Hertz (together with Mauss and even Durkheim) were better known to some anthropologists and ethologists a long and largely senseless debate might have been avoided. Unfortunately, there were too many 'ifs' and Hertz's notion that bodily behaviour is* both *culturally and biologically significant has been lost in the confusion of battle.*

While Hertz straddled the fence between inheritance and learning, his colleague Marcel Mauss presented in 1935 the classic case for regarding bodily expression as learnt. Thus a rough configuration is formed, with

Darwin on one side, Mauss on the other, and Hertz in between – neatly pulling together both arguments. While Darwin's specific subject was 'the expression of the emotions' and Hertz's was the tendency towards right-handedness, Mauss chose to investigate 'The techniques of the body', dealing with physical activities such as swimming, digging, spitting and sitting. It is unfortunate that Darwin, Hertz and Mauss did not deal with the same specific subject, but they all dealt with the same general question – bodily expression – and came to radically different conclusions.

Marcel Mauss:
'The techniques of the body' (excerpts)

From 'Les Techniques du corps', *Journal de psychologie normale et pathologique*, 32 (1935). English translation by Ben Brewster in *Economy and Society*, 2, 1 (February 1973), 70–88. These excerpts are taken from pp. 72, 73, 74, 85, 85. See the Introduction to the present volume for further comments.

I think I can . . . recognize a girl who has been raised in a convent. In general she will walk with her fists closed. And I can still remember my third-form teacher shouting at me: 'Idiot! why do you walk around the whole time with your hands flapping wide open?' Thus there exists an education in walking . . .

In all these elements of the art of using the human body, the facts of *education* were dominant.

In a book by Elsdon Best that reached here in 1925 there is a remarkable document on the way Maori women (New Zealand) walk . . . 'Native women adopted a peculiar gait . . . that was acquired in youth, a loose-jointed swinging of the hips that looks ungainly to us, but was admired by the Maori. Mothers drilled their daughters in this accomplishment, termed *onioni* . . . This was an acquired, not a natural way of walking.' To sum up, there is perhaps no 'natural way' for the adult.

In group life as a whole there is a kind of education of movements in close order.

In every society, everyone knows and has to know and learn what he has to do in all conditions.

For copyright reasons as well as problems of space in the present volume, only a few brief excerpts of Mauss's essay can be presented here. Mauss's work is now translated and readily available. The reader is urged to investigate the essay in its entirety, particularly the first and last sections.

The argument, started by Mauss, that bodily expression is learnt and social rather than inherited and biological, surfaced in America as anthropological fieldworkers became more and more convinced of the cultural (read: social) determinants of human behaviour in general. An attack gradually developed against the Darwinian assumption that biological inheritance determines bodily expression and behaviour. The following brief selection by Clyde Kluckhohn introduces most of the principal participants in this trend. As we switch our attention from France to the US and make another leap forward in time, it is sad to note that very few of the people involved in solving this problem in America appear to have been aware that Mauss and Hertz had prepared the ground for them.

Clyde Kluckhohn:
'*Motor habits*' (excerpt)

From Gardner Lindzey, ed., *Handbook of Social Psychology*, vol. II, *Culture and Behavior*, Addison-Wesley, Reading, Mass., 1954, p. 930.

Any observant traveller notes large and small variations in the gestures and other motor habits of different regions. For example, in the state of Jalisco in Mexico the height of a child, object or animal is indicated with the palm of the hand at right angles to the ground – not with the palm parallel to the ground as is customary with the same gesture in the United States. Many anthropologists have noted the astonishment of American Indians when whites would put a pinched finger in the mouth. Jane Belo,[1] Flora Bailey,[2] and Devereux,[3] have provided rather comprehensive accounts of characteristic motor habits among the Balinese, Navaho and Mohave respectively. Astrov[4] has attempted to relate Navaho motor habits to language, mythology, and other aspects of Navaho culture. Birdwhistell[5] has pointed to regional variations in motor habits within American culture. LaBarre[6] gives a survey, rich in excellent detail, of variations in gestures and their meanings throughout the world. If further proof were required that motor habits are culturally learned, this is conclusively supplied by Efron.[7] He shows with great specificity, using large samples and full quantitative treatment, that assimilated Eastern Jews and assimilated Southern Italians in New York City differ greatly from unassimilated members of the same two populations and tend to resemble each other. He also demonstrates that some American-born Jews continue to follow traditional gestural behaviour, while others from the same biological population exhibit the more generalized American habits. Finally, he makes it clear that gestures vary with cultural context in the same individual. Men speaking Yiddish or Hebrew would gesture in the traditional manner; speaking English a few minutes later their gestures were 'American'.

The development of motor habits is ... culturally patterned ...

Notes

1. JANE BELO, 'The Balinese temper', *Character and Personality*, 4 (1935), 120–46.
2. FLORA L. BAILEY, 'Navaho motor habits', *American Anthropologist*, 44 (n.s.), 2 (1942), 210–34.
3. G. DEVEREUX, 'Mohave Indian verbal and motor profanity', G. Roheim, ed., *Psychoanalysis and the Social Sciences*, International University Press, New York, 1951, vol. III, pp. 99–127.
4. MARGOT ASTROV, 'The concept of motion as the psychological Leitmotif of Navaho life and literature', *Journal of American Folklore*, 63 (1950), 45–56.
5. R. L. BIRDWHISTELL, 'Body motion research and interviewing', *Human Organization*, 11 (1952), 37–8.
6. W. LABARRE, 'The cultural basis of emotions and gestures', *Journal of Personality*, 16 (1947), 49–68.
7. D. EFRON, *Gesture and Environment*, King's Crown Press, Morningside Heights, N.Y., 1941.

Margaret Mead and Frances Cooke Macgregor:
Growth and Culture: A Photographic Study of Balinese Childhood ('Conclusions')

G. P. Putnam's Sons, New York, 1951. All illustrations are taken from *Growth and Culture* except those (with captions) from Gregory Bateson and Margaret Mead, *Balinese Character: A Photographic Analysis*, ed. Wilbur G. Valentine, Special Publications of the New York Academy of Sciences, 1942, vol. II, which are marked as such.

Margaret Mead and Gregory Bateson, after conducting field research together in Bali, assembled a verbal and photographic account of Balinese life which was published in the book Balinese Character. *Frances Macgregor and Margaret Mead later analysed Bateson's photographs for the purpose of comparing the development of Balinese children with the development of children in New Haven, Connecticut, as studied by Arnold Gessell and Frances Ilg. Mead found a few striking variations in the bodily development of Balinese children as compared to American children and her summary is printed below. What is particularly important about this study is that it reveals that* parts *of developmental behaviours (as well as complicated, formal gestures — as in dance, for example) are learnt and parts are social in nature.*

This research set out to answer a variety of questions of different theoretical levels. We have brought to bear a battery of insights and analyses and invoked large bodies of research materials in the hope of illuminating, through a particular study of eight children in a Balinese cultural setting, our knowledge of growth in culture.

7.

6.

On the basis of this analysis, our general findings are:

1. Balinese Bajoeng Gedé children seem to go through the same general stages of behaviour as American New Haven children, but significant and consistent differences can be identified in one sequence on which there was adequate material, the sequence from creeping to walking. Where the American children go from frogging to creeping on all fours, then to standing and walking, with squatting

8.

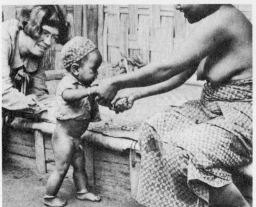

9.

10.

coming after standing, the Balinese children, who do much less creeping (and spend most of the period when American children are moving actively about either sitting or being carried) combine frogging (Fig. 6), creeping (Fig. 7), and all-fours behaviour (Fig. 8) simultaneously in a flexible, interchangeable state, from which they go from sitting to squatting to standing (Figures 9 and 10). The distinctive elements here are: (a) the much greater activity of the

American child, for whom creeping and all-fours behaviour is a stage that is prepared for by the earlier stages of crawling, a stage that is precluded in the Bajoeng Gedé children because of the way they are handled; (b) the greater prolongation of the frogging posture, which may be at least partly attributable to the many hours spent each day astride a human hip; and (c) the way in which the Balinese child can rise to a squat and from a squat to standing, combined with the great amount of

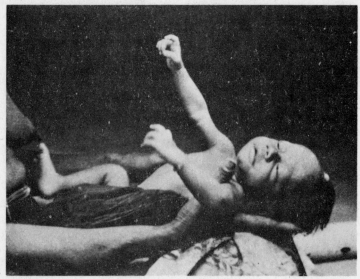

11.

hyperextension. Seen in terms of the spiral analysis of development, the Balinese neglect the possibilities of the crawling stage and give very partial play to the creeping stage as contrasted with our pattern of cultural facilitation of crawling and creeping, but they reinforce the frogging–squatting sequence that we neglect by their methods of carrying the child on the hip and by the postures of the parents.

2. A second area of contrast is found in the Balinese emphasis upon extension (Figure 11) and outward rotation (Figure 12), greater eversion (Figure 13), and use of the ulnar side of the hand, as opposed to the greater inward rotation, inversion, and use of the thumb, with good volar opposition between thumb and forefinger, of American children. This is associated in Balinese culture with flexible and partial adjustment to peripheral stimuli, and dependence upon supporting forms, calendrical, spatial, and so on, to give orientation and continuity to the personality.

12.

13.

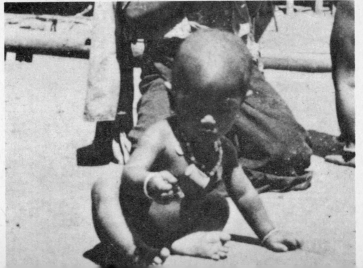

3. An area of contrast is found in the persistence in the Balinese children of a type of meandering tonus, characteristic of the foetal infant, with an accompanying very high degree of flexibility, and a capacity for the maintenance of positions of greater discrepancy, in which parts of the whole body or of the hand or the foot are simultaneously partly in flexion and partly in extension (Figures 14 and 15). The same children are able to assume, in the space of a few moments, postures of highly integrated or tense motor attention and of complete flaccidity (Figures 16 and 17).

With these three major findings in the analysis of the development of motor activity, we then attempted to find the specific ways in which the low tonal organization of the Balinese child was maintained, as this appeared to be central to the compliant sitting as contrasted to the great motor activity of American children, to the lower development of volar opposition and of the thumb in general,

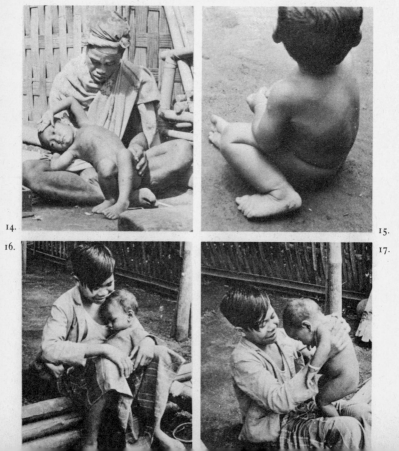

14.   15.

16.   17.

so that a more plastic, relaxed type of grasping obtained in Balinese children, and to the extraordinary flexibility and ability to maintain postures of toes and fingers, arms, legs, and head, that are found in foetal and very young infants but seldom persist beyond a few weeks here, such as the cupped and fanning hands in Figures 18 and 19. Balinese adult postures have been illustrated in this book only as adults in association with children have manifested them, but they are illustrated in variety in *Balinese Character* (Figure 20).

This low tonal organization, which Dr Gesell describes as 'meandering tonus', seems, then, to be a crucial feature of the behaviour of these Balinese children. If it is looked at strictly in terms of the physique of the individual children, it might be attributed to physical stock and so be regarded as a genetic characteristic peculiar to some proportion of the people of Bali, or as a nutritional effect, which would have to be explored much further with special attention to the variations in diet in different parts of Bali, because this demeanour is

18.   19.

common to the babies whom we have observed in other parts of Bali also.

When we add a cultural analysis, we can say that if the low tonus of the Balinese infant, which seems to resemble closely the tonus of the newborn, is taken as given, our task is to analyse the conditions under which it persists and becomes an important component in motor organization in later life. If we refuse the facile and unsatisfactory type of interpretation which is content with saying that children learn from parents and flexible parents will produce flexible children, and seek for the specific nexus between adult and infant behaviour,

20. A carver strikes a pose to show the posture he intends for his carving representing the leader (*dag*) of a modern dance (*djanger*). (*Balinese Character*)

the way in which Balinese adults carry and handle children seems to be crucial. The sling permits the child to be attached to the mother or the child nurse without either person's making any active effort whatsoever once the sling is fastened, and when the sling is absent, the Balinese arm imitates it in relaxed inattention. This very light tie between child and carrier, tactually close, but without grasping by either one, seems to establish a kind of communication in which peripheral responsiveness predominates over grasping behaviour or purposeful holding on. Furthermore, the child is carried on the left hip, leaving its left hand free to grasp, but since receiving anything in the left hand is bad manners, the child's efforts to grasp are continually frustrated as the mother or the carrier pulls back the reaching left hand and pulls out the hitherto passive right hand that was lying relaxed against her body. It is furthermore possible to suggest that the persistence in the child of its low tonal organization is a continuing stimulus to the adult for the maintenance of the type of handling of the child that perpetuates this low tonus, so that while the habitual method of handling a child is passive and involves minimal interaction (Figure 21), even when the child is held firmly it is with a firmness that evokes passivity rather than co-operative activity (Figure 22), and is transformed in learning situations into a functional inter-relation in which the low tonus becomes high flexibility, capable of absorbing the pattern of activity that the teacher is imparting. This interpretation brings together the discussions of kinaes-

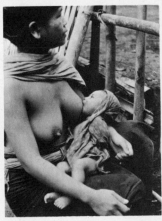 

21.   22.

thetic learning in *Balinese Character* (Figures 23–30), my original hypothesis that whole-body learning and total skin contact would be found to be of great significance in Balinese character formation, Frances Macgregor's original focus when, without any background information, she responded spontaneously to the photographs, and a recognition by the Gesell group that the relaxed, inattentive behaviour of the mothers was of unusual interest.

This combined analysis highlights the importance of dealing with the living members of a society, young and old together, as an ongoing system, seeing the behaviour of the infants evoked by and evoking the handling they receive as an integral part of the culturally regular behaviour of the adults. Whether the origination of this type of low tonal organization is to be placed hundreds of years ago in some change in child care, some change in nutrition, some shift in temperamental model for the whole population, or is to be regarded

23. The pupil dances alone while Mario watches in the background. Note the imperfect development of the pupil's finger posture.

24. Mario comes forward to show the pupil how it should be danced.

27. Mario takes the pupil by the wrists and swings him across the dancing space.

28. Mario makes his pupil dance correctly by holding his hands and forcing him to move as he should. Note that Mario is actually dancing in this photograph, and that he postures with his fingers even while holding the pupil's hands. The position of Mario's left elbow in these photographs is characteristic of the tensions developed in this dance.

as reconstituted in each new generation of infants by some genetic predisposition or biochemical prenatal environment, if it is to persist and be translated into the particular patterns of motor-activity characteristic of the Balinese, the interaction between the infant with initial infantile flexibility and the adult in whom this flexibility is highly patterned is essential. We hypothesize that Balinese babies taken away soon after birth and reared by adults who lacked this

25. Mario urges the pupil to straighten up the small of his back. Note that this instruction is given by gesture rather than by words.

26. Mario's hand position and facial expression while demonstrating.

29. Mario even assumes the conventional sweet impersonal smile of the dancer while he moves the pupil's arms and holds the pupil tightly between his knees to correct his tendency to bend the small of his back.

30. Mario again tries to correct the pupil's tendency to bend his back.

(Figures 23–30 from *Balinese Character*)

flexibility would lose it also, and that Balinese adults presented with six-month-old New Haven infants, in attempting to handle them would themselves be modified, although not as drastically, as hands that expected limpness were met with tension and hands that attempted to teach through sensitive light tactile communication, and an expectation of co-operative bodily surrender to a movement pattern, would meet instead with wriggling, struggling intractability.

We know that when individuals migrate from one culture to another, their children to some degree, their grandchildren to a greater degree, their great-grandchildren even more, approximate to the new posture and gesture patterns of the new culture. Only by identifying which particular systems of communication, between adult and infant and between child and child, are operative in which changes can we begin to plan responsibly to rear children who do not merely repeat the behaviour of previous generations but can initiate new behaviours that will in turn alter the behaviour even of their grandparents. The focus of planned cultural change lies in learning, and the learning of the infant and the child and the response-evoking aspect of the child constitute one exceedingly important point where disciplined human intelligence can intervene constructively in the process of moulding a culture closer to the needs and the capacities of all those who live within it.

Within our own existing culture, the extreme isolation of each individual home, while in many ways a handicap and a liability for the child's development, also makes it possible for individual pairs of parents to study the developmental pattern of each of their few highly cherished children. Instead of fitting each child to the procrustean bed of cultural expectations – modelled in Bali on a child that will have low tonal organization and be hyperextended, outwardly rotated, and ulnarly emphasized, with a high development of kinaesthetic and kinaesthetically modelled visual learning ability, modelled in the United States on a child who will be extremely active, focused, able to learn mostly by doing – the modern parent can begin to fit the way the child is handled to the particular sequences of growth, the particular readiness, the particular innate sensitivities and innate insensitivities, of a given child. It is probable that for every gifted individual whose innate potentialities have been fortunately elaborated, either because these potentialities fitted the cultural expectations or because those individuals who cared for him were specially congenial or skilful in evoking his abilities at the crucial moment, hundreds of equally gifted individuals remain mediocre or are deeply hurt by the lack of fit between a culturally stylized handling of developmental phases and the child's own rhythms.

We can attempt to alter our whole culture, and especially our child-rearing patterns, so as to incorporate within them a greater freedom for and expectation of variations. This is done, for instance, in the idea of reading readiness – that reading should not be taught until the child is ready to read and that for each child there is such a time. If the concept of spiral development as set forth by the Gesell group is added to this, it should be possible to chart out for each child when the next moment of readiness will come if something has miscarried at the first moment when a child could have learned most felicitously. A missed opportunity becomes the guide to the next opportunity as the child's individual rhythm of growth is interpreted within the human growth pattern as stylized by our cultural requirements and expectations.

Such a study as this both sets limits and points to new possibilities. To the extent to which Balinese peculiarities can be attributed to using as a model a particular physical type – as may perhaps be the case in the apparent greater proportional length of the little finger as contributory to the emphasis on the ulnar side of the hand (Figures 31–3), or in the use of the high-breasted woman as the model for

31.   32.   33.

carrying–suckling behaviour (Figures 34–7) – we can see the way in which a society can institutionalize for all those within it the special potentialities of some particular type. To the extent that individual children, however, continue to respond with such a high degree of individuality, even in the homogeneous, static culture of Bajoeng Gedé in 1936, we can see the enormous role that is played by the particular constitutional and temperamental endowment with which the child is born. We can develop our culture to allow play for each specific human gift, and provide elaboration for each generalized human potentiality, if we take into account both the special gift and the general gift, letting each inform and supplement the other.

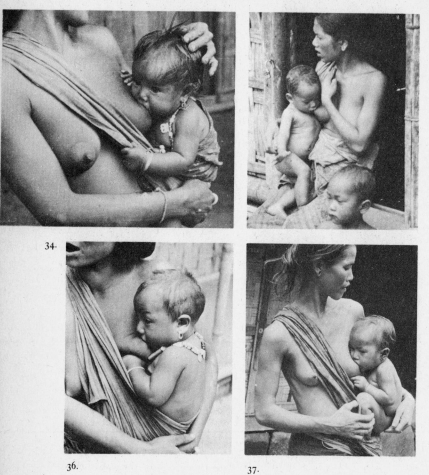

34· 35· 36. 37·

Weston LaBarre:
'*The cultural basis of emotions and gestures*'
From *Journal of Personality*, 16 (1947), 49–68.

Eibl-Eibesfeldt (see Chapter 2, p. 109 of this volume) has criticized Weston LaBarre's 'The cultural basis of emotions and gestures' by saying that the evidence that LaBarre presents is 'anecdotal'. This is, in fact, quite true, but it is equally true that LaBarre's impressive list of ethnographic anecdotes has, since it appeared in 1947, given much cause for thought about whether Darwin was right when he said 'many of our most important expressions have not been learnt'.

The text below is printed in full. A central section which deals with vocal expression (and its written transcription) might seem 'out of place in a study of the body, but as David Crystal has pointed out in his essay 'Paralinguistics' (in J. Benthall and T. Polhemus, eds., The Body as a Medium of Expression, *Allen Lane; Dutton, New York, 1975), vocal, verbal communication can also be considered as part of bodily communication.*

Psychologists have long concerned themselves with the physiological problems of emotion, as, for example, whether the psychic state is prior to the physiological changes and causes them, or whether the conscious perception of the inner physiological changes in itself constitutes the 'emotion'. The physiologists also, notably Cannon, have described the various bodily concomitants of fear, pain, rage and the like. Not much attention, however, has been directed towards another potential dimension of meaning in the field of emotions, that is to say the *cultural* dimension.

The anthropologist is wary of those who speak of an 'instinctive' gesture on the part of a human being. One important reason is that a sensitivity to meanings which are culturally different from his own stereotypes may on occasion be crucial for the anthropologist's own physical survival among at least some groups he studies, and he must at the very least be a student of this area of symbolism if he would avoid embarrassment.[1] He cannot safely rely upon his own culturally subjective understandings of emotional expression in his relations with persons of another tribe. The advisability and the value of a correct reading of any cultural symbolism whatsoever has alerted him to the possibility of culturally arbitrary, quasi-linguistic (that is, non-instinctual but learned and purely agreed-upon) meanings in the behaviour he observes.

A rocking of the skull forward and backward upon its condyles, which rest on the atlas vertebra, as an indication of affirmation and the rotation upon the axis vertebra for negation have so far been accepted as 'natural' and 'instinctive' gestures that one psychologist at least[2] has sought an explanation of the supposedly universal phenomenon in ascribing the motions of 'yes' to the infant's seeking of the mother's breast, and 'no' to its avoidance and refusal of the breast.

This is ingenious, but it is arguing without one's host, since the phenomenon to be explained is by no means as widespread ethnologically, even among humans, as is mammalian behaviour biologically.

Indeed, the Orient alone is rich in alternatives. Among the Ainu of northern Japan, for example, our particular head noddings are unknown: 'The right hand is usually used in negation, passing from right to left and back in front of the chest; and both hands are gracefully brought up to the chest and gracefully waved downwards – palms upwards – in sign of affirmation.'[3] The Semang, pygmy Negroes of interior Malaya, thrust the head sharply forward for 'yes' and cast the eyes down for 'no'.[4] 'The Abyssinians say "no" by jerking the head to the right shoulder, and "yes" by throwing the head back and raising the eyebrows. The Dyaks of Borneo raise their eyebrows to mean "yes" and contract them slightly to mean "no". The Maori say "yes" by raising the head and chin; the Sicilians say "no" in exactly the same manner.'[5] A Bengali servant in Calcutta rocks his head rapidly in an arc from shoulder to shoulder, usually four times, in assent; in Delhi a Moslem boy throws his head diagonally backward with a slight turning of the neck for the same purpose; and the Kandyan Singhalese bends the head diagonally forward towards the right, with an indescribably graceful turning-in of the chin, often accompanying this with a cross-legged curtsey, arms partly crossed, palms upward – the whole performance extraordinarily beautiful and ingratiating. Indeed, did my own cultural difference not tell me it already, I would know that the Singhalese manner of receiving an object (with the right hand, the left palm supporting the right elbow) is not instinctive, for I have seen a Singhalese mother *teaching* her little boy to do this when I gave him a chunk of palm-tree sugar. I only regretted, later, that my own manners must have seemed boorish or subhuman, since I handed it to him with my right hand, instead of with both, as would any courteous Singhalese. Alas, if I had handed it to a little Moslem beggar in Sind or the Punjab with my *left* hand, he would probably have dashed the gift to the ground, spat, and called me by the name of an animal whose flesh he had been taught to dislike, but which I have not – for such use of the left hand would be insulting, since it is supposed to be confined to attending to personal functions, while the right hand is the only proper one for food.

Those persons with a passion for easy dominance, the professional dog-lovers, must often be exasperated at the stupidity of a dog which does not respond to so obvious a command as the pointed forefinger. The defence of man's best friend might be that this 'instinctively' human gesture does not correspond to the kinaesthesias of a non-handed animal. Nevertheless, even for an intelligent human baby, at the exact period when he is busily using the forefinger in exploring the world, 'pointing' by an adult is an arbitrary, sublinguistic gesture which is not automatically understood and which must be *taught*. I am the less inclined to berate the obtuseness to the obvious of either dog or baby, because of an early field experience of my own. One day I asked a favourite informant of mine among the Kiowa, old Mary Buffalo, where something was in the *ramada* or willow-branch 'shade' where we were working. It was clear she had heard me, for her eighty-eight-year-old ears were by no means deaf; but she kept on busying both hands with her work. I wondered at her rudeness and repeated the request several times, until finally with a puzzled exasperation which matched my own, she dropped her work and fetched it for me from in plain sight: she had been repeatedly pointing with her lips in approved American Indian fashion, as any Caucasian numbskull should have been able to see.

Some time afterwards I asked a somewhat naive question of a very great anthropologist, the late Edward Sapir: 'Do other tribes cry and laugh as we do?' In appropriate response, Sapir himself laughed, but with an instant grasping of the point of the question: in which of these things are men alike everywhere, in which different? Where are the international boundaries between physiology and culture? What are the extremes of variability, and what are the scope and range of cultural differences in emotional and gestural expression? Probably one of the most learned linguists who have ever lived, Sapir was extremely sensitive to emotional and sublinguistic gesture – an area of deep illiteracy for most 'Anglo-Saxon' Americans – and my present interest was founded on our conversation at that time.

Smiling, indeed, I have found may almost be mapped after the fashion of any other culture trait; and laughter is in some senses a geographic variable. On a map of the south-west Pacific one could perhaps even draw lines between areas of 'Papuan hilarity' and others where a Dobuan, Melanesian dourness reigned. In Africa, Gorer noted that 'laughter is used by the Negro to express surprise, wonder, embarrassment and even discomfiture; it is not necessarily, or even often, a sign of amusement; the significance given to "black laughter" is due to a mistake of supposing that similar symbols have identical meanings'.[6] Thus it is that even if the physiological behaviour be present, its cultural and emotional functions may differ. Indeed, even within the same culture, the laughter of adolescent girls and the laughter of corporation presidents can be functionally different things; so too the laughter of an American Negro and that of the white he addresses.

The behaviourist Holt 'physiologized' the smile as being ontogenetically the relaxation of the muscles of the face in a baby replete from nursing. Explanations of this order may well be the case, if the phenomenon of the smile is truly a physiological expression of generalized pleasure, which is caught up later in ever more complex conditioned reflexes. And yet, even in its basis here, I am not sure that this is the whole story: for the 'smile' of a child in its sleep is certainly in at least some cases the grimace of *pain* from colic, rather than the relaxation of pleasure. Other explanations such as that the smile is *phylogenetically* a snarl suffer from much the same *ad hoc* quality.

Klineberg writes:

It is quite possible, however, that a smile or a laugh may have a different meaning for groups other than our own. Lafcadio Hearn has remarked that the Japanese smile is not necessarily a spontaneous expression of amusement, but a law of etiquette, elaborated and cultivated from early times. It is a silent language, often seemingly inexplicable to Europeans, and it may arouse violent anger in them as a consequence. The Japanese child is taught to smile as a social duty, just as he is taught to bow or prostrate himself; he must always show an appearance of happiness to avoid inflicting his sorrow upon his friends. The story is told of a woman servant who smilingly asked her mistress if she might go to her husband's funeral. Later she returned with his ashes in a vase and said, actually laughing, 'Here is my husband.' Her White mistress regarded her as a cynical creature; Hearn suggests that this may have been pure heroism.[7]

Many in fact of these motor habits in one culture are open to grave misunderstanding in another. The Copper Eskimo welcome strangers with a buffet on the head or shoulders with the fist, while the northwest Amazonians slap one another on the back in greeting. Polynesian men greet each other by embracing and rubbing each others' back; Spanish-American males greet one another by a stereotyped embrace, head over right shoulder of the partner, three pats on the back, head over reciprocal left shoulder, three more pats. In the Torres Straits islands 'the old form of greeting was to bend slightly the fingers of the right hand, hook them with those of the person greeted, and then draw them away so as to scratch the palm of the hand; this is repeated several times'.[8] The Ainu of Yezo have a peculiar greeting; on the occasion of a man meeting his sister, 'The man held the woman's hands for a few seconds, then suddenly releasing his hold, grasped her by both ears and uttered the Aino cry. Then they stroked one another down the face and shoulders.'[9] Kayan males in Borneo embrace or grasp each other by the forearm, while a host throws his arm over the shoulder of a guest and strokes him endearingly with the palm of his hand. When two Kurd males meet, 'they grasp each other's right hand, which they simultaneously raise, and each kisses the hand of the other'.[10] Among the Andaman Islanders of the Gulf of Bengal:

> When two friends or relatives meet who have been separated from each other for a few weeks or longer, they greet each other by sitting down, one on the lap of the other, with their arms around each other's necks, and weeping or wailing for two or three minutes till they are tired. Two brothers greet each other in this way, and so do father and son, mother and daughter, and husband and wife. When husband and wife meet, it is the man who sits in the lap of the woman. When two friends part from one another, one of them lifts up the hand of the other towards his mouth and gently blows on it.[11]

Some of these expressions of 'joy' seem more lugubrious than otherwise. One old voyager, John Turnbull, writes as follows:

> The arrival of a ship brings them to the scene of action from far and near. Many of them meet at Matavai who have not seen each other for some length of time. The ceremony of these meetings is not without singularity; taking a shark's tooth, they strike it into their head and temples with great violence, so as to produce a copious bleeding; and this they will repeat, till they become clotted with blood and gore.

The honest mariner confesses to be nonplussed at this behaviour. 'I cannot explain the origin of this custom, nor its analogy with what it is intended to express. It has no other meaning with them than to express the excess of their joy. By what construction it is considered symbolical of this emotion I do not understand.'[12] Quite possibly, then, the weeping of an American woman 'because she is so happy' may merely indicate that the poverty of our gamut of physiological responses is such as to require using the same response for opposite meanings. Certainly weeping does obey social stereotypes in other cultures. Consider old Mary Buffalo at her brother's funeral: she wept in a frenzy, tore her hair, scratched her cheeks, and even tried to jump into the grave (being conveniently restrained from this by remoter relatives). I happened to know that she had not seen her brother for some time, and there was no particular love lost between them: she was merely carrying on the way a decent woman should among the Kiowa. Away from the grave, she was immediately chatting vivaciously about some other topic. Weeping is *used* differently among the Kiowa. Any stereotypes I may have had about the strong and silent American Indian, whose speech is limited to an infrequent 'ugh' and whose stoicism to pain is limitless, were once rudely shattered in a public religious meeting. A great burly Wichita Indian who had come with me to a peyote meeting, after a word with the leader which I did not understand (it was probably permission to take his turn in a prayer) suddenly burst out blubbering with an abandon which no Occidental male adult would permit himself in public. In time I learned that this was a stereotyped approach to the supernatural powers, enthusiastic weeping to indicate that he was as powerless as a child, to invoke their pity, and to beseech their gift of medicine power. Everyone in the tipi understood this except me.

So much for the expression of emotion in one culture, which is open to serious misinterpretation in another: there is no 'natural' language of emotional gesture. To return a moment to the earlier topic of emotional expression in greetings: West Africans in particular have developed highly the ritual gestures and language of greeting. What Gorer says of the Wolof would stand for many another tribe:

> The gestures and language of polite intercourse are stylized and graceful; a greeting is a formal litany of question and answer embracing everyone and everything connected with the two people meeting (the questions are merely formal and a dying person is stated to be in good health so as not to break the rhythm of the responses) and continuing for several minutes; women accompany it with a swaying movement of the body; with people to whom a special deference is due the formula is resumed several times during the conversation; saying goodbye is equally elaborate.[13]

But here the sublinguistic gesture language has clearly emerged into pure formalisms of language which are quite plainly cultural.

The allegedly 'instinctive' nature of such motor habits in personal relationships is difficult to maintain in the face of the fact that in many cases the same gesture means exactly opposite, or incommensurable things, in different cultures. Hissing in Japan is a polite deference to social superiors; the Basuto applaud by hissing, but in England hissing is rude and public disapprobation of an actor or a speaker. Spitting in very many parts of the world is a sign of utmost contempt; and yet among the Masai of Africa it is a sign of affection and benediction, while the spitting of an American Indian medicine man upon a patient is one of the kindly offices of the curer. Urination upon another (as in a famous case at the Sands Point, Long Island, country club, involving a congressman since assassinated) is a grave insult among Occidentals, but it is part of the transfer of power from an African medicine man in initiations and curing rituals. As for other opposite meanings, Western man stands up in the presence of a superior; the Fijians and the Tongans sit down. In some contexts we put on more clothes as a sign of respect; the Friendly Islanders take them off. The Toda of South India raise the open right hand to the face, with the thumb on the bridge of the nose, to express respect; a gesture almost identical among Europeans is an obscene expression of extreme disrespect. Placing to the tip of the nose the projecting knuckle of the right forefinger bent at the second joint was among the Maori of New Zealand a sign of friendship and often of protection;[14] but in eighteenth-century England the placing of the same forefinger to the right side of the nose expressed dubiousness about the intelligence and sanity of a speaker – much as does the twentieth-century clockwise motion of the forefinger above the right hemisphere of the head. The sticking-out of the tongue among Europeans (often at the same time 'making a face') is an insulting, almost obscene act of provocative challenge and mocking contempt for the adversary, so undignified as to be used only by children; so long as Maya writing remains undeciphered we do not know the meaning of the exposure of the tongue in some religious sculptures of the gods, but we can be sure it scarcely has the same significance as with us. In Bengali statues of the dread black mother goddess Kali, the tongue is protruded to signify great raging anger and shock; but the Chinese of the Sung dynasty protruded the tongue playfully to pretend to mock terror, as if to 'make fun of' the ridiculous and unfeared anger of another person.[15] Modern Chinese, in South China at least, protrude the tongue for a moment and then retract it, to express embarrassment at a *faux pas*.

Kissing, as is well known, is in the Orient an act of private love-play and arouses only disgust when indulged in publicly: in Japan it is necessary to censor out the major portion of love scenes in American-made movies for this reason. Correspondingly, some of the old *kagura* dances of the Japanese strike Occidentals as revoltingly overt obscenities, yet it is doubtful if they arouse this response in Japanese onlookers: Manchu kissing is purely a private sexual act, and though husband and wife or lovers might kiss each other, they would do it stealthily since it is shameful to do in public; yet Manchu mothers have the pattern of putting the penis of the baby boy into their mouths, a practice which probably shocks Westerners even more than kissing in public shocks the Manchu.[16] Tapuya men in South America kiss as a sign of peace, but men do not kiss women because the latter wear labrets or lip plugs. Nose-rubbing is Eskimo and Polynesian; and the Djuka Negroes of Surinam[17] show pleasure at a particularly interesting or amusing dance step by embracing the dancer and touching cheek to cheek, now on one side, now on the other – which is the identical attenuation of the 'social kiss' between American women who do not wish to spoil each other's makeup.

In the language of gesture all over the world there are varying mixtures of the physiologically conditioned response and the purely cultural one, and it is frequently difficult to analyse out and segregate the two. The Chukchee of Siberia, for example, have a phenomenal quickness to anger, which they express by showing the teeth and growling like an animal – yet man's snout has long ceased being functionally useful in offensive or defensive biting as it has phylogenetically and continuously retreated from effective prognathism. But this behaviour reappears again and again: the Malayan pagans, for example, raise the lip over the canine tooth when sneering and jeering. Is this instinctual reflex or mere motor habit? The Tasmanians stamped rapidly on the ground to express surprise or pleasure; Occidentals beat the palms of the hands together for the same purpose ordinarily, but in some rowdier contexts this is accompanied by whistling and a similar stamping of the feet. Europeans 'snort' with contempt; and the non-Mohammedan primitives of interior Malaya express disgust with a sudden expiration of the breath. In this particular instance, it is difficult to rid oneself of the notion that this is a consciously controlled act, to be sure, but nevertheless at least a 'symbolic sneeze' based upon a purely physiological reflex which does rid the nostrils of irritating matter. The favourite gesture of contempt of the Menomini Indians of Wisconsin – raising the clenched fist palm down up to the level of the mouth, then bringing it swiftly downwards, throwing forth the thumb and first two fingers – would seem to be based on the same 'instinctual' notion of rejection.

However, American Indian gestures soon pass over into the undisputedly linguistic area, as when two old men of different tribes who do not know a word of each other's spoken language, sit side by side and tell each other improper stories in the complex and highly articulate intertribal sign-language of the Plains. These conventionalized gestures of the Plains sign-language must of course be learned as a language is learned, for they are a kind of kinaesthetic ideograph, resembling written Chinese. The written Chinese may be 'read' in the Japanese and the Korean and any number of mutually unintelligible spoken Chinese dialects; similarly, the sign language may be 'read' in Comanche, in Cheyenne, or in Pawnee, all of which belong to different language families. The primitive Australian sign-language was evidently of the conventionalized Plains type also, for it reproduced words, not mere letters (since of course they had no written language), but unfortunately little is known in detail of its mechanisms.

Like the writing of the Chinese, Occidental man has a number of ideographs, but they are sublinguistic and primarily *signs to action* or *expressions of action*. Thus, in the standard symbolism of cartoons, a 'balloon' encircling print has signified *speaking* since at least the eighteenth century. Interestingly, in a Maya painting on a vase from Guatemala of pre-Columbian times, we have the same speech 'balloons' enclosing ideographs representing what a chief and his vassal are saying, though what that is we do not know.[18] In Toltec frescoes speech is symbolized by foliated or noded crooks or scrolls, sometimes double, proceeding out of the mouths of human figures, although *what* is said is not indicated.[19] In the later Aztec codices written on wild fig-bark paper, speech is conventionalized by one or more little scrolls like miniature curled ostrich feathers coming out of the mouths of human beings, while motion or walking is indicated by footprints leading to where the person is now standing in the picture.[20] In American cartoons the same simple idea of footprints is also used. The ideograph of 'sawing wood' indicates the action of *snoring* or *sleeping*. A light bulb with radial lines means that a 'bright idea' has just occurred in the mind of the character above whose head it is written. While even children learn in time to understand these signs in context, no one would maintain that the electric-light 'sign' could naturally be understood by an individual from another tribe than our own. Birds singing, a spiral, or a five-pointed star means unconsciousness or semiconsciousness through concussion. A dotted line, if curved, indicates the past trajectory of a moving object; if straight and from eye to object, the action of seeing. None of these visual aids to understanding are part of objective nature. Sweat drops symbolize surprise or dumbfounding, although the physiology of this sign is thoroughly implausible. And]%!*/=#?[¢& very often says the unspeakable, quite as ? signifies query and ! surprise.

Many languages have *spoken* punctuation marks, which English grievously lacks. On the other hand, the speakers of English have a few *phonetic* 'ideographs', at least two of which invite to action. An imitation of a kiss, loudly performed, summons a dog, if that dog understands this much of English. A bilateral clucking of the tongue adjures a horse to 'giddyap', i.e., to commence moving or to move more smartly; and in some parts of the country at least, it has a secondary semantic employment in summoning barnyard fowl to their feeding. The dental–alveolar repeated clicking of the tongue, on the other hand, is not a symbolic ideophone to action, but a *moral comment* upon action, a strongly critical disapprobation largely confined in use to elderly females preoccupied with such moral commentary. These symbolic ideophones are used in no other way in our language; but in African Bushman and Hottentot languages, of course, these three sounds plus two others phonetically classified as 'clicks' (as opposed to sonants like b, d, g, z and surds like p, t, k, s, etc.) are regularly employed in words like any other consonants. It is nonsense to suppose that dogs, horses or chickens are equipped for 'instinctive' understanding or response to these human-made sounds, as much as that speakers of English have an instinctive understanding of Hottentot and Bushman. Certainly the sounds used in the Lake Titicaca plateau to handle llamas are entirely different.[21]

Sublinguistic 'language' can take a number of related forms. Among the Neolithic population of the Canary Islands there was a curious auxiliary 'language' of conventionalized whistles, signals which could be understood at greater distances than mere spoken speech. On four bugle tones, differently configurated, we can similarly order soldiers to such various actions as arising, assembling, eating, lowering a flag and burying the dead. The drum-language of West Africa, however, is more strictly linguistic than bugle calls. Many West African languages are tonemic, that is, they have pitch-accent somewhat like Chinese or Navaho. Drum-language, therefore, by reproducing not only the rhythm but also the tonal configurations of familiar phrases and sentences, is able to send messages of high semantic sophistication and complexity, as easily recognizable as our 'Star-Spangled Banner' sung with rhythm and melody, but without words. The Kru send battle signals on multiple-pitched horns, but these are not conventional tunes like our bugle calls, but fully articulated sentences and phrases whose tonemic patterns they reproduce on an instrument other than the human vocal cords. The Morse and International telegraph codes and Boy Scout and Navy flag communication (either with hand semaphores or with strings of variously shaped and coloured flags) are of course mere auditory or visual alphabets, tied down except for very minor conventionalized abbreviations to the *spelling* of a given language. (The advantages of a phonetic script, however, are very evident when it comes to sending messages via a Morse-like code for Chinese, which is written in ideographs which have different phonetic pronunciations in different dialects; Japanese has some advantage in this situation over Chinese in that its ideographs are already cumbrously paralleled in *katakana* and *hiragana* writing, which is quasi-phonetic.) Deaf-and-dumb language, if it is the mere spelling of words, is similarly bound to an alphabet; but as it becomes highly conventionalized it approaches the international supralinguistic nature of the Plains Indian sign-language. Of this order are the symbols of mathematics, the conventionalizations on maps for topography, the symbol language for expressing meteorological happenings on weather maps, and international flag signals for weather. Modern musical notation is similarly international: a supralinguistic system which orders in great detail what to do, and with what intensity, rhythm, tempo, timbre and manner. Possibly the international nature of musical notation was influenced by the fact that medieval neume notation arose at a time when Latin was an international lingua franca, and also by the international nature of late feudal culture, rather than being an internationally agreed-upon consensus of scientific symbolism. Based on the principles of musical notation, there have been several experimental attempts to construct an international system of dance notation, with signs to designate the position and motions of all parts of the body, with diacritical modifications to indicate tempo and the like. But while the motions of the classical ballet are highly stereotyped, they are semantically meaningless (unlike *natya* dancing in India and Ceylon, and Chinese and other Asiatic theatrics), so that this dance notation is mere *orders to action* like musical notation, with no other semantic content. Western dancing as an art form must appear insipid in its semantic emptiness to an Oriental who is used to articulate literary *meaning* in his dance forms. This is not to deny, however, that Occidental kinaesthetic language *may* be heavily imbued with great subtleties of meaning: the pantomime of the early Charlie Chaplin achieved at least a pan-European understanding and appreciation, while the implicit conventionalizations and stereotypes of Mickey Mouse (a psychiatrically most interesting figure!) are achieving currently an intercontinental recognition and enjoyment.

If all these various ways of *talking* be generously conceded to be purely cultural behaviour, surely *walking* – although learned – is a purely physiological phenomenon since it is undeniably a panhuman trait which has brought about far-reaching functional and morphological changes in man as an animal. Perhaps it is, basically. And yet, there would seem to be clear evidence of cultural conditioning here. There is a distinct contrast in the gait of the Shans of Burma versus that of the hill people: the Kachins and the Palaungs keep time to each step by swinging the arms from side to side in front of the body in semicircular movements, but the Shans swing their arms in a straight line and do not bring the arms in front of the body. Experts among the American missionaries can detect the Shan from the Palaung and the Kachin, even though they are dressed in the same kinds of garment, purely from observing their respective gaits, and as surely as the character in a Mark Twain story detected a boy in girl's clothes by throwing a rat-chunker in his lap (the boy closed his legs, whereas a girl would spread her skirt). If an American Indian and an adult American male stride with discernible mechanical differences which may be imputed to the kinds of shoes worn and the varying hardness of the ground in woods or city, the argument will not convince those who know – but would find it hard to describe – that the Singhalese and the Chinese simply and unquestionably just do walk differently, even when both are barefooted. Amazonian tribes show marked sexual contrasts in their styles of walking: men place one foot directly in front of the other, toes straight forward, while women walk in a rather stilted, pigeon-toed fashion, the toes turned inward at an angle of some thirty degrees; it is regarded as a sign of power if the muscles of the thighs are made to come in contact with each other in walking. To pick a more familiar example, it is probable that a great many persons would agree with Sapir's contention that there does exist a peculiarly East European Jewish gait – a kind of kyphotic Ashkenazim shuffle or trudge – which is lost by the very first generation brought up in the United States, and which, moreover, may not be observed in the Sephardic Jews of the Iberian Peninsula. Similar evidence comes from a recent news article: 'Vienna boasts that it has civilized the Russians . . . has taught them how to walk like Europeans (some Russians from the steppes had a curious gait, left arm and left foot swinging forward at the same time).'[22] The last parenthesis plays havoc with behaviouristic notions concerning allegedly quadrupedal engrams behind our 'normal' way of walking!

It is very clear that the would-be 'natural' and 'instinctive' gestures of actors change both culturally and historically. The back-of-the-hand-to-the-forehead and sideways-stagger of the early silent films to express intense emotion is expressed nowadays, for example, by making the already expressionless compulsive sullen mask of the actress one shade still more flat: the former technique of exaggerated pantomime is no doubt related to the limitations of the silent film, the latter to the fact that even a raised eyebrow may travel six feet in the modern close-up. The 'deathless acting' of the immortal Bernhardt, witnessed now in ancient movies, is scarcely more dated than the middle-Garbo style, and hardly more artificially stylized than Hepburn's or Crawford's. Indeed, for whatever reason,

Bernhardt herself is reported to have fainted upon viewing her own acting in an early movie of *Camille*.[23] There are undoubtedly both fashions and individual styles in acting, just as there are in painting and in music composition and performance, and all are surely far removed from the instinctual gesture. The fact that each contemporary audience can receive the communication of the actor's gestures is a false argument concerning the 'naturalness' of that gesture: behaviour of the order of the 'linguistic' (communication in terms of culturally agreed-upon arbitrary symbols) goes far beyond the purely verbal and the spoken.

That this is true can be decisively proved by a glance at Oriental theatrics. Chinese acting is full of stylized gestures which 'mean' to the audience that the actor is stepping over the threshold into a house, mounting a horse, or the like; and these conventionalizations are just as stereotyped as the colours of the acting masks which indicate the formalized personalities of the stock characters, villains or heroes or supernaturals. In Tamil movies made in South India, the audience is quickly informed as to who is the villain and who the hero by the fact that the former wears Europeanized clothing, whereas the latter wears the native *dhoti*. But this is elementary: for the intricate *natya* dancing of India, the postural dance dramas of Bali, and the sacred *hula* of Polynesia are all telling articulated stories in detailed gestural language. That one is oneself illiterate in this language, while even the child or the ignorant countryman sitting beside one on the ground has an avid and understanding enjoyment of the tableau, leaves no doubt in the mind that this *is* a gestural language and that there *are* sublinguistic kinaesthetic symbolisms of an arbitrary but learnable kind.

Hindu movies are extraordinarily difficult for the Occidental man to follow and to comprehend, not only because he must be fortified with much reading and knowledge to recognize mythological themes and such stereotypes as the *deus-ex-machina* appearance of Hanuman the monkey-god, but also because Americans are characteristically illiterate in the area of gesture language. The kinaesthetic 'business' of even accomplished and imaginative stage actors like Sir Laurence Olivier and Ethel Barrymore is limited by the rudimentary comprehension of their audiences. Americans watch enthusiastically the muscular skills of an athlete in *doing* something, but they display a proud muckerism towards the dance as an art form which attempts to *mean* something. There are exceptions to this illiteracy, of course, notably among some psychiatrists and some ethnologists. Dr H. S. Sullivan, for example, is known to many for his acute understanding of the postural tonuses of his patients. Another psychiatrist,

Dr E. J. Kempf, evidences in the copious illustrations of his 'Psychopathology' a highly cultivated sense of the kinaesthetic language of tonuses in painting and sculpture, and can undoubtedly discover a great deal about a patient merely by glancing at him. The linguist, Dr Stanley Newman, has a preternatural skill in recognizing psychiatric syndromes through the individual styles of tempo, stress and intonation.[24] The gifted cartoonist, Mr William Steig, has produced, in *The Lonely Ones*, highly sophisticated and authentic drawings of the postures and tonuses of schizophrenia, depression, mania, paranoia, hysteria, and in fact the whole gamut of psychiatric syndromes. Among anthropologists, Dr W. H. Sheldon is peculiarly sensitive and alert to the emotional and temperamental significance of constitutional tonuses.[25] I believe that it is by no means entirely an illusion that an experienced teacher can come into a classroom of new students and predict with some accuracy the probable quality of individual scholastic accomplishment – even as judged by other professors – by distinguishing the unreachable, unteachable *Apperceptions masse*-less sprawl of one student, from the edge-of-the-seat starved avidity and intentness of another. Likewise, an experienced lecturer can become acutely aware of the body language of his listeners and respond to it appropriately until the room fairly dances with communication and counter-communication, head-noddings and the tenseness of listeners soon to be prodded into public speech.

The 'body language' of speakers in face-to-face conversation may often be seen to subserve the purposes of outright linguistic communication. The peoples of Mediterranean origin have developed this to a high degree. In Argentina,[26] for example, the gesture language of the hands is called *ademanes* or 'with the hands'. Often the signs are in no need of language accompaniment: 'What a crowd!' is stated by forming the fingers into a tight cluster and shaking them before you at eye level; 'Do you take me for a sucker?' is asked by touching just beneath the eye with a finger, accompanying this with appropriate facial expressions of jeering or reproach as the case might be; and 'I haven't the faintest idea' is indicated by stroking beneath the chin with the back of the palm. One Argentine gentleman, reflecting the common notion that *ademanes* have the same vulgarity and undignified nature as slang – appropriate only for youngsters or lower-class folk – nevertheless, within five minutes of this statement, had himself twirled an imaginary moustache ('How swell!') and stroked one hand over the other, nodding his head wisely ('Ah ha! there's hanky-panky going on there somewhere!'). Argentine gesture-language is nearly as automatic and unconscious as spoken language itself, for when one attempts to collect a 'vocabulary' of *ademanes*, the

Argentine has to stop and think of situations first which recall the *ademanes* that 'naturally' follow. The naturalness of at least one of these might be disputed by Americans, for the American hand-gesture meaning 'go away' (palm out and vertical), elbow somewhat bent, arm extended vigorously as the palm is bent to a face-downward horizontal position (somewhat as a baseball is thrown and in a manner which could be rationalized as a threatened or symbolic blow or projectile-hurling), is the same which in Buenos Aires would serve to summon half the waiters in a restaurant, since it means exactly the opposite, 'Come here!' When the Argentines use the word *mañana* in the familiar sense of the distant and improbable future, they accompany the word by moving the hand forward, palm down, and extending the fingers lackadaisically – a motion which is kinaes-thetically and semantically related perhaps to the Argentine 'come here!' since this symbolically *brings*, while *mañana pushes off*. Kissing the bunched fingertips, raising them from the mouth and turning the head with rolled or closed eyes, means 'Wonderful! Magnificent!', basically perhaps as a comment or allusion to a lady, but in many remotely derived senses as well. 'Wonderful!' may also be expressed by shaking one of the hands smartly so that the fingers make an audible clacking sound, similar to the snapping of the fingers, but much louder. But this gesture may signify pain as well as enjoyment, for if one steps on an Argentine's toes, he may shake his fingers as well as saying *Ai yai!* for 'ouch!' The same gesture, furthermore, can be one of impatience, 'Get a move on!' Were one to define this gesture semantically, then, in a lexicon of *ademanes*, it would have to be classified as a nondescript intensificative adverb whose predication is indicated by the context. In fast repartee an Argentine, even though he may not be able to get a word in edgewise, can make caustic and devastating critiques of the speaker and his opinions, solely through the subtle, timed use of *ademanes*.

A study of conventional gesture languages (including even those obscene ones of the *mano cornuta*, the thumbed nose, the *mano fica*, the thumbnail snapped out from the point of the canine tooth, and so forth,[27] as well as those more articulated ones of the Oriental dance dramas), a study of the body language of constitutional types (the uncorticated, spinal-reflex spontaneity and *legato* feline quality of the musclebound athletosome, his body knit into rubbery bouncing ton-uses even in repose; the collapsed colloid quality of the epicurean viscerotonic whose tensest tonus is at best no more than that of the chorion holding the yolk advantageously centered in the albumen of an egg, or the muscle habituated into a tendon supporting a flitch of bacon; and the multiple-vectored, tangled-stringiness of the complex 'high-strung' cerebrotonic, whose conceptual alternatives and nuances of control are so intricately involved in his cortex as to inhibit action), and the study of psychiatric types (the Egyptian-statue grandeur and hauteur of the paranoiac's pose; the catatonic who offers his motor control to the outsider because he has withdrawn his own executive ego into an inner, autistic cerebral world and has left no one at the switchboard; the impermanent, varying, puppet-on-a-string, spastic tonuses of the compulsive neurotic which picture myotonically his ambivalence, his rigidities and his perfectionism; the broken-lute despair of the depressive; and the distractable, *staccato*, canine, benzedrine-muscledness of the manic) – all might offer us new insights into psychology, psychiatry, ethnology and linguistics alike.

Notes

1. The notorious Massey murder in Hawaii arose from the fact that a native beach boy perhaps understandably mistook the Occidental 'flirting' of a white woman for a *bona fide* sexual invitation. On the other hand, there are known cases which have ended in the death of American ethnographers who misread the cultural signs while in the field.

2. E. B. HOLT, *Animal Drive and the Learning Process*, New York, 1931, p. 111, and personal conversations.

The idea is originally Darwin's, I believe (Charles Darwin, *The Expression of the Emotions in Man and Animals*, New York, 1872), but he himself pointed out that the lateral shake of the head is by no means universally the sign of negation. Holt has further noted the interesting point that in a surprising number of languages, quite unrelated to each other, the word for 'mother' is a variant of the sound 'ma'. One can collect dozens of such instances, representing all the continents, which would seem to confirm his conjecture: the genuinely universal 'sucking reflex' which brings the lips into approximation (m), plus the simplest of the simple open vowel sounds (a), are 'recognized' by the mother as referring to her when the baby first pronounces them; hence they become the lexical designation of the maternal parent. Although this phenomenon becomes a linguistic one, it is only on some such physiological basis that one can explain the recurrence of the identical sound combinations in wholly unrelated languages referring to the same person, the mother. But there is no absolute semantic association involved: one baby boy I have observed used 'mama' both to connote and to denote older persons of either sex.

3. A. H. S. LANDOR, *Alone with the Hairy Ainu*, London, 1893, pp. 6, 233–4.

4. W. W. SKEAT and C. O. BLAGDEN, *Pagan Races of the Malay Peninsula*, 2 vols., London, 1906.

5. OTTO KLINEBERG, *Race Differences*, New York, 1935, p. 282.

6. GEOFFREY GORER, *Africa Dances*, New York, 1935, p. 10.

7. LAFCADIO HEARN, 'The Japanese smile', *Glimpses of Unfamiliar Japan*, 2 vols., New York, 1894, quoted in Klineberg, op. cit.

8. *Report on the Cambridge Expedition to the Torres Straits*, ed. A. C. Haddon, 5 vols., Cambridge, 1904, vol. IV, p. 306; Thomas Whiffen, *The North West Amazons*, London, 1905, p. 259.

9. R. HITCHCOCK, 'The Ainos of Yezo', *Papers on Japan*, pp. 464–5. See also Landor, loc. cit.

10. J. PERKINS, 'Journal of a tour from Oroomish to Mosul, through the Koordish Mountains, and a visit to the ruins of Nineveh', *Journal of the American Oriental Society*, 2 (1851), 101; Charles Hose and William MacDougall, *The Pagan Tribes of Borneo*, 2 vols., London, 1912, vol. I, pp. 124–5.

11. A. R. RADCLIFFE-BROWN, *The Andaman Islanders*, Cambridge, 1922, pp. 117, 74n.1.

12. JOHN TURNBULL, *A Voyage Round the World*, London, 1813, pp. 301–2.

13. GORER, op. cit., p. 38. Cf. Hollis, *The Masai, Their Language and Folklore*, Oxford, 1905, pp. 284–7; E. Torday and T. A. Joyce, *Notes éthnographiques sur les peuples communément appelés Bakuba, ainsi que sur les peuplades apparentées, les Bushonga*, Brussels, 1910, pp. 233–4, 284, *passim*. West Africans have developed the etiquette and protocol of greeting to a high degree, adjusting it to sex, age, relative rank, relationship degrees, and the like. Probably there is more than a trace of this ceremoniousness surviving in American Negro greetings in the South.

14. KLINEBERG, op. cit., pp. 286–7, citing J. Lubbock, *Prehistoric Times*, New York, 1872; E. Best, *The Maori*, 2 vols., Wellington, N.Z., 1924; R. H. Lowie, *Are We Civilized?*, New York, 1929; and Hollis, op. cit., p. 315.

15. *Chin P'ing Mei*, Shanghai, n.d., introduction by Arthur Waley. The sixteenth-century Chinese also had the expressions to act 'with seven hands and eight feet' for awkwardness, and 'to sweat two handfuls of anxiety'.

16. S. M. SHIROKOGOREFF, *Social Organization of the Manchus*, extra vol. III, North China Branch, Royal Asiatic Society, Shanghai, 1924, pp. 122–3.

17. M. C. KAHN, 'Notes on the Saramaccaner Bush Negroes of Dutch Guiana', *American Anthropology*, 31 (1929), 473.

18. GEORGE C. VAILLANT, *The Aztecs of Mexico*, Garden City, New York, 1941, plate 7, top.

19. ibid., plate 24.

20. ibid., plates 42, 57, 61.

21. WESTON LABARRE, *The Aymara Indians of the Lake Titicaca Plateau*, Memoir 68, American Anthropological Association, Menasha, Wisconsin, 1947. All the tribes of the Provincia Oriental of Ecuador had the 'cluck of satisfaction' (Alfred Simpson, *Travels in the Wilds of Ecuador and Exploration of the Putumayo River*, 1886, p. 94), which among the tribes of the Issa and Japura rivers is a 'sign of assent and pleasure' (Whiffen, op. cit., p. 249).

22. PAULA HOFFMAN, 'Twilight in the Heldenplatz', *Time*, 49, 23 (9 June 1947), 31. A related kind of motor habit – which is of course conscious – was that of the Plains Indian men who wore the buffalo robe 'gathered . . . about the person in a way that emphasized their action or the expression of emotion' (*Handbook of American Indians North of Mexico*, Bulletin 30, Bureau of American Ethnology, Washington, D.C., 1907–10; 2 vols.). For the Amazonians, see Whiffen, op. cit., p. 271.

23. MAURICE BARDÈCHE and ROBERT BRASILLACH, *The History of Motion Pictures*, New York, 1938, p. 130.

24. STANLEY S. NEWMAN, 'Personal symbolism in language patterns', *Psychiatry*, 2 (1939), 177–84; 'Cultural and psychological features in English intonation', *Transactions New York Academy of Sciences*, ser. II, 7 (1944), 45–54; (with Vera G. Mather), 'Analysis of spoken language of patients with affective disorders', *American Journal of Psychiatry*, 94 (1938), 913–42; 'Further experiments in phonetic symbolism', *American Journal of Psychology*, 45 (1933), 53–7; 'Behavior patterns in linguistic structure, a case history' in *Language, Culture and Personality, Essays in Honor of Edward Sapir*, Menasha, Wis., 1931, pp. 94–106. The Witoto and Bororo have a curious motor habit: 'When an Indian talks he sits down – no conversation is ever carried on when the speakers are standing unless it is a serious difference of opinion

under discussion; nor, when he speaks, does the Indian look at the person addressed, any more than the latter watches the speaker. Both look at some outside objects. This is the attitude also of the Indian when addressing more than one listener, so that he appears to be talking to someone not visibly present.' A story-teller turns his back on the listener and talks to the wall of the hut (Whiffen, op. cit., p. 254).

25. W. H. SHELDON, *The Varieties of Temperament*, New York and London, 1942. The argument of one variety of athletosome or somatotonic scientist that Sheldon is unable or unconcerned to muscle his findings into manageable, manipulable statistical forms wherewith to bludgeon and compel the belief of the unperceiving, is of course peculiarly irrelevant. The psychiatrist soaked in clinical experience is similarly helpless in his didactic relations with a public which either has not, or cannot, or will not see what he has repeatedly observed clinically.

26. ARTHUR DANIELS, 'Hand-made repartee', *New York Times*, 5 October 1941.

27. The only place I have seen this discussed recently is in an article by Sandor Feldman, 'The blessing of the Kohenites', *American Imago*, 2 (1941), 315–18. In the same periodical is an exquisitely sensitive interpretation of one person's interpretation of the signs of the zodiac in terms of positions and tonuses of the human body (Doris Webster, 'The origin of the signs of the zodiac', *American Imago*, 1 (1940), 31–47). Other papers of the few which could be cited with relevance to the present problem would include: Macdonald Critchley, *The Language of Gesture*, Arnold, 1939; G. W. Allport and P. E. Vernon, *Studies in Expressive Movement* (1933), Hafner, New York, 1968; F. C. Hayes, 'Should we have a dictionary of gestures?', *Southern Folk-Lore Quarterly*, 4 (1940), 239–45; Felix Deutsch, 'Analysis of postural behavior', *Psychoanalytical Quarterly*, 16 (1947), 195–213; Paul Schilder, *The Image and Appearance of the Human Body: Studies of the Constructive Energies in the Psyche*, Psyche Monographs, London, 1935; International Universities Press, New York, 1935, 1950; T. Pear, 'Suggested parallels between speaking and clothing', *Acta Psychologica*, 1 (1935), 191–201; J. C. Flugel, 'On the mental attitude to present-day clothing', *British Journal of Medical Psychology*, 9 (1929), 97; La Meri, *Gesture Language of the Hindu Dance*, New York, c.1940; Rudolf von Laban, *Laban's Dance Notations*, New York, c.1928.

David Efron:

Gesture, Race and Culture: A tentative study of some of the spatio-temporal and 'linguistic' aspects of the gestural behaviour of Eastern Jews and Southern Italians in New York City, living under similar as well as different environmental conditions (excerpts)

Mouton, The Hague, 1972.

David Efron's Gesture, Race and Culture (*previously published as* Gesture and Environment, *King's Crown Press, Morningside Heights,*

N.Y., 1941) is a classic study of bodily expression. Kluckhohn has described it as 'conclusive proof' that gestural expression is learnt, cultural and social.

After a theoretical and historical introduction, Efron explains the special problem and method which constitute the core of his book. His problem is simply whether the gestural expressions of Jews and Italians in New York City change as they become assimilated into American society and culture. After comparing the gestural systems of the two groups (see Chapter 7), Efron concludes that the gestures of these two groups do change and that they change in proportion to the degree of social and cultural assimilation. This has been interpreted by anthropologists to imply that bodily expression is learnt and not inherited as Darwin and others have argued. It needs bearing in mind, however, that Darwin and Efron were dealing with two separate aspects of bodily expression: the former with facial expression and the latter with manual gesturing.

Below are:

1. A quotation from Franz Boas's foreword to Efron's book (p. 20).

2. Efron's statement of his problem and material (pp. 65–6).

3. Efron's conclusions (pp. 159–60).

A quotation from Franz Boas's foreword

The present publication deals with the problem of gesture habits from the point of view of their cultural or biological conditioning. The trend of this investigation as well as that of the other subjects investigated indicate that, as far as physiological and psychological functioning of the body is concerned, the environment has such fundamental influence that in larger groups, particularly in the subdivisions of the white race, the genetic element may be ruled out entirely or almost entirely as a determining factor. This does not preclude that individually a biological element may be of importance in regard to many aspects of anatomical form and partly also of behaviour, but the great variations of genetic characteristics in members of each group make it, so far as these are concerned, an insignificant factor. The behaviour of the individual depends upon his own anatomical and physiological make-up, over which is superimposed the important influence of the social and geographic environment in which he lives.

Efron's statement of his problem and material

The problem

The object of our investigation was (a) to discover whether there are any standardized group differences in the gestural behaviour of two different 'racial' groups, and if so, (b) to determine what becomes of these gestural patterns in members and descendants of the same groups under the impact of social assimilation.

The material

The scene of our investigation was chiefly New York City. Part of the study was also carried out at several summer resorts in the Adirondacks, the Catskills, and the town of Saratoga.

Among the various groups available for study the following were selected: Eastern Jews (of Lithuanian and Polish origin) and Southern Italians (from the vicinity of Naples and from Sicily). In each case the specific ethnic extraction of the individual was established by noting the particular dialect used. In doubtful cases this was supplemented by direct interrogation after the gestural behaviour had been recorded.

For the first of the two questions involved in our inquiry, 'traditional'* Jewish and Italian subjects were used. For the second, 'assimilated'† individuals of the same descent.

All our material was obtained in absolutely spontaneous situations in the everyday environments of the people concerned, who never knew that they were subjects of an investigation.

The material was secured at the following places: 'Traditional' Jews: the lower East Side (streets, parks, markets, theatres, synagogues, homes, restaurants and social meetings); also the orthodox Jewish Yeshiva College (Amsterdam Avenue at 188th Street). 'Traditional' Italians: 'Little Italy' (streets, parks, markets, restaurants, social meetings, homes and public games); also Southern Italian meetings at the Teatro Venezia (7th Avenue at 59th Street). 'Assimilated' Jews: summer resorts in the Adirondacks and the Catskills, Saratoga race-track and hotels, Columbia University (students and professors), City College (students), Townsend Harris High School (students),

* By 'traditional' is meant both foreign and American-born individuals who have retained the language and mores of the original group, remaining relatively impervious to the influence of the American environment.

† By 'assimilated' is meant those individuals of the same descent who have more or less broken away from the customs of their respective original groups, identifying their general behaviour with that of the American.

Fieldston Ethical Culture School (students), Syracuse University (students), Temple Emanu-El, New York City (Junior Society), West Side Jewish restaurants, social gatherings, homes, political meetings (Jewish-American speakers), and the Board of Aldermen (Jewish-American speakers). *'Assimilated'* Italians: Columbia University (students), Casa Italiana, Columbia University (student fraternity meetings and gatherings of Italian-American societies), City College (students), homes, political gatherings (Italo-American speakers).

Efron's conclusions

Generally speaking our findings may be summarized as follows: Both from the standpoint of number of people gesturing and of frequency and manner of gesticulation in those people who do gesture, the assimilated Eastern Jews and the assimilated Southern Italians in New York City (a) *appear to differ greatly from their respective traditional groups*, and (b) *appear to resemble each other*.

The data obtained on the assimilated groups seem to indicate that the gestural 'characteristics' found in the traditional Jew or traditional Italian disappear with the social assimilation of the individual, Jew or Italian, into the so-called Americanized community. On the whole, gesticulation appears to be less frequent in such assimilated groups, there being a diminution of movement as compared with the traditional groups. The more assimilated the individual, the less Jewish or Italian gestural traits was he found to possess. The fully assimilated Jews (as, for instance, the Temple Emanu-El youngsters) and Italians do not show the wide differences found in the traditional groupings and both resemble gesturally the specific American group to which they have become assimilated. In general the gestural assimilation of the Jews appears to be conditioned by the particular social and economic stratum to which they have become adapted. Thus, certain Jewish groups of the upper social strata show great restraint in their motions, when movement is present at all, even when engaged in heated argument, and resemble gesturally the so-called Anglo-Saxons of the same or similar socioeconomic environment. On the other hand, assimilated Jewish groups belonging to a different social milieu may exhibit gestural movement in conversation, although unlike that of the traditional Jewish groups.

The differences in gestural behaviour between traditional groups and the lack of such differences between assimilated groups cannot be explained in terms of immigrant versus American-born. It was found, for example, that the American-born students at Yeshiva College, a traditional Jewish school in New York City, exhibited traditional gestural behaviour similar to that found in the ghetto, while the American-born Jewish subjects obtained at an exclusive Fifth Avenue club were gesturally assimilated, showing no 'orthodox-Jewish' gestural characteristics.

Lastly our observations of 'hybrid' gesticulation indicate that the same individual may, if simultaneously exposed over a period of time to two or more gesturally different groups, adopt and combine certain gestural traits of both groups.

These results, tentative as they are, point to the fact that gestural behaviour, or the absence of it, is, to some extent at least, conditioned by factors of a socio-psychological nature (the question as to what specific factor may have been operative in patterning each of the gestural characteristics described above goes beyond the scope of this book and calls for a separate, and probably very difficult, inquiry). They certainly do not bear out the contention that this form of behaviour is determined by biological descent. They have been presented here for what they may be worth, in the expectation that they will stimulate further investigation in this particular field.

2. Is Bodily Expression Universal or Relative?

38. 'The two figures differ markedly in postural tonus. The one on the left (the "Slopper"), with rounded shoulders and legs which are not fully extended, can be seen to be unresponsive; he might in addition be depressed, drowsy or even ill. The Scout on the right is ready at any moment to respond. An appropriate facial expression would make him threatening, instead of merely confident.' Picture from R. Baden-Powell, *Scouting for Boys*, Arthur Pearson, 1929. Caption and picture in R. J. Andrew, 'The information potentially available in mammal displays', in R. A. Hinde, ed., *Nonverbal Communications*, Cambridge University Press, 1972, pp. 179–206.

Intertwined with Darwin's hypothesis that bodily expression in man and animals is inherited, was and is an assumption that bodily expression is universal – that all of the world's peoples exhibit the same physical expressions. For Darwin, the later issue of universality was important only as a proof that bodily expression is inherited and not learned (see Chapter 1). Since *The Expression of the Emotions in Man and Animals* was written, the question of the universality of bodily expression has become a somewhat separate and distinct subject of investigation, and a debate has evolved between the 'universalists' and the 'relativists' – the relativistic argument being usually expressed by social scientists, particularly ethnographers.

Darwin had originally approached the problem of universality in a very anthropological manner by dispatching a questionnaire to British persons living in remote parts of the world (see below). In this regard, Darwin might be considered a pioneer of ethnographic field methods. But since he sent out his questionnaire, the issue of whether bodily expression is universal (read: the same in all societies throughout the world) or relative (read: cross-culturally variable) has developed into a perhaps unnecessary and somewhat misguided debate between social scientists and students of animal behaviour. It may well be the case that the entire debate is fruitless since it is by no means clear precisely what type of data could possibly serve to resolve the issues. Present research has still to adequately overcome the problems of method which confronted Darwin. The question of the *interpretation* of the meanings ascribed to bodily expression, for example, remains a particularly frustrating problem. How could those who responded to Darwin's questionnaire be certain that the natives whom they observed attached the same interpretations or meanings to the movements of facial muscles that they themselves did? And there are many within the social sciences who would argue that we are no closer to dealing with this problem of interpretation than were Darwin and his helpers. However, some clarification of the problem has come from a division of the issue of universality into two separate questions:

1. Do all of the world's peoples make the same muscular movements which we do when we communicate non-verbally?
2. Do all of the world's peoples attach the same symbolic or communicative meanings to these muscular movements as we do?

This division has a precedent in Hertz's handling of the subject of right-handedness (see Chapter 1), but instead of resolving the debate, the division has primarily served only to transform a single debate into two separate (but still confusing) debates. Often social and cultural anthropologists have devoted themselves to the first question without considering that their research is operating outside the bounds of sociological or socio-cultural anthropological theories and methods. And students of physical anthropology, ethnology, animal communication, etc. have often delved into the problem of the interpretation of the meaning of bodily expression without fully appreciating the methodological and theoretical problems involved in the study of human social non-verbal expression. This is hardly surprising in light of the fact that social scientists have themselves often chosen to ignore the problems of interpretation and to side-step the task of 'getting into the native's head'. And this is not very surprising either, since the problem of the interpretation of the meanings natively attached to bodily expression is all too central to the criticism of ethnographic field methods raised by ethno-scientists and others.

There is not room here to go into this problem in any detail but a simple illustration might be appropriate. Let us say that we are government administrators residing in Bongo-bongo land. We receive in the post a questionnaire from a certain C. Darwin. He asks us: 'When in good spirits do the eyes [of the natives] sparkle, with the skin a little wrinkled round and under them, and with the mouth a little drawn back at the corners?' We look around Bongo-bongo land and are about to reply in the affirmative when it occurs to us that it is just possible that although we have often observed the muscular movements of the eyes and mouth that Darwin describes, we may have been in error ever since we arrived in interpreting these movements as being reflective of a state of 'good spirits'. Unlike Darwin's helpers we resolve to actually *ask* a native of Bongo-bongo land if in fact he is in good spirits when he moves his facial muscles in the described fashion. Now the problem is a linguistic one and we cannot be certain that given the peculiar language of Bongo-bongo land it is possible to accurately translate the term 'good spirits' into native speech. After all, we cannot assume that the distinction happy/sad is itself universal. Furthermore, we have (since Darwin's letter arrived) begun to notice that the natives of this strange land seem to communicate a great range of complex information by using the muscles of the face which the British (that is, upper-class, educated British people like Charles Darwin) use in order to express a simple state of 'good spirits'. We give up on the questionnaire, never reply to Darwin, never get mentioned in his book (he thanks everyone on pages 19 to 26) and are forced to leave our government posts when we admit to our superiors that we could never begin to communicate with a group of people who communicate with each other by using complex combinations of movements of facial muscles. (Never, of course, suspecting that even back in England it is not as simple as C. Darwin would have us believe.)

Aside from a certain feeling of hopelessness at the impossible task of 'getting inside the native's head' and interpreting *as he does* his bodily expressions, one thing is clear – the only hope of approaching a valid understanding of the interpretative meaning of the bodily expressions of peoples from cultures other than our own is by study-ing facial expression, gestures, postures, etc. from *within* the social context, and *through* the social customs, world-view, status and role arrangements, etc. of the society in question.

In this regard, it is interesting to compare the two articles which follow the excerpts taken from Darwin's work. Both authors, Gordon Hewes and Raymond Firth, take posture (rather than facial expres-sion – Darwin's primary concern) as the subject of their research.

Hewes indexes and compares postures throughout the world. Firth compares postures (*and* the meanings natively attached to them) in Tikopia with postures and their respective social meanings in Britain. Hewes addresses himself to the first question of universality – the question of whether bodily expression is *physically* variable in various socio-cultural contexts. His evidence points towards a relativistic and anti-universalistic position, but in taking on the subject of posture rather than facial expression, and in not directly addressing himself to the ethologists, Hewes makes his research somewhat irrelevant to the 'universalists'' debate which has focused on specific facial expressions and which has evolved its own language and form of discussion. Firth's research, on the other hand, is aimed at the second question of universality – that of the variability of the meanings attached to the variability of physical postures which Hewes outlines so thoroughly. Research such as Firth's points the way towards more properly *sociological* analysis of postures, gestures and expression: his study integrates postural variability and factors of socio-cultural variability. From research of this type might emerge a new understanding of the term 'universal' so as to allow for the possibility of learned, socio-cultural universal correlations of bodily expression and sociocultural characteristics.

Charles Darwin:
The Expression of the Emotions in Man and Animals (excerpts)

First published in 1872; republished in 1965, ed. Francis Darwin, University of Chicago Press, Phoenix Books, Chicago, Ill. and London, pp. 14–17, 359–60, and plates 1, 2 and 3.

In Chapter 1 I presented quotes from The Expression of the Emotions in Man and Animals *which deal with the question of whether bodily expression is genetically inherited or learned. The two quotes presented in this section, on the other hand, relate to the question of whether bodily expression is universal or relative. The first quote is taken from Darwin's introduction and the second is taken from his conclusion.*

Introduction

It seemed to me highly important to ascertain whether the same expressions and gestures prevail, as has often been asserted without much evidence, with all the races of mankind, especially with those who have associated but little with Europeans. Whenever the same movements of the features or body express the same emotions in several distinct races of man, we may infer with much probability, that such expressions are true ones – that is, are innate or instinctive. Conventional expressions or gestures, acquired by the individual during early life, would probably have differed in the different races, in the same manner as do their languages. Accordingly I circulated, early in the year 1867, the following printed queries with a request, which has been fully responded to, that actual observations, and not memory, might be trusted. These queries were written after a considerable interval of time, during which my attention had been otherwise directed, and I can now see that they might have been greatly improved. To some of the later copies, I appended, in manuscript, a few additional remarks:

1. Is astonishment expressed by the eyes and mouth being opened wide, and by the eyebrows being raised?
2. Does shame excite a blush when the colour of the skin allows it to be visible? and especially how low down the body does the blush extend?
3. When a man is indignant or defiant does he frown, hold his body and head erect, square his shoulders and clench his fists?
4. When considering deeply on any subject, or trying to understand any puzzle, does he frown, or wrinkle the skin beneath the lower eyelids?
5. When in low spirits, are the corners of the mouth depressed, and the inner corner of the eyebrows raised by that muscle which the French call the 'Grief muscle'? The eyebrow in this state becomes slightly oblique, with a little swelling at the inner end; and the forehead is transversely wrinkled in the middle part, but not across the whole breadth, as when the eyebrows are raised in surprise.
6. When in good spirits do the eyes sparkle, with the skin a little wrinkled round and under them, and with the mouth a little drawn back at the corners?
7. When a man sneers or snarls at another, is the corner of the upper lip over the canine or eye tooth raised on the side facing the man whom he addresses?
8. Can a dogged or obstinate expression be recognized, which is

chiefly shown by the mouth being firmly closed, a lowering brow and a slight frown?

9. Is contempt expressed by a slight protrusion of the lips and by turning up the nose, and with a slight expiration?

10. Is disgust shown by the lower lip being turned down, the upper lip slightly raised, with a sudden expiration, something like incipient vomiting, or like something spit out of the mouth?

11. Is extreme fear expressed in the same general manner as with Europeans?

12. Is laughter ever carried to such an extreme as to bring tears into the eyes?

13. When a man wishes to show that he cannot prevent something being done, or cannot himself do something, does he shrug his shoulders, turn inwards his elbows, extend outwards his hands and open the palms; with the eyebrows raised?

14. Do the children when sulky, pout or greatly protrude the lips?

15. Can guilty, or sly, or jealous expressions be recognized? though I know not how these can be defined.

16. Is the head nodded vertically in affirmation, and shaken laterally in negation?

Observations on natives who have had little communication with Europeans would be of course the most valuable, though those made on any natives would be of much interest to me. General remarks on expression are of comparatively little value; and memory is so deceptive that I earnestly beg it may not be trusted. A definite description of the countenance under any emotion or frame of mind, with a statement of the circumstances under which it occurred, would possess much value.

To these queries I have received thirty-six answers from different observers, several of them missionaries or protectors of the aborigines, to all of whom I am deeply indebted for the great trouble which they have taken, and for the valuable aid thus received. I will specify their names, etc., towards the close of this chapter, so as not to interrupt my present remarks. The answers relate to several of the most distinct and savage races of man. In many instances, the circumstances have been recorded under which each expression was observed, and the expression itself described. In such cases, much confidence may be placed in the answers. When the answers have been simply yes or no, I have always received them with caution. It follows, from the information thus acquired, that the same state of mind is expressed throughout the world with remarkable uniformity; and this fact is in itself interesting as evidence of the close similarity in bodily structure and mental disposition of all the races of mankind.

Conclusion

I have endeavoured to show in considerable detail that all the chief expressions exhibited by man are the same throughout the world. This fact is interesting, as it affords a new argument in favour of the several races being descended from a single parent-stock, which must have been almost completely human in structure, and to a large extent in mind, before the period at which the races diverged from each other. No doubt similar structures, adapted for the same purpose, have often been independently acquired through variation and natural selection by distinct species; but this view will not explain close similarity between distinct species in a multitude of unimportant details. Now if we bear in mind the numerous points of structure having no relation to expression, in which all the races of man closely agree, and then add to them the numerous points, some of the highest importance and many of the most trifling value, on which the movements of expression directly or indirectly depend, it seems to me improbable in the highest degree that so much similarity, or rather identity of structure, could have been acquired by independent means. Yet this must have been the case if the races of man are descended from several aboriginally distinct species. It is far more probable that the many points of close similarity in the various races are due to inheritance from a single parent-form, which had already assumed a human character.

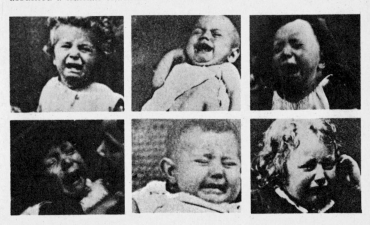

39. Weeping.

40. Obliquity of the eyebrows. (Top row: normal. Bottom row: oblique.)

41. Joy. (Bottom row: Left, 'usual passive condition'; Centre, 'smiling naturally'; Right, 'unnatural smile caused by galvanization'.)

Gordon Hewes:
'*World distribution of certain postural habits*' (excerpts)

From *American Anthropologist*, 57 (n.s.), (1955), 231–44. The article appears here in edited form. Only material from the following pages has been used: 231–3, 241–4.

Gordon Hewes has written two articles on the subject of posture with which I am familiar. Below is an edited version of his article which appeared in the American Anthropologist: *I have edited out the rather detailed centre section which simply lists, describes and geographically locates various separate postures. The other article, 'The anthropology of posture', appeared in* Scientific American (*196 (February 1957), 123– 32) and is quite similar to that part of the* American Anthropologist *article which is presented here. Both articles deal with what Hewes calls 'the borderline between culture and biology' and as such provide a response to Darwin's research and to the work of those who have followed in the universalist tradition.*

For a long time it has been suspected that certain standing and sitting postures might be culturally significant.[1] Although some[2] have doubted that such behaviours are consistent enough to enable anyone to draw useful conclusions about them, others have not hesitated to deal in systematic fashion with the postural habits of particular cultures.[3] For example, following a discussion of Mohave sitting postures, Kroeber[4] asserted, 'this [posture] is one of the most interesting matters in the whole range of customs . . .' However, in spite of this interest, there have been almost no attempts to bring the scattered data together into a comprehensive worldwide framework. Mauss's 'Les techniques du corps' was a stimulating program for such an undertaking – nothing more.

Human postural habits have anatomical and physiological limitations, but there are a great many choices, the determinants for which appear to be mostly cultural. The number of significantly different body attitudes capable of being maintained steadily is probably of the order of one thousand. Certain postures may occur in all cultures without exception, and may form a part of our basic hominid heritage. The upright stance with arms at the sides, or with hands clasped in the midline over the lower abdomen, certainly belongs in this category. A fourth of mankind habitually squats in a fashion very similar to the squatting position of the chimpanzee, and the rest of us might squat this way too if we were not trained to use other postures beyond infancy. Anthropoid postures may shed some light on the problem of which human ones are most likely to be 'natural' or pre-cultural, although ape limb proportions would deter us from relying too heavily on such evidence.

Of factors which affect postures, aside from the biological substrata, we might start with sex-differentiating conditions such as pregnancy and lactation, which possibly render certain sitting positions more frequent among adult females, and nutritional conditions (not wholly independent of culture), which may determine the amount of fat accumulated in posturally strategic parts of the body. Fear of genital exposure, whatever its etiology, seems to play an important role in postural customs (or at least in their rationale) in many cultures. Clothing and footgear, such as heavy boots and tight-fitting skirts, doubtless exert their effects on ways of sitting. Artificial supports – whether logs, rocks, stools, pillows, back-rests, benches or chairs – are highly significant, with complex histories and manifold cultural interconnections. There is also a relation of types of house-construction to posture.

The influence of techniques and activities like textile-weaving, fire-making, wood-carving, food-grinding, playing of musical instruments, canoe-paddling or the use of gaming devices, all requiring the maintenance of particular bodily attitudes, cannot be denied. Nearly every new tool or machine must be adjusted to some body posture or sequence of postures. The push-button represents the ultimate attenuation of environmental control through postural adjustments; vocal-cord vibration to actuate servomechanisms, though still neuromuscular, cannot be described as postural.

Terrain and vegetation may influence out-of-door sitting or standing habits. In some regions the existence of high grass may force herdsmen to watch their flocks from a standing position, whereas in a short-grass or tundra region herders may watch the stock while squatting or sitting down. In our own culture, moist, snowy or muddy ground clearly inhibits sitting down, whereas a reasonably dry lawn may invite us to do so.[5]

Habitual excretory or burial postures may become tabooed in other situations. It is altogether possible that the rarity of the deep squat in our culture is due to this kind of repression.

Finally, several writers suggest that infant-carrying customs may affect the postural maturational sequence, and the ease or difficulty with which children or adults can assume certain postures. If tight swaddling or cradling can influence later postural habits to anything like the degree that some authorities have claimed is the case with personality, the effects on sitting and standing behaviours should be indeed remarkable.

Some other ramifications of the cross-cultural study of postural habits can only be touched upon. Animal research on the infra-primate level seems unlikely to yield much of direct interest, since Magnus,[6] DeKleyn and Sherrington have shown how the primitive postural reflexes are normally suppressed by cortical centres in the higher mammals. Bull[7] and others have been working on the relation of reflex-related postural tensions and emotion, however, and there is a psychiatric interest in posture exemplified by the work of Schilder,[8] Feldenkrais[9] and Quackenbos.[10] *Psychological Abstracts* contains about forty items dealing with the relationships of bodily posture to such diverse topics as visual acuity, lateral dominance, psychoanalysis, fatigue and metabolic rate. Research on the metabolic efficiency of various postures has to date been restricted, because of our cultural traditions, to standing, chair-sitting and recumbent positions.[11]

The foregoing remarks suggest that anthropologists and others with opportunities to make cross-cultural observations of human postural habits could organize their data in terms of several levels of relevance. The first level is that of applied physical anthropology or 'biotechnology'.[12] In recent years, the demands of machine and vehicle design have stimulated research in an interdisciplinary field where information on postural habits in different cultures might be very useful. Human engineers might profitably experiment with postural patterns borrowed from outside our own cultural tradition.

The second level of relevance is that of functional inter-relations of postures and non-postural cultural phenomena, discussed above in connection with techniques and activities, terrain and vegetation, clothing, status and role differences, etc. Are there cross-cultural regularities in these functional relationships? Some of the data to follow suggest that there are.

A third level concerns psychological and psychiatric implications of postural behaviours. Findings in this area would of course feed back to the applied anthropology and physiology level.

A fourth level of relevance is culture-historical, along the lines indicated by Boas[13] in a discussion of criteria for historical reconstruction: 'Certain motor habits . . . may be stable over long periods.' It is possible that postural habits could be used like other culture elements in reconstructing past diffusions and contacts. The Samoan occurrence of a special cross-legged position (Fig. 42) which is else-where apparently linked with religious diffusions from India into South-East and eastern Asia may be a case in point. More precise determinations of the distributions of various postures might reveal definite blocs of postural tradition which could have deep culture-historical meaningfulness.

A fifth and final level of interest is phylogenetic. The role of postures and their functional inter-relations with environment (cultural as well as non-cultural) seem to have been important. The development of the upright stance and of bipedal locomotion took place well before the simian brain-case and face had been modified into essentially human features,[14] which suggests that standing, sitting, squatting and recumbent postures preceded the emergence of fully human behaviour. Here efforts could be made to bring together the results of studies of anthropoid ape postural behaviours, including those on maturation, on limb bones and joints of the pre- and proto-hominids, and theoretical syntheses such as Orione's,[15] on the inter-connections of eye, hand, posture and symbol-using capacities in mammalian evolution.

In the following discussion, I have recorded information on about one hundred of the commonest postures, chiefly of the sitting, kneeling, crouching and squatting varieties. Only about ten standing positions are included; many upright stances seem to be human universals, for which reason I soon ceased to record information on them. Sleeping or reclining postures have been entirely omitted, owing to the paucity of data.[16] Maturational aspects of posture and the pathology of posture (as in Parkinsonism or catatonic schizophrenia) have not been considered here. Dance positions have also been excluded, perhaps arbitrarily; for the most part they are held for only a few seconds at a time, whereas the attitudes dealt with here are maintained for minutes, at least. Finger and hand gestures, ways of holding the head, facial expressions, the tone of the abdominal musculature and many other interesting aspects of posture have also had to be left out of this paper.

In the middle section of 'World distribution of certain postural habits' Hewes describes and illustrates various postural types and outlines the geographic distribution of each type. Some sample illustrations are presented below and the reader is referred to the American Anthropologist *for the detailed descriptions. Figure 43 shows the world distribution of several of the postures which are drawn in Figure 42. Below are Hewes's concluding remarks.*

In spite of the tentative nature of my information, I think there is good reason to believe that many postures are not only culturally determined, but will exhibit the kinds of geographic distributions we have come to expect for other features of cultural behaviour. While some human postures may be archetypical or precultural, others have probably been

42. 'A portion of the postural typology used in the compilation of data . . . Drawings are for the most part based on photographs in the ethnographic literature. Head and arm positions, unless stated otherwise in the accompanying discussion, are not typologically significant. No. 23, for example, could be standing with his left hand on his hip, or resting it on his left shoulder, and his standing posture would be considered the same for present purposes.'

diffused like other items of culture. A note on the diffusion of a posture (the cross-legged sitting position) comes from Quain's Fiji study, in which he reported that older inland natives of Vanua Levu could recall when this fashion was introduced from Tonga,[17] first as a chiefly prerogative and only later as a custom of commoners.

The extent and vigour of postural etiquette evidently varies from one culture or area to another, with some societies going to great lengths to ensure postural propriety on all public occasions. Many cultures maintain careful distinctions in posture on the basis of sex, and there are others which emphasize age and status considerations in the manner of sitting or standing. Postural conformity is enforced as a rule by the same methods as conformity to other rules of etiquette – by ridicule (mentioned in several sources), verbal scolding or by physical punishment where deviation from the postural norms verges on lese-majesty or deliberate indignity to a superior. While our culture has perhaps relaxed its postural codes since the nineteenth century, certain areas of it preserve archaic postural etiquettes backed up by formidable sanctions, as in the military drill regulations. Postural deviations may also have a positive significance, as Blackwood mentions for the Buka Passage area, Northern Solomons, where a woman who sits with legs stretched out is regarded as openly inviting sexual intercourse.[18]

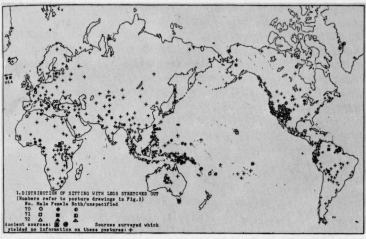

1. DISTRIBUTION OF SITTING WITH LEGS STRETCHED OUT
(Numbers refer to posture drawings in Fig.1)
   No. Male Female Both/unspecified
   70   ○   ◐   ●
   71   □   ◧   ■
   72   △   ▲   ▲
Ancient sources: ▣ ●   Sources surveyed which
yielded no information on these postures: +

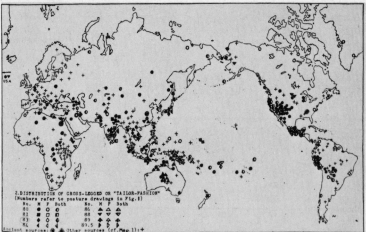

2. DISTRIBUTION OF CROSS-LEGGED OR "TAILOR-FASHION"
(Numbers refer to posture drawings in Fig.1)
   No. M   F   Both   No.   M   F   Both
   80   ●   ○   ◐   86   △   △   ▲
   81   ■   □   ◧   88   ▽   ▽   ▼
   83   ◆   ◇   ◈   89   ▲   ▲   ▲
   84   ◀   ◁   ◀   89.5 ▶   ▷   ▶
Ancient sources: ● ▲ Other sources (cf. Map 1): +

43. Examples of world distribution of various postural types as shown in 'postural typology' in Figure 42.

In our culture, the armament of science has been concentrated on normative efforts directed against a rather narrow band of our common postures, to the general neglect of many other postures which we use more frequently and with greater socio-economic effect. Physiologists, anatomists and orthopaedists, to say nothing of specialists in physical education, have dealt exhaustively with a few 'ideal' postures – principally the fairly rigid attention stance beloved of the drillmaster, and student's or stenographer's habits of sitting at desks. The English postural vocabulary is mediocre – a fact which in itself inhibits our thinking about posture. Quite the opposite is true of the languages of India, where the yoga system has developed an elaborate postural terminology and rationale, perhaps the world's richest.

In conclusion I should like to stress the deficiencies in our scientific concern with postural behaviour, many of which arise simply from the all too common neglect (by non-anthropologists) of cross-cultural data.

Notes

1. MARCEL MAUSS, 'Les techniques du corps', *Journal de psychologie normale et pathologique*, 32 (1935), 271–93.

2. HAROLD DRIVER, 'Culture element distributions: VI, southern Sierra Nevada', University of California Anthropological Records 1, 2 (1937).

3. TATSUKICHI IRIZAWA, 'Nihonjin no suwari-kata ni tsuite', *Shigakuzasshi* 31, 8 (1920–21); Margaret Mead and Frances Cooke Macgregor, *Growth and Culture: A Photographic Study of Balinese Childhood*, G. P. Putnam's Sons, New York, 1951; Flora L. Bailey, 'Navaho motor habits', *American Anthropologist*, 44 (n.s.), 2 (1942), 210–34.

4. A. L. KROEBER, *Handbook of the Indians of California*, Bureau of American Ethnology, Washington, D.C., Bulletin 78 (1925), 728.

5. MAUSS, op. cit., 280, 286.

6. R. MAGNUS, 'Animal posture', *Proceedings of the Royal Society*, 98B (1925), 339–553.

7. NINA BULL, 'The attitude theory of emotion', *Nervous and Mental Disease Monographs*, 81, New York, 1951.

8. PAUL SCHILDER, *The Image and Appearance of the Human Body: Studies of the Constructive Energies in the Psyche*, Paul, Trench, Trubner, 1935.

9. M. FELDENKRAIS, *Body and Mature Behavior: A Study of Anxiety, Sex, Gravitation and Learning*, International Universities Press, New York, 1949.

10. H. M. QUACKENBOS, 'Archetype postures', *Psychiatric Quarterly*, 19 (1945), 589–91.

11. R. H. TEPPER and F. A. HELLEBRANDT, 'The influence of the upright posture on the metabolic rate', *American Journal of Physiology*, 122 (1938), 563–8; Eleanor Larsen, 'The fatigue of standing', *American Journal of Physiology*, 150 (1947), 109–21.

12. ROBERT M. WHITE, 'Applied physical anthropology', *American Journal of Physical Anthropology*, 10 (n.s.), 2 (1952), 193–9; H. T. E. Hertzberg and Gilbert S. Daniels, 'Air Force anthropology', *American Journal of Physical Anthropology*, (n.s.), 2 (1952), 201–8; Barry G. King, 'Measurements of man for making machinery', *American Journal of Physical Anthropology*, 6 (n.s.), 3 (1948), 341–51.

13. FRANZ BOAS, 'Relationships between north-west America and north-east Asia' in Diamond Jenness, ed., *The American Aborigines: Their Origin and Antiquity*, University of Toronto Press, 1933.

14. S. L. WASHBURN, 'The new physical anthropology', *Transactions of the New York Academy of Sciences*, series 2, 13, 7 (1951), 298–304.

15. JULIO ORIONE, *Teoría visual espacial*, N. Zielony, Buenos Aires, 1950.

16. H. R. H. PETER, Prince of Greece and Denmark, 'Peculiar sleeping postures of the Tibetans', *Man*, 53 (1953), 145.

17. BUELL QUAIN, *Fijian Village*, Chicago, University of Chicago Press, 1948, p. 19.

18. BEATRICE BLACKWOOD, *Both Sides of Buka Passage*, Oxford University Press, New York, 1935, p. 125.

References that are mentioned in those sections which have been edited have been removed.

The reader may also want to see A. M. Hocart's 'Methods of sitting' (letter to the editor of Man, *66 (May 1927), 99–100), Gregory Bateson and Margaret Mead's* Balinese Character: A Photographic Analysis *(Special Publications of the Academy of Sciences, vol. II, New York, 1942) as well as sections of Mauss's 'The techniques of the body' (see Chapter 1).*

Raymond Firth:
'Postures and gestures of respect'

From *Échanges et Communications; mélanges offerts à Claude Lévi-Strauss à l'occasion de son 60ème anniversaire,* collected by Jean Pouillon and Pierre Maranda, Mouton, The Hague, 1970, pp. 188–209.

One of the most outstanding contributions to British ethnography is Raymond Firth's research into the customs of the Tikopia of Melanesia. It is particularly valuable, therefore, that Firth has in 'Postures and gestures of respect' given us a detailed account of postures and the meanings which attach to them in Tikopia – valuable in that we now have one society where information is available about the society in general and about posture in particular. The article is presented in full below (except for the opening sentence, which relates to the volume in which it first appeared).

Recent work in ethology has tended to bring home to anthropologists the essentially animal basis of much human behaviour. This is markedly so in regard to posture and gesture. The instrumental use of the human body is important in many technical procedures involved in social relationships. In a rugby football scrum or tackle, in the police control of throngs of people or in boarding a crowded train in the summer holidays, bodily impact and limb movement may be important technical aids in the achievement of social aims. Such procedures may be routinized and as such they may serve as signals, but in the cases I mention their signalling functions are less important than their physical effect. For anthropologists, however, it is the signalling functions of bodily actions which are of most interest.

Posture and gesture are closely related, and historically in English have tended to be equated in some senses. But for convenience they may be broadly distinguished – posture as a structured arrangement of the body in space, a state or position of the body as a whole, and gesture as a structured movement of a part of the body, as e.g. an alteration of position of a limb or head.

Human postural and gestural habits show a great variety, with much cultural determination.[1] In European society gesture is thought of as being made by hands or by head, but over the range of human societies almost any feature of the body may serve. In some Oriental contexts stretching out one's feet towards someone may indicate contempt, but to Europeans this would be a meaningless gesture. In the West the lips are used a great deal for interaction gestures of greeting and affection, but Europeans do not use their noses in this way. Polynesians do not use their lips for interaction,[2] but they do use their noses.

Whereas gesture is commonly regarded as having semantic value, posture is often regarded as being semantically neutral. Gesture is often thought to express emotion, posture to express physical needs. But in fact posture may be as emotionally expressive as gesture. In social terms both posture and gesture, although patterned, may be informal, insignificant, irrelevant, unoriented. A custom of Nilotic men in a relaxed position (occurring also among Australian aborigines and others) is to stand on one leg with the foot sole of the other resting against the side of the knee – a stork-like posture. This posture does not appear to be part of any elaborate, formal sequence. With this may be compared the English army postures of relaxation – 'stand at ease', 'stand easy', which are not only patterned but bear a strict, formal relationship to the contrasting patterns of tension. Again, posture and gesture may be specifically oriented, and this orientation may be of high significance. A modern Roman Catholic practice of the priest facing the congregation in the Mass is felt by many people to be important as indicating greater closeness. In Britain, though said to be popular in poor parishes, it has been a matter of some controversy among the well-educated, some of whom prefer the traditional orientation of the priest to the altar. In such formal conditions posture and gesture are ritualized, constituting part of a routine sequence of behaviour regarded as of social significance and power.[3]

Ethologists, psychologists and communication theorists have contributed significantly to examination of posture and gesture as interaction signals related to situations such as those of dominance and submission. Ethologists in particular have developed sensitive quantitative methods of studying the patterns underlying the diversity of such interaction behaviour, and have begun to apply their findings to the study of non-verbal communication in human beings. Anthropologists might seem to have an advantage in this field since the association of non-verbal behaviour patterns with language gives them a clue to what are regarded as the more significant sets of movements. Lacking such linguistic clues, the ethologist must investigate every detail of behaviour to note the response, whereas the anthropologist can focus on those blocks or configurational units whose significance has been established by linguistic evidence. But this is a field where one needs to go beneath language to the raw material of observation, of non-verbal signs.

While Hertz's essay[4] on right-handedness and left-handedness drew attention to the significance of social, especially ritual, elements in a gesture differentiation often thought to be a matter of biological endowment, and Mauss's synoptic study[5] on the techniques of the use of the human body provided a framework for broad inquiry, few anthropologists have devoted much interest to the subject.[6] (The records of sign-language are in a special category; the signalling code is very specific.) In the more general field the analytical study of posture and gesture has been developed greatly by Birdwhistell[7] as part of his investigation of kinesics. Hewes[8] has examined the distribution of certain major types of posture on a world basis. Hall,[9] under the term 'proxemics', has studied inter-culturally how man unconsciously structures micro-space in his daily transactions and in his technological relationships; Watson and Graves[10] have endeavoured to give quantitative precision to such behaviour by comparative study. In what has been called non-verbal semiotics, there have been few studies of the meaning of posture and gesture in any one society. Among these, the pioneer work of Efron[11] stands out, in its comparison of characteristic gestures of eastern Jews and southern Italians in New York. Even in this study, clearly motivated in part by the wish to demonstrate that standardized gesture is not ethnically determined but varies according to cultural conditions including the impact of social assimilation, the treatment is itemistic rather than integrative.

The present essay has the aim of examining some aspects of posture and gesture in the context of respect behaviour in one society with which I have some familiarity – Tikopia – and drawing some quick analogies from another society – Britain. If the idea of such comparison seems far-fetched, I defend it on the grounds that it is in such fields of bodily behaviour above all that our common humanity and our common animal heritage are brought home to us – the physical basis of some of our social categories, despite enormous cultural differences.

1. Space and society in Tikopia

Posture and gesture refer to position and movement of the body or parts of it in space. In trying to understand the significance of

Tikopia patterns of posture, gesture, their significance of respect, I first examine briefly Tikopia space conceptions in a general social context.

The Tikopia like all human beings utilize space concepts for social discrimination. Of major significance are the notions of 'around' and 'up and down', for which there are direct natural referents. On a map of the Pacific Ocean Tikopia appears as a tiny dot surrounded by a great empty space. To see this has surprised the Tikopia, to whom their island, though relatively small, is an extensive solid area, the seat of their community life and containing within it a range of natural features and social features.[12] But the contrast between their island home as focus of orientation and the great ocean around is constantly present to them. The villages are set around the coast so that much of the daily life is carried on in terms of this contrast between land and sea. Such a contrast tends to be in concentric circle form because of the roughly circular shape of the island and the unbroken horizon with the absence of any other visible land. Hence seawards is the outer ring and landwards the inner ring. 'Seawards' and 'landwards' are referents for social action which occur very frequently in their conversation. Localization of objects on the floor of a house is made by such expressions, and even personal reference can be couched in such terms, e.g. 'there is a spot of mud on your seaward cheek'.[13]

Just as nature provides circularity as an initial feature to the Tikopia, so indices to vertical distances are also provided. The mountain of Reani, rising steeply to 1,200 feet from the lake and the ocean on the northern side, gives a vertical criterion against which the height of trees, cliffs and houses can be judged. Sea and lake fishing with long lines give depth criteria. In some contexts the Tikopia translate vertical into lateral distance: the tops of the palm trees on the lowlands, the tops of the cliffs, the shoulders of the mountain and the ultimate peak itself are used as means of measurement of increasing ocean distance. As points on the vertical scale are lost to sight by a receding vessel, or raised above the sea by an oncoming one, so the Tikopia judge their outward distance from their home.

Yet it is the domestic rather than the landscape setting of space concepts which is so significant to the Tikopia in their respect behaviour.

If *circularity* in Tikopia space concepts is given by nature, *rectangularity* is provided by culture. Recognition of wind points[14] can give angles, but connectedness of angles in rectangular form is essentially presented by house shape. The Tikopia house is traditionally a rectangular building with four corner posts and two end posts to take the ridgepole; very large buildings have a centre post as well. The shape of the house is clearly a cultural feature because it could have been of circular form, as were traditionally some houses in the Santa Cruz group a couple of hundred miles away. The rectangularity of the Tikopia house space is a matter of social significance. Posts are used as back-rests for men of seniority, and traditionally some posts were ritual symbols and sites for offering. The traditional Tikopia house is low – able to withstand violent winds, it is said, although modern houses are constructed higher without apparent deleterious effect. A person enters a traditional Tikopia house on hands and knees. This is a posture dictated by the height of the doorway; it is also consonant with the general patterns of Tikopia respect. In general, people move about in a Tikopia house on hands and knees or in a crouching position. This is partly a matter of prudence – not to bang one's head – and partly a matter of custom. So whereas some aspects of bodily *orientation* in Tikopia society can use categories initially given by nature, individual *level of bodily movement* has its categories specifically given by culture.

But natural space orientation too in Tikopia is also linked closely with house shape.

2. Space arrangements in a Tikopia house

Tikopia houses have only one room. But although the privacy of separate rooms as Europeans know it is unknown, spatial divisions allocate different parts of the house floor to different usages. On entering a Tikopia house one looks around as if reading a chart: there are areas in which the visitor can navigate, others he must avoid, before coming to anchorage, that is, sitting down. In a European room the allocation of space follows no regular rules; furniture is disposed partly according to the dictates of room shape and partly according to the wish of the owner. Seating has certain patterns on formal occasions. At table the chairman or the host's seat may be clearly indicated, and the 'sofa rule' was stringent in parts of Central European traditional society. But the Tikopia go much further. The floor space of a house traditionally is divided into two sides, *mata paito* and *tuaumu*. The former is the seaward side, the latter the landward side of the house. The former faces the scene of activity with canoes, the latter that with ovens. The former faces towards the sphere of fish, the latter towards the sphere of vegetable food. (Even now the Tikopia have practically no animal meat.) On *mata paito* traditionally the dead are buried, *tuaumu* is the scene of social activity. The former side has the 'dead mats' marking the graves where the dead sleep, the latter the 'bed mats' where the living sleep. On *mata paito* men sit, on *tuaumu* women sit. There is here then a regular patterned contrast between the spheres of sea and land, men and women, sacerdotal and secular – in a sense it is the classical opposition of the sacred and the profane. Yet the divisions are amorphous, not rigidly defined by any markers on the house floor. There is also a middle division of general usage where men and women mingle, where both sexes sleep and where much daily activity takes place. Moreover, the division between *mata paito* and *tuaumu* is largely ignored at funerals, that is, in that ambiguous sphere where the dead and the living may be said to intermingle.

Since the *mata paito* of nearly all houses faces to seawards, one can formulate the concept of a double ring of Tikopia activity, one facing outwards to the ocean, the other inwards to the land and the cultivation. But this concept is not overt among the Tikopia. Since in an abstract sense Tikopia dwellings, scattered around much of the lowland, may be conceived as forming a ring around the island, one may conceptualize the fusion of nature-given circle and culture-given rectangle. But this concept too is quite unrecognized by the Tikopia.[15]

As compared with the disposition of space in a European room, that in a Tikopia house refers not only to seating but also to mode of entry (doorways are differentiated by function) and to general orientation. Moreover, these patterns are observed on informal as well as formal occasions. (Judging by conditions as late as 1966, these patterns of use of house floor still obtain, but as the influence of Christianity becomes more strong it is likely that the distinction between *mata paito* and *tuaumu* will tend to disappear.)

Movement in a Tikopia house is governed largely by reference to this spatial division. Respect is shown by going about on hands and knees, by not sitting on *mata paito*, by not turning one's back on it and by sleeping with head towards it.

3. Space and social status

Relative status need not imply the physical confrontation of persons, but often does so. With the Tikopia, as with most if not all other communities, space relations in personal contacts are translated into status relations. These have both a vertical and a lateral dimension.

The lateral dimension of status relations involves three elements, proximity, precedence and focus or orientation.

(a) *Proximity*. Proximity implies likeness in status: 'He who is close to me is like me, he who is unlike me should be distant.' In Tikopia when persons meet on a path, women stand aside for men, juniors for seniors, commoners for chiefs. When persons are sitting in a house the host, or a man of superior rank, will invite a person of standing who enters to draw near. The visitor usually on entering the house sits down at some distance from the principal person present. He is then enjoined 'Sosoa mai' (draw nearer), an expression based upon the term soa (friend). In other words 'become more friendly towards me'. So in Tikopia idiom nearness is equivalent to higher status and farness to lower status. Note, however, that in this idiom actual distance is not particularly relevant.[16] Moreover, the Tikopia attach no particular importance to the side on which a person sits. They differentiate right- and left-handedness, and persons who are regularly left-handed may be so nicknamed. But in general they attach no ritual or symbolic importance to such differences.[17]

(b) *Precedence.* Frontness and rearness are very important in Tikopia alignment generally. Personally the back or the foot of a person is socially very significant in contrast to his face. So the frontness and rearness of persons is an index of relative status. At a public gathering the chiefs are in front (seated, see below) with their faces towards the object of interest and their backs towards their followers, whose faces likewise for the most part are turned towards their chiefs (Figure 44). The frontness and rearness of *space occupied* is also significant. Tikopia normally do not sit upon the ground but upon coconut-leaf mats, coconut fronds or billets of wood. On formal occasions the seating arrangements involve specific laying of coconut-leaf mats adapted to the positions which the principal men will occupy. Not only are the mats themselves ranked as it were in seating order but also the tapering and shape of the mat lends itself to status identification. The broad end of the mat is the 'head', the narrow end the 'tail' and the seat of ranking status is at the head irrespective of the way in which the occupants are facing.[18]

Yet status may sometimes be indicated by a reversal of such usages. A chief or other man of rank walking on a path may say to his companions who would ordinarily follow him 'You go ahead'. Here the critical element is not the actual space relations but the *control* of space relations. The control of physical precedence is the indicator of social precedence. (There is some European analogy here – when a host ushers a guest first through the door his exercise of courtesy may not derogate from him his admitted superior status.)

Except for such reversal with the assumption of control, the general Tikopia proposition is 'My front to the rear of a person indicates he is of higher status than I. My rear to his front indicates that I am of higher status than he.'

44. Addressing Tikopia chiefs at a public meeting. The chiefs are the only Tikopia seated on stools; the Tikopia interpreter for the European government officer crouches before them at the furthest distance at which low conversation can be heard. (I am greatly indebted to my colleague Torben Monberg for permission to reproduce this striking photograph, taken in 1966.)

(c) *Orientation*. By this is meant direction towards a central status figure or object of interest. Generally this involves a combination of proximity and precedence, but it may apply in conditions where there is no close contact. For example, in some traditional Tikopia religious rites the person performing the rite at sea or in the cultivations will orient himself generally towards his chief, who may be a mile or so away, and call upon him to utter the appropriate formula. (That the chief does not respond directly to this invitation is immaterial. The important thing is that at some point in the whole proceedings, whenever he thinks the time is right, he recites the formula.)

Orientation is significant for social status even when the object concerned is not visible. At many pagan religious rites the chief turned towards the spot where the god was thought to be sitting in acknowledgement of his status.

In the vertical plane degree of elevation is a very important Tikopia status index. In Tikopia language there is a direct correlation between physical elevation and social elevation. The term *mau runga* indicates either higher above the ground or superior socially or both. Consequently, in bodily posture in an immediate personal context standing is ordinarily superior to sitting, squatting, crouching or kneeling. Standing children are continually told 'Sit down' in the presence of adults who are sitting. Sitting is superior to crouching, squatting, kneeling or crawling on hands and knees. When a chief is seated in a house people will crawl over the floor in his vicinity.[19] When it is necessary for a person to stand up in order to take down some fishing-line or a bowl stored in the rafters, an apology is made to the man of rank or head of the house if he is sitting near by. Two points should be made here. In Tikopia the sitting and kneeling postures of men and women differ considerably (see *We, the Tikopia*, and Figures 44–6, herewith). Again, senior men, but not women, sometimes use coconut-grating stools or other objects as seats which raise them off the ground. On public occasions such seats are reserved for chiefs.

There is a difference between interpretation of laterality and of vertical relations in social terms. The lateral relation is discontinuous or non-cumulative. Its significance increases as the advancing person nears the focal person and then diminishes. The vertical relation is continuously accreting. As distance below is decreased so the status of the advancing person is increased. But as distance above increases so the status of the person concerned increases. Hence vertical relation gives a series of immediately applicable order to status ranking. The most extreme examples occur in the religious field. Gods, like men, participated in a status system and were also given vertical

45. The Ariki Kafika ties a ritual necklet on a crouching woman. Other women, half-kneeling, face him as they work. (Photograph: Raymond Firth, 1952)

46. Ritual offering. The Ariki Kafika, seated, returns a kava cup to a crouching server. (Photograph: Raymond Firth, 1952)

differentiation, in a scheme of heavens. The Christian God too partakes of this scheme, being regarded as at the apex of all relationships in the heavens. (In 1952, when spirit mediumship was still current, even for pagan mediums God was regarded as being so far above in the heavens that on their spiritual journeyings they never saw His face, but only heard His voice calling down.)

Degree of elevation applies not only to the body as a whole but also to such members as head and hand. A sitting chief bowed his head in obeisance as he addressed his gods, and raised his hand to the level of his brow in offering the cup of *kava* before pouring libations. This balanced opposition of head and hand can be interpreted as raising the offering to the highest level of the officiant before being transmuted to the god.

One can epitomize action in respect of a person of superior status in terms of these spatial criteria in the following Table (composed from the point of view of a high-ranking person):

Action

Lateral	F	F	F	F	N	N	N	N
Vertical	L	L	H	H	L	L	H	H
Orientation	O	B	O	B	O	B	O	B
Judgement	+ +	+	+	±	+	−	−	− −

N	Near position	O	Face orientation
F	Far position	B	Back orientation
L	Low posture	+	Approved
H	High posture	−	Disapproved

In judgement of the relevance of posture for social status, the combination of criteria has a cumulative or intensified effect. So somebody who is crouching far off facing a chief (Figure 44) is in a highly approved position; somebody who is standing far off likewise is showing respect, but not extremely so; someone who is standing far away but turning his back is on the borderline of respect; whereas someone who is close at hand standing with his back turned is definitely disrespectful, i.e. not acknowledging the status of the other person.

Spatial or orientation expressions may be used symbolically as well as for actual physical relationships. The Tikopia do not describe 'near' and 'distant' kin as we do in English, with a spatial referent generally. But they do have expressions for kin who are genealogically less close to be described as 'set aside' or 'in another place'. The expression of turning one's back on someone is used figuratively to indicate disrespect or lack of communication, as when an uncooperative daughter-in-law is said to 'turn her back' metaphorically on her husband's relatives.

4. Respect postures and gestures

So far I have discussed the social significance of elevation of the body in general Tikopia terms. I now examine it in terms of posture and gesture.

The Tikopia use various bodily points (in what the Maori anthropologist Peter Buck once described as anatomical topography) as status indices in gesture. These key points are particularly nose, wrist, knee and foot. From the point of view of interpersonal action they may all be viewed as projections on the body. Other features are used in Tikopia systems of ritual not particularly involving respect. When a woman has given birth to a child, turmeric is smeared on the top of her head. The breast is also used as a location for smearing on turmeric and coconut oil in various ritual contexts. The shoulder is regarded as the place upon which a spirit descends for mediumistic communication. The sex characters also have their place in the aesthetic system.

Gestures of respect involving bodily contact may be most simply considered as movement of an initiator towards a recipient, though there is always some mutual interaction.

The organ of prime initiation for a bodily gesture of Tikopia respect is the nose. The hands are used primarily as ancillaries. (In traditional Tikopia society the handshake was not used as a gesture of greeting, though it has now come into vogue with European contact.) Pressing the nose to a part of another's body is the prime gesture of proximity, establishment of contact and emotional expression among the Tikopia – as of course it is among the Maori. Tikopia do not ordinarily use the lips for such purpose; if not immobile, they are at least disregarded. This gesture with the nose is termed *songi* and is often accompanied by a kind of gentle inhalation, a sniffing indicative of emotional involvement and reminiscent of the preliminary sounds made before crying when a mourning wail is raised. (One might interpret this as a kind of figurative disruption of part of the personality of the recipient of the gesture, but this interpretation is speculative in the Tikopia context. The inhalation seems to be understood by the Tikopia as sniffing, not smelling.) In all these gestures it is the *bodily* expression which is of primary significance. The expression of the *face* which is so important to Westerners is almost immaterial to the Tikopia in this context. Indeed, gestures which imply respect and affection may be made with the face of the initiator concerned almost forbidding. This may be, or may purport to be, indicative of emotional strain, but it probably also relates to the fact that laughter may seem derogatory in the presence of a person of high status. What is important is the use of the body as an *instrument* on the one hand and as a *point of reception* of gesture on the other.

Gestures with the nose directed to different parts of the body indicate different status relationships or evaluations (see Figure 47a–d). The pressing of nose to nose and cheeks indicates a relationship

47. Tikopia postures and gestures of respect:
(a) Nose to nose – greeting between equals.
(b) Nose to wrist – greeting junior to senior.
(c) Nose to knee – follower to chief/apology.
(d) Nose to nose – acknowledgement of fealty or apology.

between equals. The pressing of nose to wrist indicates respect to someone of seniority, e.g. a woman to the head of a lineage. (This was commonly the gesture of *songi* to me by women, whereas my peers, chiefs and elderly men *songi*'d to my face.) Pressing of nose to knee is an acknowledgement of status superiority of very definite kind. It takes place particularly from commoner to chief in circumstances of considerable formality, such as when a man is taking leave to go abroad or wishes to proffer a request of some importance. It is also the gesture made by close male kin of a bridegroom to the male kin of a bride in apology for taking away the woman of their group.

Whereas nose to wrist and to knee is not uncommon in the more formal circumstances of Tikopia social life, nose to foot is very rare. Indeed, while theoretically it is an abject bodily apology made by someone who has insulted a chief, it is rather a verbal expression used to indicate that apology; it is figurative rather than actual. In this form it was used as a token of respect by a chief addressing his traditional gods.

Ethologists can find parallels between such behaviour and respect behaviour of animals. But there is one marked difference. With human beings, and this is evidenced by the Tikopia, there may be a very considerable time separation between the initial stimulus and the response. A case which I observed in 1966 illustrates this. As I was sitting in the house talking privately with my host one evening, he suddenly stopped and said 'Wait, people are approaching.' Suddenly in through all the entrances men crawled, about a score in all, and began pressing their noses in turn to my host's knee. As this proceeded someone said, referring to me, 'Father is sitting there, bring him in too,' and a number of the crowd included me in this gesture of respect. This lasted about five minutes and they then departed. When I asked the reason of this irruption my host, who obviously had known what was coming, said, 'A marriage has taken place.' This 'crawling' (*toro* as the Tikopia call it) was the formal apology of the man's kin to the bride's kin. I asked when and where was the wedding because I had not heard of it. It was explained this was a marriage that had occurred some time ago in Honiara 600 miles away, and the news had just been brought by a ship which had called. A month or so later I was in Nukufero, a Tikopia settlement many hundreds of miles away from Tikopia and distant also from Honiara. When I arrived I saw huge piles of bananas and other green food standing about, and on inquiring the reason was told, 'A feast is about to take place because of a marriage – in Honiara.' Here then was both an extended time interval of more than a month and an extended space interval of hundreds of miles between the initial event, the marriage in Honiara, the 'crawling' apology in Tikopia and the feast and exchange of goods in Nukufero.

I have mentioned that between initiator and recipient of such gestures there is mutual interaction. The common pattern is for one who has been the recipient of nose-to-knee pressing to lift up the head of the other person and then press nose to nose. This is what the Tikopia describe as 'making the face good' (*fakamatamata laui*) – the 'saving face' metaphor which the English have taken over from the Chinese. In the case of the marriage apology just discussed this gesture of bringing up the face of the initiator to equality with that of the recipient was followed. A chief too likewise lifts up the head of a man who has pressed nose to knee that they may press nose to nose. So a respect gesture in acknowledgement of superior status which is relevant to one situation may demand an equalization gesture in acknowledgement.

Such bodily gestures of respect are signals, in that they release other actions by both parties. But they are not simply signals to advise other parties of appropriate action, as they might be in the animal world; they are symbolic of ideational and emotional patterns. Physical principles are used in the service of society, acts on a simple scale of vertical distance being basic to the interpretation of degrees of status and respect, in accordance with the social context. The relation of these acts to language is complex.[20] They can be described in language, they are initiated by verbal as well as non-verbal behaviour, and many of the clues to their meaning are given by language. The sudden irruption of a crowd of men into a house might be a warlike attack – it is by linguistic expression, the 'crawling for the woman', that the quickest explanation is given to the householders. To some degree such postures and gestures are a supplement and alternative to language, but in themselves they have a significance, a propriety, a restorative effect, a kind of creative force which words alone cannot give.

5. Some British analogies

So far I have described some of the social implications for status relations in what may be regarded as a technologically primitive society. But we must realize that this kind of analysis can be applied also in Western societies. In sophisticated as in primitive communities the human body is used very simply, almost crudely, as an instrument of expression of respect relationships. Each society appears to have its own stereotyped differences of bodily posture and its own rules for interpreting these differences in status terms. Yet while the precise interpretations are clearly not universal, Hewes's postulate that some general values do appear to attach to distance, verticality and orientation in bodily posture seems reasonable.

One might think that sophisticated societies would avoid the more extreme postures in formal social intercourse. To some extent this is so. But they still use very simple physical positions or movements as a code for elaborate and deeply felt distinctions in respect behaviour. I take my examples from the society where I live, Britain.

Direct comparison with Tikopia is not simple. To begin with the distribution of personal contact, of body touching, in social contact is very different in Britain and in Tikopia. British young women do not press their noses to the wrists of ageing men – though men of Continental background sometimes make pretence of kissing the hands of elder married women. When a British young man marries, his brothers and uncles do not go in a body and crawl in apology to the knees of the bride's father – rather they crack jokes as they drink champagne at the bride's father's expense at the wedding breakfast. (This too has its Tikopia analogy.) The techniques as well as the occasions of apology in Britain are very different from those in Tikopia. Apology, a kind of submission, involves in Britain a lowering of the *idea* of the self, not of the *physical* self. In Britain it is a verbal process, not as it is in Tikopia a bodily process. Yet while it might seem that the more sophisticated a society the more it translates non-verbal into verbal behaviour, there is still an ambiguity here – an apology, though it must be admitted in words – often a most difficult admission – is expected to be backed up by deeds. Acts not words are regarded as the true indicators of attitude. And to the Tikopia it is acts that count most of all.

But despite difficulties of comparison the physical analogies of body inclination and body lowering are still there, if in somewhat different form.

Bowing, kneeling and prostration all have some place in British social usages. To bow is to incline the body and/or head in salutation, acknowledgement or respect. This is still a usage in polite society, although it has come to be less generally practised during the present century. In the nineteenth century the bow tended to be the male signal; the female equivalent was the curtsy.

In modern British society the bow has become more generalized. If such a gesture of politeness is made, women as well as men bow, to equals and to nearly all superiors. (A brief inclination of the head, almost a nod, is a common salutation.) Ritually, the bowing of the head is still extremely common, as in prayer. But in non-ritual contexts the gesture is relatively neutral. It is a recognition signal and an indicator of status, but it may indicate an acknowledgement of equality at least as often as a concession to superior status, and it may be very difficult to construe the signal as indicating one rather than the other. The bow also may indicate recognition in the sense of condescension, an acknowledgement of some other service.

Of special interest here is the curtsy (curtsey). Originally 'courtesy', a general movement of politeness in the sixteenth century, this came to have a more specialized significance – the particular movement of respect made by bending the knees and lowering the body. Moreover, it came to be regarded as a peculiarly feminine movement.[21] What is of particular note here is that while the bow merely lowers the head, the curtsy lowers the whole body. But it is in effect an intermediate posture, halfway to kneeling and unstable, not able to be maintained for any length of time. It is significant also that this is the most difficult posture to achieve with dignity, and is the only one which has been the object of special training. It was in conformity with nineteenth-century views on the subordinate position of women that this posture then was regarded as appropriate to women, especially young unmarried women. Nowadays in Britain only to royalty does a woman curtsy, and then only on the occasion of a formal presentation.

If the status significance of the bow is general, not indicating precisely the relative position of the parties, postures on formal occasions which involve lowering the body as a whole may very definitely indicate status inferiority. In British society this does not refer to sitting relative to standing, since the relaxation of bodily tension is a significant social factor. Hence in such conditions the higher posture, if performed or maintained in some degree of tension, is a respect gesture, e.g. by rising when a senior person enters the room where others are sitting, or by offering one's seat to a lady in a crowded bus.

In modern British society kneeling as a formal posture is rare, at least in public. But it occurs in ceremonial and ritual contexts – at the Coronation of the Sovereign (Figure 48); when a man receives

48. High Church dignitaries kneel in homage before the seated Sovereign. (Noble secular officeholders stand behind. Note the stepped platform.)

49. The accolade. The recipient kneels on the 'knighting stool' (with handrail). The Sovereign stands on a platform.

the accolade of knighthood from his Sovereign (Figure 49); when a grave social undertaking such as marriage is solemnized by a major church rite; on a religious occasion such as prayer; on presentation at the communion table.[22]

Further abasement of the body is still possible. In some oriental societies, bending over to touch the feet of a person of superior status is a method of salutation still practised. But this is not a British practice. Bending over to touch the feet of another involves lowering the head of the person making the gesture. Lowering of the head in more extreme form is characteristic of the Chinese practice of *k'o-t'ou*, known in English as *kowtow* or *kotow*, and used as a figurative expression for obsequious conduct. Literally meaning 'knock the head', this custom of touching the ground with the forehead as an expression of respect, submission or worship was an integral part of formal social intercourse with superiors in traditional China. Such behaviour is alien to British and to other Western societies. The attempted insistence of the Chinese Imperial Court on Western ambassadors observing this practice was the cause of considerable difficulty in the early period of European contact.[23]

Yet prostration of the body with head to ground is not a completely unfamiliar procedure in Britain. As a formal posture it seems to be a sign of humility in any society in which it occurs. In general, the term 'prostration' indicates lying at full length, but in stricter use in English it implies lying with face to the ground, a posture which in

50. Prostration before the altar. Other participants kneel and stand.

itself implies submission. As a ritual posture prostration does not ordinarily occur in Christianity, in contrast to Islam, where it is an integral part of the prayers. But although rare in British society it does occur as part of ordination rites in the Catholic Church. For instance, a recent public report (with photograph)[24] described how a Roman Catholic dignitary, during his consecration as Bishop, prostrated himself before the altar (Figure 50). The adoption of such a posture is sociologically interesting because it indicates not merely extreme submission of man before God, but also the appropriateness for a man about to assume a high sacramental position in God's service to preface this assumption by an acknowledgement before men of his own humility.

As a general trend in British society and presumably in other Western societies it would seem that the more elaborate postures and gestures of respect, involving lowering of the body, have been reduced in scope. They have been transferred from the more generally social situations to more purely formal occasions, especially in a ritual context. One may infer that this movement has been associated with an egalitarian trend in modern social relations, tending to reduce the degree of bodily disturbance and, by implication, the degree of status differential.

In this essay I have not attempted to give any very precise analysis, but rather to indicate some general points which an anthropologist may observe. When ethologists devote more attention to the field of human behaviour, much more exact formulation of the problem and observation of material may be expected.

Material such as I have described above reminds one of similarities between animal and human behaviour in the field of dominance and submission relations. However, there are certain fairly marked differences. Human beings, as compared with animals, may plan their formal postures and gestures well in advance of their execution. Correspondingly, as I have indicated in the example of Tikopia marriage behaviour, a set of postures and gestures may be anticipated on the basis of remote clues, and this anticipation may be a cardinal factor in the interpretation of them when they occur. The sudden brusque entry of a mass of men into a house could be treated not as aggression but as apology, since the fact of the marriage was already known and their pattern of behaviour could be construed accordingly. Hence, human posture and gesture may be not only signals to indicate performance, but also may have their performance predictable at long range. Again, the complexity of status relations in space terms may be such that actions may be undertaken in respect of persons not present but whose presence is anticipated or who may be known to be remaining at a distance. Orientation towards someone who is not present suggests the analogy of the notion of a mental space or territory as well as of a physical space or territory. Further, the use of language allows of a whole series of verbal equivalences to posture and gesture which may equally, or almost equally, convey status relations. To some extent language can provide an easy way out, relieving one from the discomfort of bodily disturbance. But provided that it is acceptable as valued currency by the person listening the expressions of respect uttered may be taken as sufficient indication of status recognition without bodily submission. The figurative use of posture signals is frequent in the ritual context of prayer and religious poetry.[25] Even such a conventional expression as 'I bow to your opinion' is a status indicator with an ultimate physical referent.

A complex factor is, that in anthropological work the observer himself to a great extent may share the behaviour of the subjects he studies. Most anthropologists follow local custom and engage in status postures and gestures with the people among whom they live. So the anthropologist tends to infer the interpretation of posture and gesture from the reaction in himself as well as that observed in others. While this personal involvement introduces an element of subjectivity it means commonly that, on the other hand, when he initiates status behaviour he can judge of the correctness of his interpretation by the manner in which it is received. It follows from this that the difficult problem of choice of units for isolation and comparison is not completely arbitrary. The anthropologist tends to choose as behavioural units those which are linguistically and thematically isolated by the people themselves in communication with him.

Notes

1. G. HEWES, 'World distribution of certain postural habits', *American Anthropologist*, 57 (n.s.), 2 (1955), 231–44, states that the number of significantly different body attitudes capable of being maintained steadily is probably of the order of one thousand.

2. In parts of Melanesia, as I myself have seen in the Solomons, the lower lip is projected as a pointer equivalent to the use of a finger.

3. Even in what some anthropologists would term ceremonial – i.e. a sign accredited with no intrinsic power – posture and gesture can still be of high social significance.

4. R. HERTZ, 'La prééminence de la main droite: étude sur la polarité religieuse' in Robert Hertz, *Death and the Right Hand*, trans. R. and C. Needham, Cohen & West, 1960.

5. MARCEL MAUSS, *Sociologie et anthropologie*, Presses Universitaires de France, Paris, 1950.

6. See report of Wenner-Gren Conference (1966), which refers to 'the very important but uncharted area of cultural information which can be learned from the way man moves his own body': 'Human movement as an expression of culture, February 25–27, Chicago', *Current Anthropology* (February–April 1967), 130; see also LaBarre, 'Paralinguistics, kinesics and cultural anthropology', in T. A. Sebeok, A. S. Hayes and M. C. Bateson, eds., *Approaches to Semiotics: Cultural Anthropology, Education, Linguistics, Psychiatry, Psychology*, Mouton, The Hague, 1964.

7. R. L. BIRDWHISTELL, *Introduction to Kinesics*, University of Louisville Press, Louisville, Ky, 1952.

8. HEWES, op. cit., pp. 231–44.

9. E. T. HALL, 'A system for the notation of proxemic behavior', *American Anthropologist*, 65 (n.s.), 5 (1963), 1003–26.

10. O. M. WATSON and T. D. GRAVES, 'Quantitative research in proxemic behavior', *American Anthropologist*, 68 (1966), 971–85.

11. D. EFRON, *Gesture and Environment*, King's Crown Press, Morningside Heights, N.Y., 1941.

12. RAYMOND FIRTH, *Social Change in Tikopia*, Allen & Unwin, 1959, p. 49.

13. RAYMOND FIRTH, *We, the Tikopia*, Allen & Unwin, 1936, p. 19.

14. Traditionally, the Tikopia did not recognize the four compass points, but took their major directions from prevailing winds. (This goes against the supposition of Audrey Richards, that there are words for north, south, east and west in all languages; 'African systems of thought: An Anglo-French dialogue', *Man*, 2 (n.s.), (1967), 290.)

15. As noted in *We, the Tikopia*, p. 79.

16. Unlike traditional practice in, e.g. Kerala, where caste status is expressed by the given number of paces or feet which a member of a lower caste should keep away from a member of the higher caste. (See A. Aiyappan, *Iravas and Culture Change*, Bulletin, Madras Government Museum, n.s., General Section, vol. v, no. 1 (1945), 38–9.)

17. cf. HERTZ, *Death and the Right Hand*, Cohen & West, 1960. One might perhaps recognize that the killing of two chiefs of Kafika by men of Raropuka, each known as Te Sema, 'The Left-handed', might involve a sinistral moral implication, though I have never heard any Tikopia express this view.

18. RAYMOND FIRTH, *The Work of the Gods in Tikopia*, London School of Economics Monographs in Social Anthropology, nos. 1 and 2, 1967, *passim*.

19. They will also be careful not to turn their backs upon him in so doing. Retreating backwards on hands and knees is a common Tikopia method of going out of the house. As a matter of ordinary courtesy this was continually done by anthropologists in Tikopia and is now adopted by instructed European visitors.

20. JOWETT'S well-known statement, 'gesture is the imitation of words' (*Oxford English Dictionary*), represents a limited if suggestive view.

21. See Jane Austen, *Pride and Prejudice* (1812), Macmillan, 1929, p. 158. 'Elizabeth merely courtesied to him'; cf. *Julius Caesar* III, i, 42. 'low-crooked curtsies, and base spaniel fawning' for the direct alignment of curtsy with status deference.

22. Actual height is of less importance than posture. But in Britain elevation of the principal character is often assisted by a special platform. A special use of bodily posture for social ends is the 'Clameur de Haro' of Guernsey, an ancient method of appealing against a decision considered unjust. An instance of this was recently reported in the newspapers, when a Guernsey hotelier, threatened with the cutting off of his water supply because of a dispute about meter readings, formally knelt in protest on the steps of the island's water board offices in St Peter Port (*The Times*, 7 June 1967).

23. The English were among those who did not conform. Lord McCartney on a mission to China in 1793 refused to *kowtow*, as also did the English ambassador Lord Amherst in 1816. With the decline of Chinese imperial power the custom waned, though recently reports indicate that Red Guards have attempted to induce some representatives of Western countries to conform in this way to give public expression to their submission.

24. As in *The Times*, 22 December 1966.

25. The Psalms contain many examples of the status significance of relative elevation: Psalm 14, ii: 'The Lord looks down from heaven upon the children of men'; Psalm 21, xiii: 'Be Thou exalted in Thy strength'; and the stirring injunction, Psalm 9, xix: 'Up, Lord, and let not man have the upper hand.'

I. Eibl-Eibesfeldt:
'Similarities and differences between cultures in expressive movements' (excerpts)

From Robert A. Hinde, ed., *Non verbal Communications*, Cambridge University Press, London, 1972, pp. 297, 299, 304, 305, 305–6, 308–9, 312.

In the 100 years since Darwin wrote The Expression of the Emotions in Man and Animals, *research has progressed in the 'universalist' tradition of studies of bodily expression which he fathered. This path of research – concentrating primarily on the physiological, non-social, non-psychological aspects of bodily expression – is (as I have said) well summarized in a recent volume entitled* Non-Verbal Communication *and edited by Robert Hinde (Cambridge University Press, London, 1972). This work of Hinde's might be considered a parallel volume to this present reader, with the distinction that* Non-Verbal Communication *moves from a base in physiologically oriented studies to include sociologically oriented studies, while the present volume takes as a starting-point what Hinde sees only as a peripheral subject – the social aspects of the body. The relationships of the social and physical aspects of expression are also explored by several contributors to that collection: Thorpe, Lyons, van Hooff, Argyle, Eibl-Eibesfeldt, etc. and the socio-cultural aspects of bodily expression are dealt with by Edmund Leach in an article entitled 'The influence of cultural context on non-verbal communication in man'. Most valuable for our present discussion is, I think, Eibl-Eibesfeldt's essay 'Similarities and differences between cultures in expressive movements' (pp. 297–314). Below are several quotes from this article which I have selected for presentation here. It is clear from this essay of Eibl-Eibesfeldt's that the universalist–relativist debate is still unresolved. It is also clear, however, that some socio-cultural variables of bodily expression do exist (even Darwin recognized this). I would like to suggest that rather than carrying on this debate* ad infinitum *the student should simply recognize that there are at least some social (i.e. non-physiological) aspects of bodily expression and that these need to be examined sociologically.*

Is there a signalling code – a language without words – common to all men? The question has been much discussed and contradictory statements have been published. As long ago as 1872 Charles Darwin pointed out certain similarities in the expressive behaviour of men with different cultural background. He interpreted these as being due to characteristics inborn in all men, but this opinion has been challenged repeatedly. For instance Birdwhistell[1] has advanced the hypothesis that no expressive movement has a universal meaning and that all movements are a product of culture and not biologically inherited or inborn.

The similarities in expressive movements between cultures lie not only in such basic expressions as smiling, laughing, crying and the facial expressions of anger, but in whole syndromes of behaviour. For example, one of the expressions people of different cultures may produce when angry is characterized by opening the corner of the mouth in a particular way and by frowning, and also by clenching the fists, stamping on the ground and even by hitting at objects. Furthermore, this whole syndrome can even be observed in those born deaf and blind.[2]

... cultural variation can result from the use of the available, probably inborn, patterns in slightly different ways. In addition there are numerous gestures which are culturally ritualized both in pattern and meaning – for example the method of saluting by tipping the rim of the hat or by lifting the hat, the latter being said to have originated from the lifting of the helmet as an expression of trust. It is interesting to note that a number of these culturally developed patterns show similarities in principle in different cultures. This suggests that the acquisition of these expressive movements may have sometimes been guided by phylogenetic adaptations involving specific learning dispositions. Whether these are for example 'innate releasing mechanisms' biasing the perception of the individual, or drive mechanisms channelling behaviour in particular ways, has yet to be explored.[3]

There are detailed cross-cultural similarities in both the meaning and the patterning of expressive behaviour. It is highly improbable that these similarities are due to chance. It remains to discuss the various possible ways in which they could have arisen. Many of the expressive behaviour patterns in man are certainly passed on by tradition. This is clear with patterns that are unique to one culture, such as the lifting of the hat. Often the historical origin of such patterns, their spread and the way in which they are learnt during ontogeny, can be followed. However, whether there are universals that are culturally traditional still needs to be explored. Since those behaviour patterns that are culturally learnt vary between cultures (for example, the development of dialects and languages),[4] it seems less probable that expressive patterns which occur as universals are culturally learnt. It is more likely that their universality is due either to common conditions in early upbringing channelling learning in a common manner, or that they are inborn.

Another argument which I once encountered in discussion was that the deaf- and blind-born individuals may have acquired information about facial expressions by the sense of touch. However, I know of three deaf- and blind-born who are thalidomide children, born without arms: they cannot acquire information in this way. They nevertheless exhibit the normal repertoire of facial expressions. Finally, I may mention that the typical facial expressions are also shown in those deaf- and blind-born who are so much brain-damaged that even intensive trials to train them to hold and guide a spoon fail. It is difficult to imagine how they could have learned social expressions without any deliberate training. If anyone insists in such cases on the learning theory, the burden of proof for such an improbable hypothesis lies on his side. It seems more reasonable to assume that the neuronal and motor-structures underlying these motor patterns developed in a process of self-differentiation by decoding genetically stored information. That would mean that the motor patterns in question are phylogenetic adaptations, which I assume they are.

The frequent repetition of the statement that all of our expressive patterns are culturally learnt, and that except for a few reflexes of the newborn 'nothing' is inborn in man,[5] proves nothing: the authors promoting such views did not even consider the contrary evidence. The study of the deaf- and blind-born at least demonstrates that phylogenetic adaptation partly determines our social behaviour, though the extent of its influence is not yet known. However, the fact that at least some basic modes of communication are inborn to man is of considerable theoretical importance.[6]

Careful analysis is needed and this means adequate documentation. If one wants to argue about the natural or 'instinctive' signalling code in man, one should not confuse the meaning of a movement and its pattern, as if they were the same. Both could be inborn but it is not necessarily so. The 'meaning' of an inborn motor pattern could be learned even when the motor pattern is a phylogenetically adapted one, and vice versa. A learned motor pattern might be shaped by a perceptual structure and often both are acquired from the culture.

Notes

1. R. L. BIRDWHISTELL, 'The kinesis level in the investigation of the emotions' in P. H. Knapp, ed., *Expressions of the Emotions in Man*, International Universities Press, New York, 1963, and 'Communication without words' in P. Alexandre, ed., *L'Aventure humaine*, Société d'Études Littéraires et Artistiques, Paris, 1967.

2. I. EIBL-EIBESFELDT, 'The expressive behaviour of the deaf and blind born' in M. von Cranach and I. Vine, eds., *Non-Verbal Behaviour and Expressive Movements*, Academic Press, 1970.

3. I. EIBL-EIBESFELDT, *Ethology: The Biology of Behavior*, Holt, Rinehart & Winston, New York, 1970, and *Liebe und Hass: Zur Naturgeschichte elementarer Verhaltensweisen*, Piper, Munich, 1970.

4. E. H. ERIKSON, 'Ontogeny of ritualisation in man', *Philosophical Transactions of the Royal Society*, B, 251 (1966), 337–49.

5. M. R. A. MONTAGU, *Man and Aggression*, Oxford University Press, New York, 1968.

6. EIBL-EIBESFELDT, 'The expressive behaviour of the deaf and blind born'.

B. The Psychological and the Social Aspects of the Body

3. Body Imagery

51. Stimuli in 'organization' or 'faceness' experiment. From M. Hershenson, W. Kessen and H. Munsinger, 'Pattern perception in the human new born', W. Wathen-Dunn, ed., *Models for the Perception of Speech and Visual Form*, M.I.T. Press, Cambridge, Mass., 1967.

Marcel Mauss, as we saw in the introduction to Part I, suggested that the human body must be studied from three separate perspectives: sociology, physiology and psychology. At the time of Mauss's writing, Robert Hertz in 'The pre-eminence of the right hand' had already pointed out that physiology and sociology need not vie with each other for the right to study the human body. In Chapters 1 and 2 we have explored the relationship of physiological and sociological approaches to the study of the body since the writings of Darwin. Now we can turn our attention to the other side of the academic triangle: the relationship of body studies in sociology and psychology.

As Seymour Fisher explains in his essay 'Body image' (printed below), the roots of psychological interest in the human body derive from diverse sources − neurological research into 'phantom limb' phenomena, etc., on the one hand, and Freudian body-symbolism research on the other. In a book about the 'Social Aspects of the Human Body' it is not appropriate that we attempt a full swing through the psychological literature. It is appropriate, however, to introduce those works in psychology which are of particular interest to the sociologist or anthropologist and to begin to explore the possibilities of finding a common ground between these two types of body studies. In 'The techniques of the body' Mauss does not make much concrete progress towards a meeting of psychology and his own discipline. He does, however, concede that the clear conclusion is that we find ourselves in the presence of 'physio-psycho-sociological' series of acts.

The real move towards a symbiotic psychology–sociology of the human body has come from the psychologists and not from the sociologists. Seymour Fisher and Sidney Cleveland in *Body Image and Personality* (which was first published in 1958) discovered in the subject of body imagery a ground in common with sociological research. Early psychologically oriented studies of body imagery were involved strictly with the neurological and psychological aspects of the subject. Fisher and Cleveland began their work from this perspective and then went on to expand the problem of body image into a social and cultural context:

> Up to this point the concept of body image has been described only in terms of its relevance for individual personality characteristics. A considerable area of personality correlates has been mapped out as bearing some relation to body image. Although such characterization has thus far been restricted to a description of individual behaviour, it seemed logical to assume that the striking individual trends uncovered should have application to group behaviour. A body-image index, such as the one being presently pursued, may be conceptualized as indicating the way in which the individual sets himself off from others. The whole concept of body-image boundaries has implicit in it the idea of the structuring of one's relations with others. It would seem to follow that if the body-image concept has something to do with the kind of defensive barriers an individual establishes about himself, an understanding of these barriers or peripheral boundaries should tell us something about the nature of that person's interactions with others. (Seymour Fisher and Sidney E. Cleveland, *Body Image and Personality*, Van Nostrand, Princeton, N.J., 1968, p.206.)

In a chapter entitled 'Cultural differences in boundary characteristics' (pp. 277–97) Fisher and Cleveland presented statistical information about variations of body-image boundary maintenance in several different cultures. The authors maintained that they were not 'sufficiently versed in anthropology to have the detailed grasp of conditions in a range of cultures' to enable them to conduct the study exactly as they would have liked. Their findings are nevertheless of interest to the anthropologist and some co-ordination of disciplines should have been, or should be, attempted. There are, for example, striking parallels between Fisher's and Cleveland's research and work done in anthropology on the subject of space. (See excerpts from E. Hall in Chapter 9 in this volume.) Fisher and Cleveland compared body-image boundary maintenance cross-culturally and Hall and others have been interested in the measurable distances between people's bodies and the fluctuations of these distances in different cultures, the former problem operating on a conceptual level and the latter on an expressive level. Watson and Graves have put Hall's theories of the cross-cultural variability of personal space to the test by a comparative study of Arab and American students ('Quantitative research in proxemic behavior', *American Anthropologist*, 68 (1966), 983). They found that 'Highly significant Arab–American differences emerged in the direction expected, with the Arab students confronting each other more directly than the Americans, moving closer together, more apt to touch each other while talking, looking each other more squarely in the eye, and conversing in louder tones.' It would be interesting to know if such cross-cultural variations of bodily expression are paralleled by similar variations at the conceptual level of body imagery as studied by psychologists such as Fisher and Cleveland.

Seymour Fisher:
'Body image'

From *International Encyclopedia of the Social Sciences*, ed. David Sills, vol. II, Collier-Macmillan, 1972; Macmillan, New York and Free Press, Glencoe, 1968, pp. 113–16.

Rather than selecting bits and pieces of Body Image and Personality *to appear in this volume, I have chosen to use the short essay that Fisher wrote for the* International Encyclopedia of the Social Sciences *entitled 'Body image'. This work also has the advantage that it deals with a wide range of theories about body imagery.* Body Image and Personality *was republished in 1968 and so is readily available. Chapters*

7, 9 and 11 are of particular interest to the sociologist or anthropologist.

'Body image' can be considered synonymous with such terms as 'body concept' and 'body scheme'. Broadly speaking, the term pertains to how the individual perceives his own body. It does not imply that the individual's concept of his body is represented by a conscious image; rather, it embraces his collective attitudes, feelings and fantasies about his body without regard to level of awareness.

Basic to most definitions of body image is the view that it represents the manner in which a person has learned to organize and integrate his body experiences. Body image concepts are important for an understanding of such diverse phenomena as adjustment to body disablement, maintenance of posture and spatial orientation, personality development and cultural differences.

At a commonsense level, the pervasive significance of the body image is evident in widespread preoccupation with myths and stories that concern body transformation (such as the change from human to werewolf form). It is evident, too, in the vast expenditure of time and energy that goes into clothing and reshaping the body (for example, plastic surgery) for the purpose of conforming to idealized standards of appearance.

Historical background

Interest in the body image appeared first in the work of neurologists who observed that brain damage could produce bizarre alterations in a person's perception of his body. Patients suffering from brain damage manifested such extreme symptoms as the inability to recognize parts of their own bodies and the assignment of entirely different identities to the right and left sides of their bodies. Interest in body image phenomena was further reinforced by observations that neurotic and schizophrenic patients frequently had unusual body feelings. Paul Schilder, neurologist, psychiatrist and early influential theorist, reported the following kinds of distortions in the schizophrenic patient: a sense of alienation from his own body (depersonalization), inability to distinguish the boundaries of his body, and feelings of transformation in the sex of his body.[1] Surgeons recorded unusual body experiences in patients with amputations and noted that amputees typically hallucinated the absent member as if it were still present. The hallucinated body member was designated a 'phantom limb'.

The neurologist Henry Head, another early influential theorist, took the view that a body schema was essential to the functioning of the individual.[2] He theorized that each person constructs a picture or model of his body that constitutes a standard against which all body movements and postures are judged. He applied the term 'schema' to this standard. His description of the body schema underscored its influence upon body orientation, but he noted also that it served to integrate other kinds of experiences.

Equally prominent in early body image formulations was the psychoanalytic work of Sigmund Freud.[3] Freud considered the body concept basic to the development of identity and ego structure. He conceived of the child's earliest sense of identity as first taking the form of learning to discriminate between his own body and the outer world. Thus, when the child is able to perceive his own body as something apart from its environs, he presumably acquires a basis for distinguishing self from non-self.

Freud's theory of libidinal development was saturated with key references to body attitudes. He conceptualized the individual's psycho-sexual development in terms of the successive localization of energy and sensitivity at oral, anal and genital body sites. It was assumed that as each of these sites successively acquired increased prominence and sensitivity, corresponding needs were aroused to seek out agents capable of providing stimulation. Presumably, too, when a person failed to mature and was fixated at one of the earlier erogenous zones (oral or anal), he was left to deal with adult experiences in terms of a body context more appropriate to the way of life of a child.

Many of Freud's concepts of personality development assign importance to changes in the perceptual and erogenous dominance of body sectors. Psychoanalytic theorists continue to focus upon body attitudes as significant in understanding many forms of behaviour deviance (for example, schizophrenia and fetishism). Indeed, psychoanalytical concepts have had a major influence upon body image theory and research.

Schilder drew attention to other body image phenomena in his book *The Image and Appearance of the Human Body*, where he formulated a variety of theoretical concepts that were phrased largely in psychoanalytic terms. He suggested that the body image is moulded by one's interactions with others, and to the extent that these interactions are faulty, the body image will be inadequately developed. Schilder's book contained rich descriptions of how the individual perceives his own body in diverse situations. He analysed body experiences that characterize awakening, falling asleep, assuming unusual body positions, ingesting certain drugs and undergoing schizophrenic disorganization. One idea he particularly emphasized was that sensations of body disintegration are likely to typify those who masochistically direct anger against themselves.

Schilder concerned himself with determining whether specific brain areas are linked with the body image. He was one of a group of neurologists who made persistent attempts to relate body image distortions observed in brain-damaged patients to the sites of the brain lesions. Considerable evidence has accumulated that damage to the parietal lobes selectively disrupts the individual's ability to perceive his body realistically.

Phantom limb. Historically, the phantom limb phenomenon has played a significant role in calling attention to the problems of organizing body perceptions. Such observers as Head and his colleagues,[4] Lhermitte[5] and Schilder[6] were puzzled by the fact that normal persons typically hallucinated the presence of body members lost through injury or amputation. Such hallucinations implied that the individual had a 'picture' of his body which persisted even when it was no longer realistically accurate. Controversy still exists about whether the phantom experience is primarily a result of a compensatory process occurring in the central nervous system or of persisting peripheral sensations evoked by injured tissue in the stump. Evidence indicates that while stump sensations play a part in the phantom experience, central factors are of greater importance. Interesting questions have been stimulated by observations of the phantom limb: for example, why does the duration of phantom experiences vary markedly between individuals? And why does the phantom not appear when body parts are gradually absorbed (as in leprosy) rather than suddenly removed?

Research

Well-controlled experiments in the area of body image are relatively new, most scientific studies having been carried out since 1945.

Human figure drawing. One of the oldest and most frequently used techniques for the study of the body image makes use of human figure drawing. It has been suggested that when an individual is asked to draw a picture of a person, he projects into his drawing indications of how he experiences his body. Some investigators have proposed that such indicators as the size of the figure drawn and difficulty in depicting specific body areas provide information about the individual's body concept. There have been claims that the figure drawing can be used to measure such variables as feelings of body inferiority and anxiety about sexual adequacy. However, despite a profusion of studies, there is no evidence that figure drawing is an effective method of tapping body image attitudes. It is true that in some instances it has proved sensitive to the existence of actual body defects. For example, individuals with crippling defects have been shown to introduce analogous defects in their figure drawings. Moreover, there have been some demonstrations that figure-drawing indicators of body disturbance are higher in schizophrenic than in normal subjects. However, no consistently successful indices of body attitudes have been derived. Indeed, the problem of using the figure drawing to evaluate body image has been enormously complicated by evidence that artistic skill may so strongly influence the characteristics of drawings as to minimize the importance of most other factors.

Attitudes towards the body. Another approach to evaluating the body image has revolved about measuring the subject's dissatisfaction with regions of his body. Procedures have been devised that pose for him the task of indicating how positively or negatively he views his body. These procedures vary from direct ratings of dissatisfaction with parts of one's body to judgements regarding the comparability of one's body to pictured bodies. It has been found that men are most likely to be dissatisfied with areas of their bodies that seem 'too small'; whereas women focus their self-criticism upon body sectors that appear to be 'too large'. Also, evidence has emerged that dissatisfaction with one's body is accompanied by generalized feelings of insecurity and diminished self-confidence.

Perceived body size. One of the most promising lines of body image research has dealt with perceived body size. This work concerns the significance to be attached to the size an individual ascribes to parts of his body. The individual's concept of his body size is often inaccurate and exaggerated in the direction of largeness or smallness as a function of either situational influences or specific body attitudes. It has been demonstrated that estimates of body size vary in relation to the total spatial context of the individual, the degree of sensory input to his skin, the nature of his ongoing activities, and many other variables.[7] For example, subjects judge their heads to be smaller when heat or touch emphasizes the skin boundary than when such stimulation is absent. It has further been shown that subjects perceive their arms as longer when pointed at an open, unobstructed vista than when pointed at a limiting wall. The subject's mood, his attitudes towards himself, his degree of psychiatric disturbance and a number of other psychological factors have been found to play a part in his evaluation of his own body size. For example, persons exposed to an experience of failure see themselves as shorter than they do under conditions of non-failure. Schizophrenic, as compared to normal, subjects unrealistically exaggerate the size of their bodies. Normal subjects who ingest psychotomimetic drugs, which produce psychotic-like disturbance, likewise overestimate the sizes of their body parts. At another level, it has been noted that the relative sizes an individual ascribes to regions of his body (for example, right side versus left side, back versus front) may reflect aspects of his personality organization.

Aside from the formal research efforts that have highlighted the importance of perceived body size as a body image variable, there is a long history of anecdotal and clinical observation supporting a similar view. Vivid experiences of change in body size have been described in schizophrenic and brain-damaged patients, in patients with migraine attacks and in various other persons exposed to severe stress demands. Clearly, there is a tendency for experiences to be translated into changes in perceived body size.

Projective techniques. Responses to ambiguous stimuli, such as ink blots, briefly exposed pictures and incomplete representations of the human form have been widely utilized to measure body attitudes. It is assumed that when a person is asked to interpret or give meaning to something as vague as an ink blot, he projects self-feelings and self-representations into his interpretations. In this vein, it has been found that persons with localized body defects focus their attention upon corresponding body areas when studying pictures containing vague representations of the human figure. The frequency of references to body sensations (such as pain, hunger, fatigue) in stories composed in response to pictures has been shown by D. J. van Lennep to vary developmentally and to differ between the sexes.[8] Females were found to show a moderate increase in body references beyond the age of 15, whereas males were typified by a pattern of decline in such references. It has been suggested by van Lennep that in Western culture men are supposed to transcend their bodies and to turn their energies toward the world. Women, on the other hand, are given approval for continuing and even increasing their investments in their bodies.

Fisher and Cleveland have developed a method for scoring responses to ink blots which measures how clearly the individual is able to experience his body as possessing boundaries that differentiate it from its environs.[9] This boundary measure has been able to predict several noteworthy aspects of behaviour, including the desire for high achievement, behaviour in small groups, the locus of psychosomatic symptomatology and adequacy of adjustment to body disablement.

Perspectives and problems

The investigation of body image phenomena has become a vigorous enterprise. One dominant fact that has emerged is that the individual's body is a unique perceptual object. The individual responds to his own body with an intensity of ego involvement that can rarely be evoked by other objects. The body is, after all, in a unique position as the only object that is simultaneously perceived and a part of the perceiver. In studying an individual's manner of experiencing and conceptualizing his body, one obtains rich data about him that is not readily available from other sources.

It is difficult to know what priorities to assign to the body image issues that still need to be clarified. Speaking broadly, one may say there is an emphatic need to ascertain the principal axes underlying the organization of the body image. It remains to be established whether the body image is built around the spatial dimensions of the body, the specialized functions of different body regions or perhaps the private and symbolic meanings assigned to body areas by the culture. There is also a need to examine the relationships between body attitudes and socialization modes in different cultures. There is evidence in the anthropological literature that body attitudes may differ radically in relation to cultural context. Another important problem for research is the assessment of the role that body image plays in the development and definition of the individual's sense of identity.

Notes

1. PAUL SCHILDER, *The Image and Appearance of the Human Body: Studies of the Constructive Energies in the Psyche*, International Universities Press, New York, 1935, 1950.

2. HENRY HEAD *et al.*, *Studies in Neurology*, 2 vols., Hodder & Stoughton, 1920. These papers consist mainly of a republication of papers published in *Brain* between 1905 and 1918.

3. SIGMUND FREUD, *Collected Papers*, 5 vols., International Psycho-analytic Library, Nos. 7-10, 34, Basic Books, New York; Hogarth, London, 1959. Translation of *Sammlung kleiner Schriften zur Neurosenlehre* and additional papers. A ten-volume paperback edition was published in 1963 by Collier Books.

4. HEAD *et al.*, op. cit.

5. JACQUES J. LHERMITTE, *L'image de notre corps*, Éditions de la Nouvelle Revue Critique, Paris, 1939.

6. SCHILDER, op. cit.

7. SEYMOUR WAPNER, H. WERNER and P. E. COMALLI, 'Effect of enhancement of head boundary on head size and shape', *Perceptual and Motor Skills*, 8 (1958), 319-25.

8. D. J. VAN LENNEP, 'Projection and personality' in Henry P. David and Helmut von Bracken, eds., *Perspectives in Personality Theory*, Basic Books, New York, 1957, pp. 259-77.

9. SEYMOUR FISHER and SIDNEY E. CLEVELAND, *Body Image and Personality*, Van Nostrand, Princeton, N.J., 1958.

Susan Postal:
'Body image and identity: A comparison of Kwakiutl and Hopi' (edited)

From *American Anthropologist*, 67 (1965), 455–60, 462.

It is significant that Seymour Fisher closes the article which appears above by stressing the need for the exploration of the social implications of the concept of body imagery. Susan Postal, an anthropologist, has taken up this challenge in her American Anthropologist *article 'Body image and identity: A comparison of Kwakiutl and Hopi'. By using mythological material from two North American Indian tribes (the Hopi and the Kwakiutl) she attempts to reconstruct and compare the notions of body imagery of these two very different cultures. In doing this, she brings us a step closer to answering Fisher's question of whether 'body attitudes may differ radically in relation to cultural context'. In Chapter 2 we saw that body behaviour is cross-culturally variable. Postal's article, plus Fisher's and Cleveland's research, make it clear that cross-cultural variability should also be expected at the conceptual level of body imagery. As I suggested in my introduction to this chapter, the next step is to see if variations of body behaviour correlate with variations of body imagery.*

Postal's study also brings us to the issues raised by Professor Mary Douglas, in her studies Purity and Danger *and* Natural Symbols, *concerning the relationship of concepts of pollution and body boundary maintenance. I suspect that Douglas would want to carry Postal's research one step further and ask what 'social facts' of Hopi and Kwakiutl social structure should predispose the Kwakiutl (but not the Hopi) to develop body image concepts which have a dominant preoccupation with the external boundaries of the body.*

Most human action can be seen to involve not only an adjustment and adaptation to the external environment, but also to an internal perceptual scheme or self concept. One integral component of a person's self concept is the perceptual structuring of his physical body, the 'body image' or schema of himself as an objective entity.

This image of the boundaries of one's body provides the basis for a sense of identity: it permits the distinction between self and the world 'out there' to be maintained.

Study of the relationship between types or variations in body image and personality has been primarily limited to the study of abnormal behaviour, for it is here where variations in boundary image were first brought to light as important aspects of psychological functioning.[1] Given this understanding of the central importance of body image in self identity formulation, the extension of some of these insights to a more general level, as has been done by Fisher and Cleveland in their recent work entitled *Body Image and Personality*,[2] has suggested possibilities for utilizing the concept of 'body image' in anthropological research. In particular, these authors present tentative cross-cultural comparisons based on Rorschach samples which indicate that although body image has its locus in the individual, general features of this perception may be culturally shared.[3]

The results of Fisher's and Cleveland's study have stimulated interest and further inquiry into those consistent attitudes towards body boundaries which seem to be characteristic within a particular culture. Analysis of types of body boundary attitudes might add another dimension in terms of which one could approach an understanding of 'world view' or 'ethos'. This paper is an attempt to explore such possibilities and to suggest a conceptual scheme for characterizing body image as a dimension useful for the study of culture.

Previous research involving the content analysis of folk-tales and the comparison of values and themes as revealed in the tales[4] indicated that attitudes towards body boundaries were quite clearly reflected in narratives from various cultures.[5] The present paper grew out of the attempt to understand more precisely and conceptualize variations in 'body image' as reflected in folk-tales. Two very well-known cultures which appear to contrast markedly in many respects have been selected for analysis: Kwakiutl and Hopi. The method is essentially that of content analysis of texts – folk-tales, myths and autobiographies – which aims at identifying those recurrent 'themes' or 'motifs' revealing attitudes towards body (or self) boundaries. Ethnographic data has been used only as a general background and for supplementary explanation. It should be emphasized that this study is, in a way, a venture into the unknown. Although original inspiration has come from Fisher's and Cleveland's work, actual analysis of cultural materials is from quite a different perspective from that these authors present. Conclusions are therefore far from complete or final.

Body boundary image has been likened to a 'screen on which is projected the individual's basic feelings about his safety in the world'.[6] One way of characterizing attitudes towards body boundaries is through an analysis of 'feelings of safety' – of what is threatening and how to protect against it – as expressed in the folk-tales of a particular group. That is we can aim at the characterization of the 'safety screen' in terms of which the self-image of individuals is reinforced. Such analysis can be made, it is here suggested, in terms of three general dimensions:

1. The focus of boundary maintenance concern as determined by the localization of threat or danger;
2. The means of protection against such threats;
3. The manner of actively overcoming potential danger by affirming self strength.

In the first instance, a fundamental distinction between types of boundary maintenance concern can be established according to the perceived source or localization of danger. In some cases one finds that concern has an external focus: there is fear of harm from incoming actions. In others, concern is internal: harm and danger are seen as emanating from the self in outgoing impulses. Protection against danger follows these distinctions. Where concern is internal protection is through containment; where it is external, it is through defence against intrusion. Similarly, modes of increasing self strength to reduce potential danger reflect the basic focus of concern. Taken together, the means of protecting against and reducing danger (2 and 3) form the content of the 'safety screen'. The type of maintenance concern (1) represents its perceived purpose of function. The specific components of these dimensions, as found through an analysis of myths and folk-tales, can be said to characterize (abstractly) the attitudes towards self-boundaries.

Content analysis of narratives from Kwakiutl and Hopi[7] reveals many quite interesting contrasts between these two cultures in terms of the three dimensions suggested. At the most general level, we find a clear contrast between the central 'theme' of the tales from the two groups. Kwakiutl tales centre on the achievement of strength or *mastery* by the 'hero'. Those qualities definitive of strength in a character are three: beauty, physical power and wealth. Weakness and consequent subjugation is attributed to a character if he is sick, blind, ugly or abandoned. Further analysis of this central theme indicates that in the Kwakiutl tales the focus of 'safety concern' is external: there is fear of danger to the self from outside sources. That is, weakness does not derive from an individual's actions *per se*, but rather has an 'ego-alien' cause. Hopi narratives, on the other hand, centre on the theme of maintaining a *'good-heart'*. Attributes of an individual with a good-heart relate to four main characteristics: knowledge, temperament, courage and awareness. Without a good-heart, individuals are unable to resist the influence of evil, and they become susceptible to the temptations of misconduct. The dependence of good actions on the maintenance of a pure 'heart' indicates that the focus of Hopi identity concern is more internal: harm to the self is seen as having its source in outgoing actions or impulses.

In the Kwakiutl tales, protection against threats to the self involves an emphasis on *'surface barriers'* against intrusion or subjugation from the outside. This emphasis centres on the external boundaries of the physical body itself. Protective elaboration of these boundaries seems to involve attempts to almost literally strengthen the skin by ritual purification, rubbing or bathing the body, or by the use of clothing or masks. Furthermore, in most of the tales the physical characteristics of a person determine his fate. The great shamefulness of sores or other deformation of the body surface and, conversely, the admiration of well-formed bodies attest to the importance of the body surface and its role in the reinforcement of identity.

The emphasis on surface barriers of protection is perhaps most vividly illustrated in the attitudes towards *clothing* found in the tales. The significance of clothing is revealed, in the first place, by the very large number of references to details of apparel, dressing and undressing: in the fifteen tales analysed there are over twenty-five different references to body covering and adornment, many of which are also repeatedly mentioned in the particular narrative. Clothing seems to function much in the same way as physical appearance: it allows for the recognition and approval of others and simultaneously serves to strengthen 'surface barriers' of protection. This is most dramatically portrayed in the tale *'Nenelkenox'* in which a boy, having decided to kill himself, dresses in blankets and earrings and starts out walking up the river. He pauses and bathes in the river, thus curing his shameful sores, and then puts down one of his blankets. He walks further, bathes again, and lays down the other blanket. This continues until he has discarded all of his garments and jewelry and bathed again. At this point, '. . . it is said that he felt different'. We find that the decision to commit suicide is followed by the boy's literal shedding of his identity as he walks along until, when naked and finally bathed, he has become something different. That a change of clothes involves a change of being is made even more clear as the story continues, for we find that his body has become that of a bird and he flies around having great influence over others. In the

Kwakiutl stories, clothing allows for recognition of one's status by others, but it also seems to determine one's real character. When shed or discarded there is a weakening of power; when replaced by something new, there is a gain in mastery.

Still another way in which identity is protected through external barriers is found in the importance of *naming* in Kwakiutl tales. Frequent naming and re-naming according to one's position acts as a kind of 'verbal clothing'. A name, like a particular garment, reinforces the boundaries between the self and the outside world: it is a device which connects an individual's image of himself with a tangible external label defining 'me'.

Another motif in the Kwakiutl tales indicative of the importance of external boundary definition is that of *incorporation*. We find, as Codere has noted, 'the general Kwakiutl attitude of disapproval and distaste of gluttony'.[8] Analysis of the tales reveals that the focus of disapproval is not on the fact of eating or over-eating *per se*, but rather on the greedy individual's inability to gain mastery over or successfully incorporate what he consumes. Thus the ridicule of the Bear, 'you ugly hollow stomach, you ugly one whose food goes from end to end', is a statement designed to demonstrate the weakness of the Bear's character – his weak external boundaries – for all to notice. Many other tales also mention 'the running of things from mouth to anus' with strong disapproval. This theme of successful incorporation is also reflected in related themes of enclosure, of being inside something larger and stronger than the self; of completion, of gathering up parts and putting them together or repairing things which have been broken.

Openings or gaps in an external barrier of protection are, in the Kwakiutl tales, something to be avoided. The themes of clothing, physical form, naming, incorporation, enclosure and completion can be viewed as cultural expressions of a concern for protection against incoming threats to the self.

In the Hopi narratives, protection against harm involves the development of an inner strength sufficient to contain dangerous action or to resist the temptation of evil 'two hearts' who may try to influence one's behaviour. Barriers which guard the self from harm have, in direct contrast to the Kwakiutl case, an inward focus. Those boundaries which limit and define an individual's character in these folk-tales are dependent on continuous and conscious *self-control*. The reality of this internal concern is quite explicitly stated by Sun Chief in his autobiography: 'You have come to examine my heart and learn what kind of a man I am . . .', and at another time a wise man tells him, 'My boy, your heart is out of order . . .'[9] Reinforcement and protection of a 'good-heart' can be seen to take place on three levels: skilful control of the body, discipline of thoughts and feelings and attention to the guidance of the supernatural. Moving from the individual's actual body outwards to his relations with others and then to the religious system, we find a series of themes which give support to the maintenance of inner discipline.

In the first instance, frequent mention of running practice to increase one's swiftness and strength, 'to make one more wide awake, capable of clearer thinking', indicates the importance of developing *skilful control* of the body. Courage and bravery are taken as objective proof that the individual may have a strong heart. In striking opposition to all that was revealed in the Kwakiutl material, we find that external forms are not only unimportant but may actually be hindrances in the growth of strength. For example, it is said in one of the myths when praising the swiftness and skill of a poor boy: 'he never wore much clothing which accounted for his strength'. Skilful control of the body is related to the more general theme of awareness, of thinking clearly and paying attention. Descriptions of men with 'good-hearts' often include such comments as, 'unwinking eyes . . . his eyes never close, he never sleeps', or 'he sat all night without sleeping'. The ability to 'run fast and never tire' is proof of control of both body and mind and thus evidence of a strong and pure heart.

The second kind of inner discipline, that of control over thoughts and feelings, is also given expression in the tales. Arguing, it is said, is never justified for it 'warms you up inside'. Patience and a *restraint* of anger are valued. Although an individual receives help and guidance in his attempts to maintain a pure heart from his Guardian Spirit, such help is never a permanent or established thing. Support in one's attempts to preserve a 'good-heart' depends on the individual's constant awareness of the efforts which he alone must make. Lack of control over one's negative thoughts and emotions results in being 'dropped' by the spirit guide.

Turning attention now from the means of protection to those of actively overcoming the possibility of danger through affirming self strength, a theme of *self-extension* frequently appears in the Kwakiutl tales. Existing perhaps as a complement to intrusion concern, one finds an emphasis on the areal extension of the self. There seems to be a reinforcement of identity in so far as there is an increase of areas under self control or an expansion of self potency. Through extension there is actual reduction of that which is external: definition of self limits comes to include power over much that is clearly outside the objective boundaries of skin. Illustrations of this feature of Kwakiutl boundary attitudes can be found in the frequent transformation of forms which takes place in the tales; the themes of resurrection from the dead by bathing or sprinkling with magic waters; and the marked concern with movements of flying, diving, and up and down directions. The bolstering of the self image through such expansion has as its goal the receipt of attention. Flying through the air, singing from the rooftop or transforming oneself or others magically all involve the visual notice of others. Weakness is derived from being unnoticed and thus abandoned.

In the Kwakiutl material, participation in a network of reciprocal attention exchange, having perhaps its most well-known and obvious manifestation in the ritualized giving of the potlatch, appears as the sign of mastery or strength. To be outside this network – to be abandoned – presents a real threat to an individual's identity. The increase of self strength through extension and consequent *receipt of attention* can be seen as further expression of the importance of firm external boundaries for the maintenance of a stable self image.

In the Hopi case, rather than increasing self strength through an expansion or extension of the limits of self, one finds just the opposite: the breaking down or removal of external appearances so that the true 'inner man' might be revealed. This feature of Hopi boundary attitudes, *self-disclosure*, is quite clearly evident in the kinds of tests or trials which give proof of a good heart. One finds frequent mention of contests, races and games designed to settle a dispute and prove the inner strength of the victor. One legend, for example, tells of the race between the Hawk and the Antelope in which the latter, being just a wobbly-legged fawn, appears to be losing from the very start when suddenly 'he decided to cast aside the fawn skin and display himself as the true antelope . . . he came dashing across the valley with great speed. He won the race.' It is perhaps most interesting to note the end of this story. The Hawk, having lost, is to be killed by the Antelope. However, because his legs are strong and his heart is brave, the Antelope cuts out the Hawk's heart and places it on a shrine called the 'heart containing' so that others might come and worship it to gain speed and courage. The disclosure of inner attributes – the true Antelope and the brave heart of the Hawk – is a central point in the story.

The theme of disclosure is given expression in many other ways in the Hopi legends. Often there is actual unveiling of the identity of the character through unmasking (often the cutting away of a series of masks). Punishment brought on the wicked is also indicative of the breaking down of external appearance as a means of overcoming evil influence. Here the theme of becoming twisted or *distorted* is frequent. When the earthquake comes to punish the people of

Palatkwabi, one myth relates, a survivor notes 'all of it was twisted . . .' The god Massau, a persistent practical joker, is said to 'twist men's faces into ridiculous shapes so that he could laugh at them'. The association of ridicule with this distortion occurs quite often, and seems to suggest that foolishness and weakness are revealed when appearances are disclosed as misshapen. For example: 'You are evil and this shall be your punishment . . . An old man found that he had only one of his own legs, while the other was a woman's; another man had one arm of natural size, and for the other that of a child; a third found a woman's head on his body; and so on . . . They were the laughing-stock of the people.'

In the Hopi tales, the physical body itself is not considered as a barrier, rather its form and strength are important in so far as the nature of what is inside is revealed. Being poor, unclothed or abandoned are often qualities of those with good hearts, for survival under these conditions requires great inner strength. With such internal concern, identity is protected through self-discipline and affirmed through disclosure.

That the differences between themes in Kwakiutl and Hopi folk-tales are striking is certainly not surprising. Selection of two cultures which, in most other respects as well, appear quite opposite was intentional. What can be learned, however, is what kinds of themes are contingent upon others, what kind of patterning there is within each culture concerning attitudes towards body boundaries and self identity as expressed in their oral literature.

Notes

1. cf. PAUL SCHILDER, *The Image and Appearance of the Human Body: Studies of the Constructive Energies in the Psyche*, Psyche Monographs, London, 1935; International Universities Press, New York, 1935, 1950.

2. SEYMOUR FISHER and SIDNEY CLEVELAND, *Body Image and Personality*, Van Nostrand, Princeton, N.J., 1958.

3. Additional evidence for cultural variations in body image perception has been brought to my attention since the writing of this paper by Marvin K. Opler. In particular, his study entitled 'Schizophrenia and culture' (in *Scientific American*, 197 (1957), 103–10) indicates striking differences between Italian and Irish schizophrenic patients in attitudes toward self boundaries and their protection.

4. B. N. COLBY, G. COLLIER and S. K. POSTAL, 'Comparison of themes in folk-tales by the General Inquirer System', *Journal of American Folklore*, 76 (1963), 318–23.

5. Content analysis of texts from five cultures (Kwakiutl, Egypt, Eskimo, India and China) using the General Inquirer System of analysis utilizing a high-speed digital computer (IBM 7090) has given tentative results which support the general conclusions presented here. Themes relating to body parts and boundaries appear to cluster in ways predicted by the theoretical assumptions of this paper.

6. FISHER and CLEVELAND, op. cit., p. 354.

7. FRANZ BOAS, 'Ethnology of the Kwakiutl', Bureau of American Ethnology, *35th*

Annual Report, Part 2, 1921, and 'Kwakiutl tales', *Columbia University Contributions to Anthropology*, XXVI, 1943; ALEXANDER STEPHEN, 'Hopi tales', *Journal of American Folklore*, 42 (1929), 1–84; WILSON WALLIS, 'Folktales from Shumopovi, Second Mesa', *Journal of American Folklore*, 49 (1936), 1–68.

8. HELEN CODERE, 'Kwakiutl society: rank without class', *American Anthropologist*, 59 (1957), 483.

9. LEO SIMMONS, *Sun Chief, the autobiography of a Hopi Indian*, Yale University Press, New Haven, 1942.

4. Psychological and Sociological Theories of Body Symbolism

52. 'The City Tonsor, *c.* 1770'. From John Woodforde, *The Strange Story of False Hair*, Routledge & Kegan Paul, 1971.

As we saw in Chapters 1 and 2, the relationship of physiological and sociological theories of body behaviour has been dominated by two inter-related and yet analytically distinct issues: firstly, whether body behaviour is relative or universal and secondly, whether the similarities and variations of body behaviour from one society to another are the result of physical or social factors. The relationship of psychological and sociological theories of body behaviour, on the other hand, is not neatly organized around issues that are so closely inter-related. The reason for this may be that *within* the framework of psychological studies of the body there has occurred a sharp division between behaviouristic studies which take as their subject the study of the perception of body imagery and, on the other hand, psychoanalytically orientated studies of body symbolism in the tradition of Freud and Jung. In Chapter 3 we examined some of the research which has been done on the subject of the perception of body imagery and we saw that there are great opportunities for integrating this type of psychological research with the study of the social aspects of the body. The relationship of the social aspects of the body and psychoanalytic theories of body symbolism, however, appears to be more problematic.

Anthropologists and sociologists have themselves often indulged in the sport of interpreting symbols. Usually this has been done with complete disregard (and often obvious disdain) for psychoanalytic theories of symbolism. In the midst of this situation, Professor Edmund Leach in his Curl Bequest Prize Essay of 1957 attempted to integrate psychoanalytic theories of the symbolic meanings of hair with ethnographic data pertinent to the subject of the ritual use of hair and anthropological theories of hair and body symbolism. Leach's essay is entitled 'Magical hair' and it first appeared in print in the *Journal of the Royal Anthropological Institute* (88, Part 2 (July–December 1958), 147–64) and has since been reprinted by Bobbs-Merrill (New York, no. A-435).

In this essay, Leach explored the thesis of the psychoanalyst Dr Charles Berg (*The Unconscious Significance of Hair*, London, 1951) that 'hair-cutting and shaving are . . . to be understood as symbolic "castration" ' (p. 149) and that 'at a pre-genital level there is a common association between hair and faeces and that, in the last analysis, head hair is used as a symbol for libidinous aggressive drives of all kinds' (ibid.). After considering a great variety of ethnographic data, Leach concludes that 'when fully investigated the symbolic pattern does turn out to be self-consistent and in accordance with [Berg's] theory' (p. 154). However, Leach then admits that he is aware 'of a small number of cases where hair is used as a ritual symbol apparently without any libidinous significance' (ibid.) but summarizes his position thus: 'Even so, an astonishingly high proportion of the ethnographic evidence fits the following pattern in a quite obvious way. In ritual situations: long hair = unrestrained sexuality; short hair or partially shaved head or tightly bound hair = restricted sexuality; close-shaven head = celibacy' (ibid.). In his conclusions, Leach also makes the following remarks which are relevant to the material in this present chapter:

> ... ethnography indicates a persistent link between hair as a symbol and the phallus as a symbol and to this extent it is appropriate that hair should be prominent in rites denoting a change in social–sexual status; but the anthropologists alone have no theory which would explain why the symbolization should take the form it does.
>
> Dr Berg's psychoanalytic arguments do provide such an explanation. In the body of the essay I have tried to show why these psychoanalytic arguments are anthropologically inadequate but I have also indicated that they are not actually in conflict with the ethnographic evidence. The anthropologist need not accept the psychoanalyst's view, but he has no good ground for rejecting it (p. 160).

We can appreciate Leach's essay 'Magical hair' as an attempt to bring together psychoanalytic and anthropological–sociological theories of body symbolism. Whether he succeeded in his attempt, however, has become a subject of much dispute. In particular, C. R. Hallpike in an essay entitled 'Social hair' criticized Leach's flirtation with psychoanalytic theories. Hallpike's essay appears below and I will let him speak for himself. I should point out, however, that Leach (in a personal communication) contends that Hallpike has misinterpreted his original argument and that some of Hallpike's ethnographic data is incorrect. In view of Hallpike's criticisms, it is to be regretted that Leach declined the invitation to give his reasons for rejecting them in this chapter. Resolving the argument once and for all is thus well beyond the scope of this present volume. The reader is referred to Leach's article which as it has been reprinted recently is readily available. And I would like to pass on Professor Leach's suggestion that two other articles be consulted for ethnographic details: J. Duncan M. Derrett, 'Religious hair', *Man*, 8 (n.s.), 1 (March 1973), 100–103, and Julian Morgenstern, *Rites of Birth, Marriage, Death and Kindred Occasions among the Semites*, 1966.

For our present purposes, however, it is hoped that the reader will consider Leach's and Hallpike's essays as two opinions of the possibilities of incorporating psychoanalytic theories of body symbolism into the sociological and anthropological study of body behaviour. Beyond the details of the disagreement between these two authors, one common theme emerges: psychoanalytic and sociological theories approach the subject of body symbolism from such radically different perspectives that it will be a long time before a common, 'ecumenical' framework of research can be elaborated for the study of body symbolism.

C. R. Hallpike:
'Social hair'

From *Man*, 4 (n.s.) (1969), 256–64

Although I have not edited this essay the author himself has been kind enough to supply some additional material which was not included in the essay as it originally appeared in Man, *and to edit the original slightly. (Changes from the original are presented in italics.)*

A central problem in the interpretation of ritual is the fact that while the participants in each society may be unable to give an explicit explanation of the meaning of the symbols involved, there is a large body of symbols and symbolic acts which is common to a wide variety of cultures, and while any particular symbol may have a multiplicity of meanings from society to society, we find that these meanings constantly recur. For example, as Turner has pointed out,[1] black, white and red are the colours most often used in ritual, where black is very often symbolic of dirt or rainclouds, white of milk or semen, and red of blood. Given, then, that there is a number of symbols, with a common signification in different cultures, *we must* try to explain the basis of this similarity.

Two different hypotheses suggest themselves. The first is that the meanings ascribed to symbols are related to the workings of the subconscious, which are assumed to be similar in members of every culture and, more specifically, to the mechanisms of the repression and sublimation of the sexual impulses. The second is that, given the common concern of all societies with survival, the nature of the physical environment, procreation, the social role of the sexes, youth and age, order and disorder, and similar basic concepts, there are certain symbols and symbolic acts which are inherently appropriate in expressing these concepts, and that this is why these symbols are so commonly found and often have the same meaning in different cultures. *All that I mean by 'inherently appropriate' is that since blood and fire, for example, are red and not green, we would expect to find that cultures which ascribe symbolic values to colours would choose red as a symbol of blood or warfare, and not green. This does not mean that only one symbol is ever appropriate to express any particular concept. For example, one culture may choose red as a symbol of death through its association with bloodshed; another might choose white through its association with bone; and a third might choose black through its association with night, and the setting of the sun. The point I am making is that we elucidate the meaning of symbolism by examining the way in which people conceptualize the associations of entities in the real world. Thus the first hypothesis mentioned above regards symbols as 'about' the subconscious, while the second hypothesis regards them as 'about' the world and man's place in it.* The object of this article is a re-analysis of Dr Leach's celebrated and stimulating essay 'Magical hair'[2] in which he advances a theory of the symbolic meaning of hair which is of the first type.

Leach examines the relationship between the significance of symbolism in the individual subconscious, as seen by a psychoanalyst, Dr Charles Berg, and the significance of symbolism in social ritual, as interpreted by ethnographers. The particular piece of symbolism which he uses as a basis for discussion is Berg's hypothesis that there is a basic symbolic equivalence between head hair and the male genitals in the subconscious, such that hair-cutting equals castration. His problem is to explain how the conclusions of psychoanalysis about the symbolic meaning of hair in individual fantasies, as a matter of fact, though without much logical or empirical justification, turn out to be closely in accord with what ethnographers have to say about the significance of hair in ritual. His conclusion is that the psychologists and the ethnographers are discussing quite different types of phenomena (the subconscious and the social), but that the psychologists can contribute to our understanding of ritual because much of its content is designed to express, and therefore to control, our potentially dangerous emotions. Phallic symbolism occurs often in ritual because 'ritual makes explicit these powerful and dangerous thoughts . . . Phallicism in ritual is thus a form of cathartic prophylaxis; it is not an expression of the repressed unconscious of the collective individual, it is a social process which serves to prevent the individual from developing sexual repressions at all.'[3] This may or may not be so; the problem with such theories is to bring them into some sort of relationship with the facts, so that they can be shown empirically to be true or false. The whole relationship between private and social symbolism is too complex to be considered here; on this occasion my immediate concern is to consider a particular symbolic theme, in the light of Leach's psychological theory, and to try to determine whether it is really true that head hair can be shown to be associated with sexuality in a wide range of societies and, more explicitly, if it is true that:

$$head = phallus$$
$$hair = semen$$
$$hair\ cutting = castration$$

and that:

$$long\ hair = unrestrained\ sexuality$$
$$short\ hair = restricted\ sexuality$$
$$close\text{-}shaven\ hair = celibacy.$$

Let us first of all consider the special characteristics of hair.

1. Like the nails it grows constantly.
2. It can be cut painlessly, again like the nails.
3. It grows in great quantity, such that individual hairs are almost numberless.
4. Head hair is apparent on infants of both sexes at birth.
5. Genital–anal hair appears at puberty in both sexes.
6. In some races, males develop facial hair after puberty, and also body hair.
7. Hair on different parts of the body is of different texture, e.g. eyelashes, pubic hair, head hair.
8. In old age hair often turns white and/or falls out.
9. Hair is a prominent feature of animals, especially monkeys, man's analogue in the animal kingdom.

Now the human body is the focus of much ritual; and it is not surprising that a physical feature with such manipulative potential as hair should be used so frequently in ritual. Moreover, in view of its manifold characteristics, which I have just set out, it would be surprising if all its ritual and symbolic manifestations could be reduced to a single origin.

One of the most frequent ritual uses of hair is in association with mourning. On this point Leach says: 'That hair rituals may have sexual associations has been apparent to anthropologists from the beginning, but mostly they have not regarded this as a matter of crucial significance.' Tylor, for example, classed ritual hair-cutting as one 'of an extensive series of practices, due to various and often obscure motives, which come under the general heading of ceremonial mutilations'. Of other such practices he mentions bloodletting and the cutting-off of finger joints. He avoids reference to circumcision, but the latter rite is clearly a 'ceremonial mutilation'.[4,5] While conceding that ritual does not reflect the psychological condition of the individual performing it, but rather that 'the structure of the social situation requires the actor to make formal symbolic statements of a particular kind',[6] he still finds Berg's hypothesis in relation to shaving the head at mourning – that loss of the loved one equals castration equals loss of hair – to be meaningful as explaining the genesis of the symbolism in the first place. Now exactly *why* people should react to grief by shaving off their hair and mutilating themselves is undoubtedly amenable to psychological explanation, but there is no *prima facie* reason to link it with castration. Certainly circumcision has no such meaning, but quite the reverse in most primitive societies.

One of the greatest weaknesses in Berg's hypothesis that shaving head hair equals castration is that women shave their heads in mourning as well as men. But what on earth does it mean to talk of 'female castration'? The notion is sufficiently bizarre to require some elucidation for readers who are not psychologists. Moreover, references to shaving the head at mourning very frequently describe other mutilations such as gashing the face and body. For example, Frazer lists,[7] besides the Jews of the Old Testament, sixty-eight societies in which some form of self-mutilation is performed at mourning, and in almost every case we find that the cutting off of the hair is accompanied by bodily laceration. In the absence of any indication to the contrary, why should we therefore assume that the cutting off of the hair is not simply a particular type of self-mutilation?

We frequently find in ethnographical literature that hair has close associations with the soul. For example, to refer to Frazer again: 'The Siamese think that a spirit called *khuan* or *kwun* dwells in the human head, of which it is the guardian spirit. The spirit must be carefully protected from injury of every kind; hence the act of shaving or cutting the hair is accompanied with many ceremonies';[8] and he cites many other instances to show the sacred character of the head and consequently the peculiar nature of head hair. Since the head is the seat of reason and the sensory organs, among other things, this is surely good reason for recognizing that it is a most appropriate seat of the soul, in primitive eyes. Leach concludes however that 'the "soul stuff" of such writers as Hutton and Wilken is not perhaps very different from the "libido" of the psychoanalysts'.[9] Not perhaps *very* different, but sufficiently different to require considerable demonstration of similarity, which we are not given.

Magic is another familiar ritual use of hair, which is treated, along with nail parings and bodily secretions, as symbolically equal to the person from whose body they came. Of this Leach says:

> The psycho-analyst, being concerned with the inner feelings of the individual, categorizes all actions which cut away part of the individual's body as symbolic equivalents of 'castration'. He then argues that these ritual acts have emotional force for the individual because they are in fact felt to be a repression of libidinous energy. In contrast, the social anthropologist is concerned with the publicly acknowledged status of social persons, and he notes that the ritual acts in which part of the individual's body is cut off are prominent in *rites de passage* . . . He might well label all such rites 'circumcision'. The social anthropologist's explanation of why rites of 'circumcision', so defined, should be emotionally charged comes from Durkheim. The ritual situation converts the symbol into a 'collective representation' of God and Society . . . These two arguments, the psycho-analytic and the Durkheimian, appear to be sharply contrasted, yet they are not contradictory. We can accept them both simultaneously together with a third argument, borrowed from Frazer, to the effect that magical power typically resides in objects which are detached from individuals in ritual situations – e.g. the blood, hair, nail parings, etc. of persons involved in *rites de passage*. We cannot simply merge these three arguments, but if we recognize that they all refer to 'the same thing', then we are led to conclude that magical potency, regarded as a social category, is something which inheres in 'circumcision' symbols, but that such symbolization is effective because for each individual the ritual situation is felt to signify 'castration'.[10]

Originally, it will be remembered, Leach was concerned to show that Berg's equation of head hair equals genitals was relevant in explaining certain ethnographical facts, but now we have gone far beyond this and are being asked to believe that *everything* cut or removed from the body has a sexual significance – specifically, castration. But if blood and body dirt as used in magic and ritual *symbolize castration, does the use of* personal names, garments, foot-prints and shadows, which are very prominent in magic, also symbolize castration? In fact, of course, there is a much simpler explanation of why hair, nails and blood, etc. are used in magic on a *pars pro toto* basis to symbolize the person from whom they were taken. In the first place, hair and nails grow constantly and this is surely a very good reason why they should be believed to be specially endowed with vitality; blood and semen, for different reasons, are also believed to be sources of vitality in primitive thought. But these considerations cannot apply to body dirt or nasal mucus, and still less to foot-prints, shadows, names and garments. In primitive thought we frequently find that the person is thought of as having extensions, of which personal names, personal belongings, shadows and foot-prints are examples. It seems likely, therefore, that there are two reasons why hair is chosen as a symbol of the whole person in magic. It is endowed *par excellence* with vitality (and may have associations with the soul if it has come from the head) and it also falls into the wider category of extensions of the person.

So far in this article I have tried to demonstrate something of the multiplicity of hair in its ritual aspects. For example, it can be thought of as associated with the soul, through the head, as having inherent vitality because it grows; it may figure in the general category of bodily mutilations; and its physical characteristics make it very appropriate, like dress, for expressing changes or differences in ritual or social status. There is thus no reason why a theory of hair in ritual should be obliged to reduce all the manifestations of hair to a single origin – symbolic castration. It is only when we realize that the ritual uses of hair are of widely differing types that we can attempt to explain any of them. But Leach's theory not only tries to provide a single explanation, but founders on three stubbornly empirical facts.

The first is one to which I have already referred. This is that women's hair, as well as men's, is frequently the focus of ritual attention. The second is that if head hair equals male genitals, why is it that comparatively little regard is paid to beards in ritual contexts? As I remarked earlier, head hair is common to both sexes and is present at birth, while the facial hair only develops in the male at puberty. Moreover, in texture the latter has more resemblance to pubic hair than to head hair. If there were any plausibility in the theory that head hair equals male genitals, and that cutting hair equals castration, one would expect beards to be more prominent than head hair in ritual; so it is surely strange that in fact beards have a comparatively minor role, even allowing for the fact that in some races males do not develop much facial hair. The third and most serious defect is one to which I have not so far alluded. This is the fact that ascetics commonly have long hair. Now of course, according to the equations: long hair equals unrestrained sexuality; short hair equals restricted sexuality; close-shaven hair equals celibacy; this is all wrong. Leach of course is aware of the problem; but his solution, in so far as he advances one, is far from adequate.

He quotes Iyer as follows: 'The *sannyasin*'s freedom from social obligation and his final renunciation of the sex life is symbolized by change of dress but above all by change of hair style. According to the mode of asceticism he intends to pursue a *sannyasin* either shaves off his tuft of hair [the isolated tuft of hair is an essential social identification mark of the male Brahmin] or else neglects it altogether, allowing it to grow matted and lousy.'[11] Berg explains the long hair as follows: 'Fakirs simply ignore altogether the very existence of their hair (cf. the ascetic tendency to ignore the existence of the genital organs). It grows into a matted lice-inhabited mass and may be as much a source of unremitting torment as the neglected penis itself. Apparently it is not permitted to exist as far as consciousness is concerned.'[12] Leach points out that far from the *sannyasin*'s behaviour being compulsive, it is socially prescribed: 'The correct hair behaviour . . . of Indian ascetics was all laid down in the *Naradaparivrajaka Upanishad* over 2,000 years ago.'[13] But he agrees with Berg that 'for the Brahmin the tonsured tuft "means" sexual restraint, the shaven head "means" celibacy and the matted head "means" total detachment from the sexual passions.'[14] But this explanation is of course quite opposed to the theory that long hair equals unrestrained sexuality.

There is a striking passage in Gibbon's *Decline and Fall of the Roman Empire* relating to long hair and asceticism.

The monks were divided into two classes; the Coenobites, who lived under a common and regular discipline; and the Anachorets, who indulged their unsocial, independent fanaticism. The most devout, or the most ambitious of the spiritual brethren, renounced the convent, as they had renounced the world . . . All superfluous incumbrance of dress they contemptuously cast away; and some savage saints of both sexes have been admired, whose naked bodies were only covered by their long hair. They aspired to reduce themselves to the rude and miserable state in which the human brute is scarcely distinguished above his kindred animals; and the numerous sect of Anachorets derived their name from their humble practice of grazing in the fields with the common herd. They often usurped the den of some wild beast whom they affected to resemble . . . The most perfect Hermits are supposed to have passed many days without food, many nights without sleep, and many years without speaking . . . [15]

This illustrates very well the hypothesis I wish to advance in this article: that long hair is associated with being outside society and that the cutting of hair symbolizes re-entering society, or living under a particular disciplinary regime within society. Of course, one may be outside society partially or wholly and I am not suggesting that long hair is appropriate only to hermits and outcasts. By being 'outside society' I do not mean therefore the total exclusion of ascetics and similar categories, but rather an attitude or condition of rejection of which the asceticism of the anchorite or *sannyasin* is the ultimate expression, or, again, the possession of certain traits such as spiritual power by reason of which the possessor is not fully amenable to social control. To be more precise, I would formulate the theory as 'cutting the hair equals social control'. Dressing the hair may also be ceremonially equivalent to cutting it.

The tonsure of the monk is a familiar aspect of Christian religious life, to which Leach refers briefly[16] and which at first sight seems to support the theory that shaven head equals celibacy. But the monk takes three vows, of which chastity is only one; the others are poverty and *obedience*. The monk in fact is under discipline, ideally of a most rigorously social type. The anchorite, as Gibbon's quotation makes very clear, is under no social discipline whatsoever and indeed represents rejection of social control in its most extreme degree; yet he, like the monk, abstains from the lusts of the flesh. The monk, of course, is not the only person under the discipline of institutional life who has his hair cut short. The soldier and the convict are other well-known examples, but nobody would suppose that soldiers are ideally intended to refrain from having sexual relations, even if convicts, by reason of their circumstances, are in practice deprived of sex. Thus the cropped head or tonsure in all three cases of monk, soldier and convict signifies that they are under discipline.

By contrast to these groups, we may consider three categories of person who are, in Western society, generally credited with long hair – intellectuals, juvenile rebels against society, and women. It is not difficult to see that in various ways they are, or are thought to be, in some respects less subject to social control than the average man. The intellectual is someone who is, by reason of his interests, remote from the concerns of everyday life, or even positively hostile to and critical of society; and enough has been written about 'hippies' to make any explanation of their long hair somewhat superfluous. But the case of women perhaps needs a little more elucidation. In the first place, they are traditionally concerned with domestic affairs and not with the running of society as a whole, and secondly, they have always been considered to be more governed by their emotions, more whimsical and less predictable than men. (Whether truly or falsely is beside the point – it is still a widely held social stereotype.) It is of course true that in past centuries men have worn long hair, but in such periods women's hair has been even longer; at the end of the eighteenth century it was not considered unmanly for men to weep publicly, but there is no indication that they outdid women in this respect.

Long hair is therefore *frequently* a symbol of being in some way outside society, of having less to do with it, or of being less amenable to social control than the average citizen. But the means by which one attains this condition are of course various. Anchorites, witches, intellectuals, hippies and women all have long hair, but there is no single quality which they have in common besides the negative one of being partially or wholly outside society. There is however one characteristic which is often associated with being outside society, for whatever reason: this is animality.

Gibbon's irony delights in emphasizing how men in their search for holiness come to resemble the beasts, and while I am not suggesting that the relationship between spiritual power and beastliness is more than outward and analogical, it is nevertheless a striking resemblance. There is considerable evidence in fact for an association of 'outside society equals hairiness equals animality'. The animal familiars of witches and the wild beasts over which the Egyptian saints had such power, come to mind in this connection. Most primitive societies give animals an important place in their cosmologies and they often symbolize the chaos of untamed nature before the process of socialization. The culture hero Dribidu of the Lugbara as described by Middleton[17] is a good example of this association. 'They [the two culture-heroes] were not human as men are now; Dribidu means "the hairy one" since he was covered with long hair over most of his body. He is also known as "Banyale" ("eater of men"), since he ate his children until he was discovered and driven out of his earlier home on the east bank of the Nile . . .'[18] '. . . In our own terms the significant differences between the two periods before and after the heroes is that in the latter the personages were ordinary human beings, who behaved as people behave now, and were members of clans, whereas in the former they behaved in a contrary manner and lived in isolation, in a world in which there were no clans.'[19]

The Bible provides considerable support for my hypothesis, but little for Leach's. Esau, the hunter of wild beasts, was a hairy man, while his brother Jacob, a herdsman dwelling in tents, was a smooth man. Esau also sold his birthright for food (Genesis xxv, 23–7). In

Leviticus it is prescribed that a sufferer from leprosy and therefore an outcast, when cured and thereby ready to be reincorporated in society, shall shave off all his hair (Leviticus XIV, 8, 9). The Nazarites, who separated themselves unto the Lord, were never allowed to cut their hair until the end of their separation, when the hair was formally shaved off at the tabernacle (Numbers VI, 1–18). *In Deuteronomy* (XXI, *10–14) it is prescribed that female captives taken in war if made wives shall pare their nails and shave their heads.* In the Book of Judges we are told that Samson's strength resided in his hair, and when he is shorn he is as weak as any other man (Judges XVI, 17–19). *2 Samuel* XIV, *26 records that Absalom only cut his hair at yearly intervals, and that at each polling of his head his hair weighed 200 shekels (estimated as* $3\frac{5}{7}$ *lbs avoirdupois, by Hastings).*[20] *He was not remarkable for his fertility, and begot only a daughter and three sons, who pre-deceased him (2 Samuel* XIV, *27; 2 Samuel* XVIII, *18). His principal claim on our attention is, of course, that he attempted to overthrow his sovereign, and his father, King David.* The description of how King Nebuchadnezzar was overthrown and made an outcast is another very clear example of the association of hairiness and the separation from society in the state of nature: '. . . and he was driven from men, and did eat grass as oxen, and his body was wet with the dew of heaven, till his hairs were grown like eagles' feathers, and his nails like birds' claws' (Daniel IV, 33). It may be significant that two major prophets, Elijah and John the Baptist, are associated with hairiness and animal clothing. In a discussion of St Paul's injunction to women to cover their heads in church, W. F. Howard says: 'It may be a sign of the husband's authority. So Stack and Billerbeck show from Rabbinical sources that the bride walked in the wedding procession with uncovered head as a token of her free maidenhood. Then, as a sign that her husband's authority was upon her, Jewish usage required that the married woman should always appear with her head covered' (1 Corinthians, XI, 3).[21] I should emphasize that I have not been partial in my selection of these Biblical examples in order to prove a point. On the contrary, the examples are a complete list of every significant mention of hair, except those passages dealing with the cutting-off of hair in mourning, an aspect of hair already discussed.

The Bible therefore provides the following associations between long hair, or cutting the hair, and social attributes:

hairiness = hunter (Esau)
hairiness = wild beasts (Nebuchadnezzar)
hairiness = physical strength (Samson)

> hairiness = rebellion (Absalom)
> hairiness = asceticism, spiritual power (Elijah, John the Baptist)
> growing long hair = separation from society to God (Nazarites)
> shaving hair = rejoining society (Nazarites, when lepers are cured)
> shaving hair = submission to captors by women
> covering hair = discipline (women's acceptance of husbands' authority).

The only marginal case among these is that of Samson, in that taken by itself it could be cited as evidence of the association of head hair and sexuality. But it fits equally well with my hypothesis.

Stith-Thompson's *Motif-index of Folk Literature*[22] also provides considerable support for my hypothesis, and little for Leach's. There are twenty instances of hairiness being associated with supernatural or half-human beings, such as fairies, dwarfs, giants, water and wood spirits, devils and mermaids; seven associations with animal–human relationships; three associations with witches; three associations with vegetable–human relations; seven associations with the soul or vitality; and six with asceticism. (I have consulted only the references to 'hair' and 'hairy'.) There were no clear references to head hair in association with sexuality, though Leach might disagree with me.

This is not to suggest that in some cases the head and its hair may not have a clear sexual significance. For example, it is evident from Onians's account of ancient Greek and Roman beliefs about the body that the head was seen as the source of seed, in the form of cerebro-spinal fluid,[23] and that the hair was an indication of sexual vigour.[24] Yet he also makes it clear that these beliefs were derived from the observation of animal and human physiology, and not the repressed workings of their subconscious minds. But such cases are not particularly common in the literature. If we are searching for the most general explanatory framework in which to place hair symbolism it would therefore seem more reasonable to treat the symbolic associations of the hair with sexuality as a special case of its more general association with animality. The chief deficiency of Leach's hypothesis however is not that it applies to a much narrower range of facts than he leads us to suppose, but that on its own ground, where social status is overtly associated with hair and with sex, it fails to provide any explanation of why long hair is associated with ascetics and with men like Samson, and why short hair is associated with monks and soldiers.

My primary objection to Leach's theory therefore is simply that it takes account of very few of the facts. But there is a more fundamental weakness in his theory, which it shares with all such psychological theories. When an anthropologist is trying to understand the rituals of an alien culture he does not concern himself with what the symbols stand for in the subconscious of each participant; indeed, he has no means of knowing this. His mode of analysis will be twofold. He will ask the natives what each symbol means (without necessarily eliciting a satisfactory answer) and make a list of the occurrences of each symbol in its ritual context. When he has collected sufficient data of this type he will try to discern the structure of the symbolism and its relation to the people's cosmology, social organization and values. A good example of this procedure is Turner's paper on symbols of *passage* in Ndembu circumcision ritual.[25] Of course, the success of the interpretation will depend on the quality of the anthropologist's intelligence, imagination and training; the facts cannot interpret themselves. But the point I am making is that once the anthropologist has discerned the structure of the symbolism in the culture he is investigating, his work is complete. The structure is *there* in the symbolism, just as the structure is *there* in a language analysed by the linguist.

The advantage of treating symbolism as 'about' the world, rather than 'about' the subconscious, is that the relations between symbols and the world are empirically verifiable, and it is accordingly possible to evaluate different explanations of a particular piece of symbolism in terms of how well they fit the facts. Thus the advantage of my theory that cutting hair equals social control is that it can be applied fairly rigorously to the logic of social situations in which hair is symbolically significant. In other words, we do not have to ask ourselves: 'What is going on in the minds of people who cut off their hair after being cured of leprosy?' (quite possibly nothing at all is going on in their minds beyond the acceptance of a social rule); we simply consider the structural form of the evidence. With psychological theories such as Leach's, however, we cannot relate a people's symbolism to the facts of their natural environment and their society, but only to one of an indefinite number of theories about the subconscious.

Notes

1. V. W. TURNER, 'Colour classification in Ndembu ritual' in M. Banton, ed., *Anthropological Approaches to the Study of Religion*, Association of Social Anthropology Monograph 3, Tavistock Publications, 1966.

2. E. R. LEACH, 'Magical hair', *Journal of the Royal Anthropological Institute*, 88, Part 2 (July–December 1958), 147–64.

3. ibid., p. 161.

4. E. B. TYLOR, *Primitive Culture*, 2 vols., 1873, vol. II, p. 403.

5. LEACH, op. cit., p. 150.

6. ibid., p. 153.

7. J. G. FRAZER, *Folklore in the Old Testament* (abridged edition), Macmillan, 1923, pp. 377-83.

8. J. G. FRAZER, *The Golden Bough* (abridged edition), Macmillan, 1922, p. 230.

9. LEACH, op. cit., p. 150.

10. ibid., p. 162.

11. ibid., p. 156.

12. ibid.

13. ibid.

14. ibid.

15. E. GIBBON, *The Decline and Fall of the Roman Empire* (abridged D. M. Low), Chatto & Windus, 1960, p. 516.

16. LEACH, op. cit., p. 154.

17. J. MIDDLETON, *Lugbara Religion*, Oxford University Press, London, 1960.

18. ibid., p. 231.

19. ibid., p. 233.

20. J. HASTINGS, *A Dictionary of the Bible*, T. & T. Clark, Edinburgh, 1902, vol. IV, p. 904.

21. W. F. HOWARD, 'ist and 2nd Corinthians', in F. C. Eiserlen *et al.*, eds., *Abingdon Bible Commentary*, Epworth Press, London, 1929.

22. J. STITH-THOMPSON, *Motif-index of Folk Literature*, Rosenkilde & Bagger, Copenhagen, 1955-8.

23. R. B. ONIANS, *The Origins of European Thought*, Cambridge University Press, 2nd edn, 1954, pp. 109-10.

24. ibid., p. 232.

25. V. W. TURNER, 'Three symbols of *passage* in Ndembu ritual' in Max Gluckman, ed., *Essays on the Ritual of Social Relations*, Manchester University Press, 1962.

PART II

Special Problems and Perspectives

Introduction

Within the bounds of the generic subject of the social aspects of the human body there are two special subjects – firstly, the artistic and secondly, the linguistic aspects of the body – which demand more detailed attention. In my introduction to Part I, I suggested that our subject as a whole has been hampered by confusion with regard to the definition and limits of the subject of 'the body'. I pointed out that we cannot assume that the human body medium and the clothing and adornment which are put on it are, for any native informant, unrelated subjects. The need to appreciate the possible structural and functional inter-relationship of 'the body' and its aids is particularly important (and particularly obvious) with regard to the specialized subjects of the body as art and the body as language.

There is a fine line between the artistic adornment of the human body medium (e.g. scarification) and the various types of bodily decoration which incorporate materials other than the body medium (e.g. body painting). It is true that in terms of artistic media we can distinguish between a stretched ear-lobe and an earring made of a metal, but in terms of artistic and visual effect the distinction may be irrelevant – indeed, the 'earring' may in fact be a weight, the function of which is to stretch the ear-lobe. (See Chapter 5, figures 92 and 93.) Furthermore, there is (as I pointed out in the Introduction to Part I) great difficulty in knowing how to define the human body medium itself. For example, there is (judging by even a quick survey of the literature) little agreement as to whether materials such as hair and fingernails should be included as part of 'the body'. The problem becomes more difficult when we appreciate that witchcraft practices and beliefs about bodily pollution indicate that some peoples assume that both hair and nail-clippings are part of 'the body' – even after these have been cut off and ritually disposed of. Also, in many societies adornment and clothing are thought of as having an intimate association with the body of the person who wears them, such that they too should in some cases be accepted as part of the body set, as the following quotations suggest:

> Prussian folklore has it that if you cannot catch a thief you may get hold of a garment he has dropped in his flight. If this is beaten soundly, the thief falls sick. [This] . . . suggests that the dress is regarded as a part of personality, or an exterior and superficial layer of personality . . . Such examples need not be multiplied, but

their interpretation cannot be found merely in the idea of contagion of physical or magical properties. For early thought it is an obvious inference that a man's nature 'inheres not only in all parts of his body, but in his dress . . .'. (Herbert Spencer as quoted in A. E. Crawley, *Dress, Drink and Drums*, Methuen, 1931, pp. 64–5; reprint of 'Dress', *Encyclopedia of Religion and Ethics*, vol. v, pp. 40–72.)

When Hanun, King of Ammon, cut off half the beard and half the clothes of David's ambassadors when he sent them back, he wanted a guarantee of friendly relations. His wise men, Sir James Frazer observes, would be muttering spells over these personal guarantees while David was on his way. (Crawley, op. cit., p. 158.)

In this volume I have tried to integrate studies of 'the body' and studies of adornment and clothing. This is particularly evident in Chapters 5 and 6 where the subject of bodily decoration is extended to include studies of adornment and clothing. And within the final section entitled Body 'Language', I have included a chapter (8) which pertains specifically to the subject of 'The Language of Dress and Adornment'.

The problem of defining 'the body' is fundamental to all areas of study regarding the social aspects of the body. There are also, however, important problems which are specifically unique to the study of either the artistic aspects or the linguistic aspects of the human body. For example, until very recently many practices of bodily modification which we would now consider 'artistic decoration' were originally dealt with as 'deformations' or 'mutilations'. Now we realize that we cannot go on labelling what we do to our bodies as 'adornment' while labelling what others do to their bodies as 'mutilation'. But we have only just begun to explore the social and cultural functions of body decoration. Why is it that bodily modification and adornment are so widely practised? Why is bodily modification often practised regardless of pain, discomfort and in some cases injury or even death? And why are practices such as scarification frequently employed in initiation rites, and finally what relationship do acts of bodily modification have to processes of socialization?

These questions and many others suggest that bodily adornment constitutes a very special type of decoration and that the artistic uses of the body constitute a very special type of art. The human body (as I suggested in my introduction to Part I) is a unique material or medium of expression in that it can serve to integrate intensely individual and, on the other hand, intensely collective levels of experience. Now we can appreciate that this characteristic is often extended to include the adornment and clothing which is put *onto* the body. The social–individual characteristics of the human body (and its 'aids') are particularly apparent when we consider the artistic aspects and uses of the body, as shown in primitive initiation rites which employ practices of bodily modification and decoration. The scars which Nuer elders, for example, cut into the foreheads of adolescent boys are traditional and collectively motivated and meaningful. Although they are placed on individual bodies, they are (in a sense) not personal or idiosyncratic but serve instead to symbolize the fact that an individual has become a member of the social group, the cultural collective, the 'social body'. These scars are, for the Nuer, symbols of the socialization process and of the collectivity of their existence.

It is relevant from both an artistic and a sociological perspective that the bodily modifications employed in initiation rites are often intended (and may often be effective) as 'permanent' rather than as transitory works of art. For example, Nuer elders apparently hope and expect that the socialization process – the process whereby initiates become members of the social group – will be irreversible and 'permanent'. Therefore, instead of merely using paint or clothing to mark the '*rite de passage*', a 'permanent' scar is made in the body of the initiate (Figure 53). This scar becomes for all concerned a symbol of the relationship of the individual and the social levels of

53. (a) Youth (Zeraf River). (b) Youth (Lou). (c) Man (Zeraf River). From E. E. Evans-Pritchard, *The Nuer*, Oxford University Press, 1940.

human behaviour. Looking at bodily adornment in this way can serve as a tool, a means by which the functional and structural operation of social systems can be better understood. We can see that artistic activities as seemingly destructive as scarification and as seemingly frivolous as fashion can perform valuable – perhaps even *in*valuable – social and socializing functions.

Similarly, studying the 'linguistic aspects' of the body can help us to appreciate the intricacies of social interaction in that it has become increasingly obvious that observing only *verbally* communicated social interaction is analogous to assuming that the entirety of an iceberg is visible above the water-level. Unfortunately, however, many studies of 'body language' have, in fact, been based more in linguistics (or more often pseudo-linguistics) than in *socio*-linguistics and little has thus far been learned about social interaction *per se*. A major focus of concern has been to demonstrate that non-verbal bodily communication is 'language-like' – the underlying assumption apparently being that verbal communication is man's most sophisticated achievement and to demonstrate that non-verbal communication is 'language-like' would elevate the subject to a more respectable status.

The problem, however, is that it cannot be presumed that we can accurately define verbal language, in a cross-cultural sense, so as to enable us to properly compare verbal language with non-verbal communication. It has been suggested (see Edward Hall in Chapter 9 of this volume) that a principal 'design feature' of language is that it is always arbitrary (e.g. 'whale' is a little word for a big object – 'micro-organism' is the reverse). Although the vast majority of words in Western languages are obviously arbitrary, I am suspicious of the general presumption that all human verbal communication is equally arbitrary. In brief, we cannot be sure what non-verbal communication would have to be like in order for it to be properly described as 'language-like'.

Personally, I believe that rather than debating this sort of issue, time would be more profitably spent by considering *both* verbal and non-verbal communication under one general heading of 'sign systems'; that these signs (regardless of whether verbal or non-verbal) should be classified according to a typology of signs (e.g. arbitrary versus motivated signs) and that the anthropologist (or sociologist) should explore whether certain types of signs are rooted in and generated by certain social situations (e.g. do particular types of social environments generate verbal *and* non-verbal sign systems which operate according to arbitrary processes of signification?). By adopting an approach of this type, the study of the linguistic aspects of the body could be moved on into the overall framework of the study of the social aspects of the body and in so doing, the social underpinnings of language and, as we saw earlier, of art, could be explored and underlined.

A. Body 'Decoration'

5. Body Alteration and Adornment: A Pictorial Essay

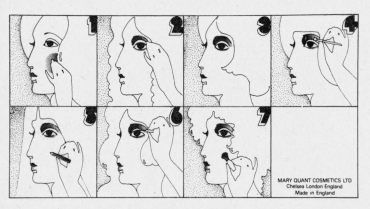

54. From Mary Quant make-up instructions leaflet, Mary Quant Cosmetics Ltd.

The majority of the illustrations in this chapter are taken from Adolfo Dembo and J. Imbelloni, Deformaciones Intencionales del Cuerpo Humano de Carácter Étnico (Humanior, Biblioteca del Americanista Moderno (José Anesil), Buenos Aires, 1938). (*The captions to these illustrations have been translated and in some cases altered by the editor.*) *Figures 56 and 64 are from Eric John Dingwall,* Artificial Cranial Deformation: A Contribution to the Study of Ethnic Mutilations (John Bale, Sons and Danielson, London, 1931), *and are specifically marked as such.*

Alterations to the body medium

Cranial 'deformation'

Figures 55–9 and 64 show some cranial 'deformations' deliberately produced by bandaging. Figures 60–63 show equipment used to produce such 'deformations' of the skull.

55. French child wearing a 'bandeau' (after Foville).

56. 'Deformed' head due to bandaging. (Dingwall)

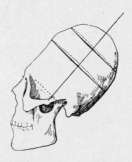

57. 'Deformed' head due to use of tight bands (after Foville).

58. Diagram showing a 'deformed' skull. (Imbelloni)

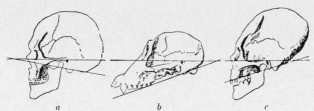

a   *b*   *c*

59. Skull shapes for (a) normal man (b) a gorilla (c) 'deformed' skull. (Imbelloni)

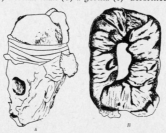

a   *B*

60. Apparatus for cranial 'deformation' from Cerro Colorado (Peru):
(a) 'Deformed' infant's skull with apparatus (after photograph by Yacovleff and Muelle).
(b) The small cushion at the back of the skull in fig. a (after Weiss).

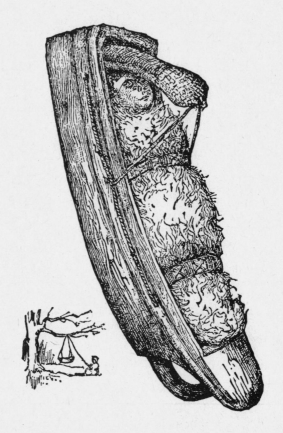

61. Chinook cradle with arrangement for flattening the forehead (after Mason).

62. Apparatus for cranial 'deformation' used by the natives of the Celebes (after Baron van Hoevell).

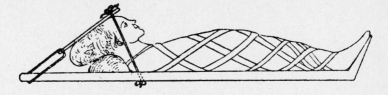

63. Cradle for cranial 'deformation' (after Meyer).

64. Peruvian child Mummy (after d'Orbigny).
(Dingwall)

Teeth-filing and incrustation

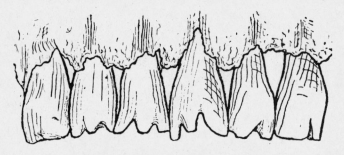

65. Filed teeth from the pre-Columbian Tarascan, Mexico (after Lumholtz).

66. Tooth found on Monte Albán, Mexico (after Batres).

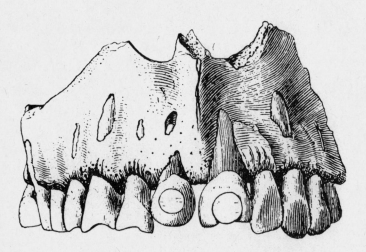

67. Inlaid and carved teeth from Esmeraldas, Ecuador (after Saville).

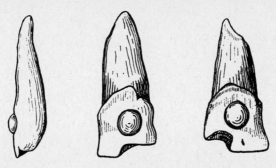

68. Filed and inlaid incisors excavated at Copan, Honduras (after Saville).

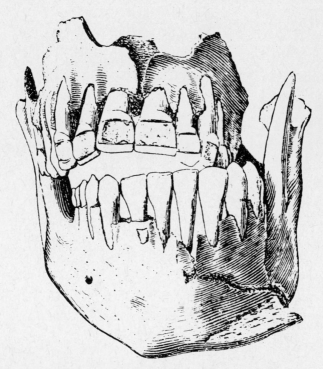

69. Teeth carved for laminated incrustations of gold from Esmeraldas, Ecuador (after Saville).

Scarification

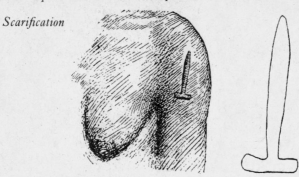

70. Scar on a woman from the island of Dauan (south-east of New Guinea) which represents the nose of a dead brother in natural size and is called *Piti tonar*.

71. Tribal insignia scarification designs on some men of the Fly River delta, New Guinea (after Bruce-Haddon).

72. Characteristic chest scars of the Saguane, Fly River delta, New Guinea (after Bruce-Haddon).

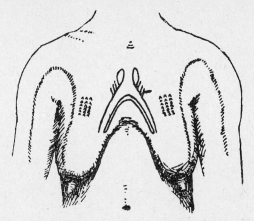

73. Variations of chest scarification designs on a Mawata woman, New Guinea (after Bruce-Haddon).

74. Congolese youth adorned with a complicated scar pattern. The Congolese use mud to obtain the raised design (after McBride).

75. Australian aborigines with designs of scarred lines on torso and extremities.

Other alterations of the body medium

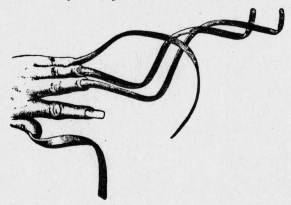

76. Long fingernails which in some societies signified wealth or asceticism (after Tylor).

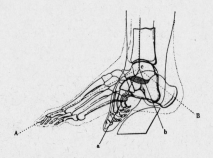

77. The planes of normal foot A, B, and the planes of a foot which has been bound (a), (b) (after Roth).

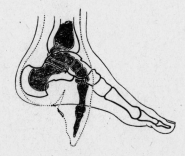

78. Comparison between a normal foot and a Chinese foot (dotted line) which has been bound (after Flower).

79. Native of New Guinea with an artificially constricted waist (after Bruce-Haddon).

80. A girl of old Calabar, West Africa, (a) before and (b) after artificial fattening (photograph by Malcolm).

Decorative additions to the body medium

Tattooing and painting

81. Hand tattoos from the Marquesas Islands (after Willowdean Chatterson Handy).

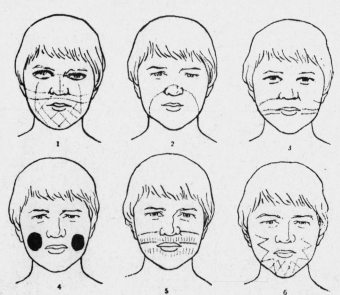

82. Face painting designs common among the Ashluslay of the Chaco (after Palavecino).

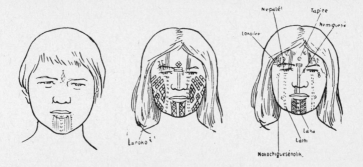

83. Facial tattoos of Pilaga women of the Chaco (after Palavecino).

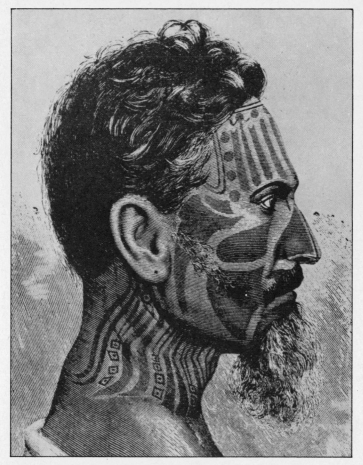

84. Tahitian facial tattooing (after Stolpe).

85. Tattooed right leg of a woman of Western Laos (Indochina) showing 1 mouse, 2 cloud, 3 dove, 4, 9, 14 vultures, 5, 10, 13 mythological animals, 6, 15, 16 lions, 7, 11 bats, 8 civet, 12 heron (after Bock).

86. Tattoos on a female of the Marquesas Islands: (a) shows the leg as seen from the front and (b) shows the back of the same leg (after Handy).

87. Body painting of the natives of the Upper Mississippi (after G. Catlin).

88. (a) Ona Indians of the Shelknam tribe, Tierra del Fuego, with ceremonial body paint. (b) Ona Indians with body paint and head-dresses (photographs by Gusinde).

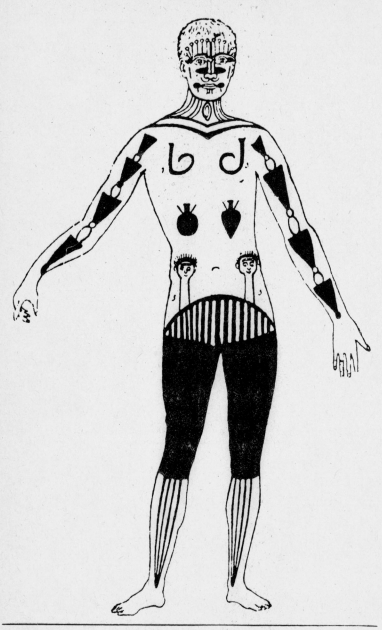

89. Tattooing on a native of Rapa-Nui, Easter Islands (after K. Routledge).

The addition of ornament

90. Nose-ring customary among the Gabili women of Timbuctu (after Huchery).

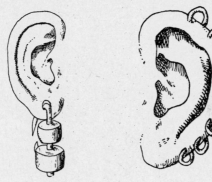

91. Ear ornamentation of the natives of the Timbuctu region (after Huchery).

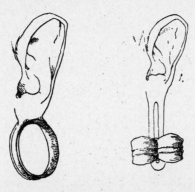

92. Stretching and ornamentation of the ear-lobes by the natives of Nias, Indonesia (after Modigliani).

93. Kikuyu girl with ear ornaments.

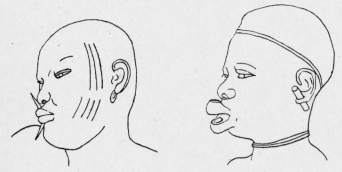

94. (*left*). Ule woman with lip ornaments made of bone (after Labouret).

95. Lobi woman with wooden lip ornaments and ears pierced with cane (after Huchery).

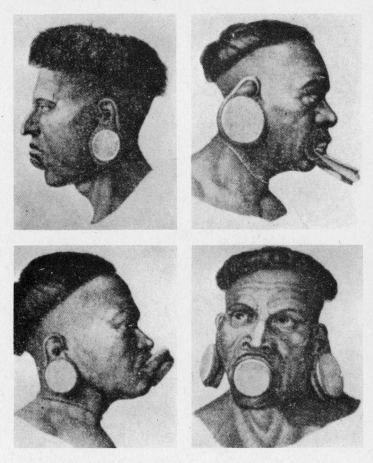

96. Botocudo, Brazil, males with ear and lip discs (photograph by de Wied).

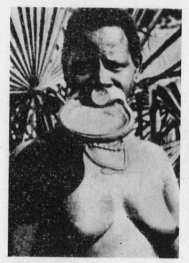

97. Sara woman with lip disc (photograph by Weinert).

98. Aino woman with characteristic tattoos round the lips and chest ornaments (photograph by Weinert).

99. Nose and chest ornaments from Melanesia (photograph by L. Schultze).

100. Masai woman of the Kilimanjaro region with metal rings around her arms and neck (photograph by Rickli).

6. Beyond the Body Medium: The Naked and the Nude

101. 'Although stark nakedness may never become socially acceptable in a Puritan country, some baubles and trinkets or a few yards of strategically placed beads may lend a semblance of being well-dressed to an otherwise unclothed body. Detail from an *Allegory on Man's Mortality* by Niklaus Manuel Deutsch.' Caption from Bernard Rudofsky, *The Unfashionable Human Body*, Hart-Davis, 1972, p. 53.

For me, the naked and the nude
(By lexicographers construed
As synonyms that should express
The same deficiency of dress
Or shelter) stand as wide apart
As love from lies, or truth from art.

Lovers without reproach will gaze
On bodies naked and ablaze;
The Hippocratic eye will see
In nakedness, anatomy;
And naked shines the Goddess when
She mounts her lion among men.

The nude are bold, the nude are sly
To hold each treasonable eye.
While draping by a showman's trick
Their dishabille in rhetoric,
They grin a mock-religious grin
Of scorn at those of naked skin.

The naked, therefore, who compete
Against the nude may know defeat;
Yet when they both together tread
The briary pastures of the dead,
By Gorgons with long whips pursued,
How naked go the sometime nude!

Poem by Robert Graves in *Robert Graves:
Selected by Himself* (Penguin Books, Harmondsworth, 1972, p. 131)

The social aspects of the human body do not necessarily end with the limits of the physical medium of the body, but often extend outwards to include all types of adornment and clothing. The distinction between nakedness, on the one hand, and nudity, on the other, helps us to appreciate the inter-relationship of the body medium and its 'aids' of clothing and adornment. A nude body clothed only in a G-string and adorned with paint and feathers – whether that of a Brazilian Indian or that of a stripper in Soho – is not naked. Very rarely is the anthropologist or sociologist justified in studying the human body *as if* it were stark naked: there are no 'naked savages' and the study of body behaviour must take this into account so as to include the clothing and adornment of the body within the study of the social aspects of the body.

An essay which deals with the Nuer, a Nilotic people who live in the Sudan, and which concentrates on the related subjects of nakedness, nudity, adornment and clothing, opens this chapter. H. Th. Fischer's 'The clothes of the naked Nuer' helps us to appreciate that the body and its adornment and clothing may constitute one unified subject of inquiry. As we can see in Figures 102 and 103 the Nuer wear what is by our standards a minimal amount of clothing. But as Fischer points out, it would be a mistake to think of them as being naked. Equally, it would be a mistake to study their meagre clothing and adornment independently of their bodily behaviour and expression.

The intimate relationship of clothing, adornment and the human body (as reflected in subtle definitions of nakedness and nudity) is not, of course, unique to the Nuer, and neither is it unique to the tribal setting. In the West, trends in fashion have continually modified our assumptions about where clothing ought to end and where the body ought to begin. Changes in hem-length, depth and width of décolletage, the exposure of the arms and shoulders, etc., have generated patterns of what the fashion historian James Laver has called 'shifting erogenous zones'. Jane Richardson and Alfred Kroeber in their now classic study 'Three centuries of women's dress fashions' quantitatively reported the changing patterns of concealment and exposure which have occurred in women's evening dress design from 1787 to 1936. There is not room here to reproduce their study in full, but even a cursory glance at two of the graphs which summarize their findings serves to demonstrate that the definition of nakedness can vary temporally just as ethnographic studies such as Fischer's demonstrate that it can vary from one part of the world to another.

102. Nuer males. From E. E. Evans-Pritchard, *The Nuer*, Oxford University Press, 1940, plate viii.

103. Nuer girl. From E. E. Evans-Pritchard, *The Nuer*, Oxford University Press, 1940, plate xiii.

104. An illustration from the Nigerian magazine *The Bureaucrat*, which appeared in 'Ian Macintyre writes about Nigeria's military regime', *The Listener*, 89, 2307 (14 June 1973).

Ali Mazrui's 'The robes of rebellion: Sex, dress and politics in Africa' brings the problem of defining nakedness and nudity back full circle to the African setting. Mazrui explores the confusion which has often occurred when Western, Westernized and tribal definitions of dress, clothing, nakedness and nudity are brought into juxtaposition in the urban centres of black Africa. As the changing hemlines of Western fashion bring the West closer to 'naked Africa', the Westernized African often finds that his own definitions of nakedness and nudity are opposed to *both* the traditional and the modern styles of dress.

The lack of a cross-culturally and temporally fixed definition of nakedness and nudity makes it clear that only an arbitrary line of demarcation can be drawn between the social aspects of the body, the social aspects of adornment and the social aspects of clothing. The essays which appear in this chapter are in a sense unique in that they ignore the traditional academic division between the subject of the behaviour of the human body and the separate subjects of adornment and clothing. Throughout this present volume (and especially in the following chapters) it is assumed that the social aspects of the body may extend beyond flesh and bones to include clothing and adornment in the fullest sense of these terms.

H. Th. Fischer:
'*The clothes of the naked Nuer*'

From *International Archives of Ethnography*, 50 (1964), 60–71.

H. Th. Fischer's essay appears below in unedited form. Parts of it relate to a somewhat dated argument concerning the 'origins' of clothing. During a certain period in anthropology and in many historical studies of clothing and fashion, various arguments were put forth to suggest that clothing began as a form of protection, for reasons of modesty, for identification or for various other reasons. Recently anthropologists and historians have recognized that it is rather foolish to suppose that one primary, worldwide, original 'function' of clothing and adornment can be found. Fischer's 'The clothes of the naked Nuer' may have helped to end this debate once and for all. This is not the only importance of Fischer's essay, however. In combining the two traditionally distinct subjects of clothing and (to borrow another phrase from James Laver) the 'clothes-peg' of the human body, Fischer's essay is important as a harbinger of a new unified science of body behaviour, bodily adornment, clothing and fashion.

Those who write about clothing nearly always want to express their opinion about its origin. Although it is clear that it is absolutely impossible to know anything about it, the pronouncements made are often very positive, this positiveness being inversely proportional to factual knowledge. Men lived hundred thousand years on earth without leaving us any trace of their cultures. The rock paintings and engravings of southern France, Spain or Bushmen, much more recent, show us naked men, but others clearly wearing clothes. Moreover the pictures show us them in a hunting situation and we know that the Fuegians of South America were always naked when hunting, while they still wore a kind of clothing when staying in their camps.

Strange enough it is so, that if we will study the phenomenon of 'clothing', the meaning of this term becomes very problematic indeed. It then becomes difficult to tell whether a person is naked or not. We ourselves wear clothes, but our hands and face are naked. In normal life European men do not have their feet or knees bare but there are situations in which one has to undress certain parts of the body to be properly dressed. A Balinese woman may have the upper part of her body uncovered, but never will appear with bare legs, while the reverse is the case with the European one, even when she wears a bikini. The leopard-skin chief of the Nuer wearing only a leopard skin around his shoulders seems to us rather naked.

If one only speaks of being dressed when a man or woman wears a loincloth it only means that one selects one of the many functions of clothing to be the real one. This means that we assume that among all others, the covering of the pudenda must be the original function of clothing.

But there certainly is no reason why one should do this. The complex phenomenon, called clothing, does not have and apparently cannot have one single origin, as nevertheless many anthropologists and psychologists seem to accept. No wonder that they differ greatly in opinion. There are among them who tell us that feelings of modesty or shame have created clothing, while others see as its oldest function that of sex-allurement. To others clothing originally must have had a practical purpose; in the beginning it was simply a protection against climate, insects, brambles or other hardships. To others the first clothing was began by being a kind of gadget for carrying necessary instruments leaving the hands free, while others think that women-clothing in the beginning had something to do with the menstrual period. To some the first clothing meant to be a protection against the evil eye or other supernatural perils, while other authors tell us that nakedness and especially the naked genitals, radiate magical powers and therefore have to be covered. To others again the first clothes were ornaments or badges.

There are still more hypotheses and each anthropologist defends his own with astounding conviction, speaking almost with contempt about dissentient opinions. The more satisfied he is, the greater his contempt. Thus e.g. Dunlap,[1] who attacks, among other hypotheses, the modesty theory of clothing, writes that this theory, which, as he puts it, troubles popular moralists and bobs up in police regulations, 'seems still to be entrenched among the ignorant'.

Those who defend the 'fig-leaf theory' are not less positive in their pronouncements. Thus the fathers Schmidt and Koppers, attacking evolutionistic theories, point at the so-called '*Urvölker*', which to them wear a shame-covering. Being obliged to concede the existence of naked pygmies, they declare them to be 'exceptions proving the rule'.[2] Without any comment they pass the 'naked' Nilotic peoples, and suggest in doing so that their nakedness is the product of degeneration.

Leaving the theories of origin for what they are, we will see now what Evans-Pritchard has to tell us about the function of clothing in Nuer culture.[3] We cannot expect to find in his monographs a special chapter or paragraph dealing with clothing[4] and such a chapter would certainly have been of less interest anyway than the scattered data which we can gather throughout his books. What he writes about Nuer clothing is exactly of value because of the context. Mentioning social institutions and behaviour he notes details about the use of clothes, and thus we learn much more about their functional values, than any special paragraph could have given us.

Evans-Pritchard's data are confirmed and amplified by Miss Huffman's *Nuer Customs and Folklore*,[5] while Evans-Pritchard himself was so kind as to give me supplementary comments on some of the passages out of his books.

On page 40 of *The Nuer* we read that the Nuer are 'stark naked' and the reader is asked 'to look at some illustrations . . . which will convey to him . . . the crudity of kraal life'. These illustrations confirm indeed the nakedness of Nuer men and women and those we find in *Kinship and Marriage* do the same. But already these pictures teach us that the Nuer are not totally devoid of clothes. In fact Evans-Pritchard has much to say on the subject of clothing which may warn us to read the assertions about the nakedness of peoples with caution and explains how it is possible that cross-cultural studies show such divergent opinions.[6]

The illustrations in Evans-Pritchard's books show us stark naked men and women, but they show us too that these naked persons wear without any exception a string or girdle round their loins. What is the function of this string? Crawley[7] assumes that this girdle, which, according to him, is very common where no clothes are worn, 'is the point of departure for the evolution of dress', and he explains its function as to be that of 'a continuous pocket'. 'The savage finds it indispensable for carrying articles which he constantly needs, and which otherwise would encumber his hands. Once fitted with a waist-string, the body, as a machine, is enormously improved, being able to carry the artificial aids of manual operations ready for use as occasion requires, without hampering the work of that universal lever, the hand.'

This is a wild story, typical for the reasoning of those who wish to construct pseudo-historical evolutions. Evans-Pritchard in his books does not say a word about the function of the waist-string and when asked about it wrote: 'I do not know what its function is. Sometimes it is a special string of mourning, when a close relative has died. The ordinary cord may have a symbolic connection with the tethering-rope of cattle.' So the only thing that can be said for the present is that, if one wishes to call the string an article of cloth, all Nuer wear clothes. To me however it seems rather pedantic to do so.

But, as has been said already, even the illustrations show that the Nuer are acquainted with clothes. Moreover it is evident that, as everywhere else, here too exists a difference between male and female clothing.

Woman's clothes

Unmarried girls go normally naked. However, if there are feasts, and girls and boys dance together, the former adorn themselves. They are decked with flowers and ornaments, anointed with oil and wear long skirts made of grass. 'The long grass skirt reaches from hip to ankle and is worn as a dance dress.'[8] This dancing-dress is not explicitly mentioned by Evans-Pritchard, but his text shows that on different occasions (especially during the marriage ceremonies) the girls are dressed in a sense. When the bride is brought to the village of her bridegroom, we read, 'Then, towards evening, takes place the rite of consummation, though there is no invariable order of events in these ceremonies and no fixed time-table. The bride retires to a hut wearing a special goatskin cap and here the bridegroom joins her. His age-mates seek him out and say to him: "Come now let the people go to bed, come and loosen the bride's girdle." '[9]

In his letter to me Evans-Pritchard wrote that by this 'bride's girdle' the Nuer meant the skirt which 'she (the bride), as well as her companions, would be wearing at the marriage ceremonies and also at all dances. This is something quite different from a married woman's skirt: it is just an ornamental attire for dancing; when dancing is over the girls take them off.'

This married woman's skirt is also mentioned by Huffman who writes: 'A woman after marriage must always wear a loincloth of some description.' It 'consists of a triangular piece of sheepskin worn over the pubic region, with a larger triangular piece of sheepskin at the back, the two pieces meeting at the waistline at each side but not overlapping to any extent' (p. 4).[10] Huffman (p. 5) also mentions a *short* grass skirt, which 'may also be worn as a garment by a married woman'.

The foregoing is supplemented by Evans-Pritchard who wrote me: 'Till marriage girls are naked. After marriage they wear a special little skirt but may take it off when they please till they have had a child. After the birth of a child only their husbands see them naked in the privacy of a hut when the spouses sleep together. After the birth of a child no woman goes naked in public again.' And also: 'One can *at once* tell a married woman (after the birth of her first child – which for Nuer completes the marriage), by her skirt. She is never without it.'

So the loincloth is for Nuer women a token of the married status. There are however more such tokens. The marriage ceremonies end with the shaving of the bride's head and this too expresses the change in her status. The Nuer call this ceremony 'the removal of the hairs of maidenhood'. At the same time the bride is 'stripped of all her ornaments, which are divided among her husband's kin, and she is arrayed in new finery provided by her husband'.[11]

The same ceremony is described by Huffman, who then however mentions the providing of the bride with the married woman's garb. 'When she is married, she gives all her ornaments to her husband's people, who in return give her the married woman's dress and such ornaments as they wish to give her.'[12]

Among the cattle given as bride-price Evans-Pritchard mentions two cows, which have to do with these ceremonies. They are called the '*yang yani*' i.e. 'cow of the skirts', the mark of the married status, and the '*yang miemne*', i.e. 'cow of the hairs' which are shaved off the bride's head at the consummation.[13]

There still is another piece of women's clothing which is mentioned by Huffman and which also is to be found among other Nilotic and Nilotic–Hamitic peoples. She writes: 'And as she (the married woman, F.) grows older, she usually wears a cloth of sheepskin over the upper part of the body, under one arm and fastened over the opposite shoulder' (p. 4). The same cloth is mentioned a second time when Huffman writes: 'The Nuer girl may or may not wear a cloth, just as it suits her. If she does wear one, it is worn under one arm and knotted over the opposite shoulder . . . But no matter how many garments she may possess, the Nuer girl – if unmarried – may discard any or all of them at will' (p. 5). It is no wonder that we don't read about this latter garment in Evans-Pritchard's monographs, since its only function seems to be that of a cover against the cold.

Man's clothes

Miss Huffman states that 'clothing is not considered essential by the Nuer man and is not usually worn' (p. 3). Nevertheless we shall see that under certain conditions it may be very essential for him.

The most spectacular piece of clothing certainly is the leopardskin, which is worn by the otherwise naked chief as a garment. It unmistakably is a badge, indicating his social status. It might be said that it is more a badge than a cloth and neither Evans-Pritchard nor Huffman mention it as such. Herbert Spencer, whose opinion it is that all clothing originated in the wearing of badges, would say that the skirt worn by the 'leopard-skin chief' is 'still' a badge and 'not yet' a true garment.

But the illustrations show other Nuer men wearing loincloths. Normally this loincloth is a wild-cat skin and both our informants[14] tell us that just as the woman's loincloth it has something to do with marriage. For a man must not appear naked before his parents-in-law, or even before those who possibly may become his parents-in-law. This rule applies, though in a lesser degree, also to other in-laws and even to the wives of his wife's close kinsmen. 'I have seen,' writes Evans-Pritchard, 'a man's wife's paternal aunt make a great fuss when unintentionally he appeared naked before her. He knelt behind another man to hide his nakedness and receive her reproaches when he became aware of his misdemeanour. On another occasion the fuss was made by a bride's paternal uncle's wife while the astonished bridegroom hastily retired into a hut.'[15]

For these stark-naked Nuer the tabu of being naked already begins before marriage. When a young man proposes officially to the people of the girl he wants to marry, he and his accompanying friends wear skins to cover their genitals.[16] One of the main features of a wedding is the discussion about the cattle of the bride-wealth and then not only the bridegroom and his friends, but even the bride's father and his 'master of ceremonies' wear wild-cat skins round their loins.[17]

It is very interesting to note that the prohibition of nakedness finds a parallel in another tabu, which however seems to have a larger radius of action. We hear that a Nuer must abstain from eating in the presence of unrelated women and vice versa. This tabu is already inculcated to rather young children. 'A small boy eats with his mother and sisters, but when he is about six he eats with the other boys of the household when the womenfolk have guests, lest they might feel embarrassed at the presence of a lad, though only a small one, and, bit by bit, he gets into the habit of eating with them regularly.'[18]

A youth is particularly careful not to be seen eating by unrelated girls: 'If he is not making love to them, he may do so some time or to one of their relatives.' When I asked whether it would matter if your sisters saw you eating, the reply was, 'Do you make love to your sisters?' Food must never be mentioned in the presence of girls, and a man will endure severe hunger rather than let them know that he has not eaten for a long time. It is a strict rule of Nuer society that the sexes, unless they are close kin, avoid each other in the matter of food. Nuer do not go near persons of the other sex when they are eating. A man may mention food but not sexual matters before kinswomen, and he may mention sexual matters but not food before unrelated girls.[19]

This eating prohibition however does not only apply to persons of the other sex. It has also to do with the in-law relationship. Thus Evans-Pritchard writes: 'Even before a young man has started to look for a bride he will not generally eat with much senior men, unless they are kin, because one of them might become his father-in-law. Once he has asked for a girl's hand in marriage he may under no circumstances eat in her home, and the prohibition continues, sometimes greatly to his discomfort, until two or three children have been born . . .'[20] Even husband and wife never eat together during the first years of their marriage.[21]

A married woman stays to live in the homestead of her own parents till after the weaning of her first child[22] or, as Miss Huffman says, during the first two years of her marriage (p. 41). Until the first child is born the husband visits his wife when everyone is asleep. He spends the night with her in the hut, given to the wife by her parents, leaving before any of the wife's people are about. The parents and kin of a young wife scarcely acknowledge her husband's existence and are supposed to know nothing of his visits;[23] the wife herself feigns annoyance or lack of interest, if told that her husband has come. She pretends 'that she is still unmarried, a shyness she keeps up with third persons, though she is at ease when alone with her husband'. We have seen that during this time she may even appear naked, i.e. without the married woman's garb.

Only after the birth of the first child the marriage is held to have become a complete union, and then the husband may visit his wife openly 'though he must continue to treat his in-laws, particularly his parents-in-law, with great respect, expressed in formal modes of address, which are reciprocal, and in other ways, most emphatically in the prohibitions on eating in their home and appearing naked before them'.[24]

It is clear that these prohibitions may be felt as a hindrance and that they have the tendency to wear out after some years. Moreover it is obvious that the rules of avoidance are even much more inconvenient for the wife and her in-laws, when, after the first two years of marriage, she lives amongst her husband's kin. First of all she will begin with sharing her husband's meal when they are alone. Soon after the wife 'has taken up residence in her husband's home it will be arranged that her husband enters as though by accident a hut in which she is eating. After this it is no longer shameful for husband and wife to see one another eating,'[25] though the wife at first will still be shy. Although nothing is said by Evans-Pritchard about the woman not eating with her parents-in-law, and no ceremony is mentioned by which this and other tabus are relaxed and abolished, we may understand that after some time many of the avoidances will be mitigated. The wife however never will appear in public without her loincloth.

The rules of avoidance regulating the behaviour between a man and his in-laws are relaxed by a formal ceremony when two or three children are born. 'The father-in-law prepares beer, kills a goat or sheep, and invites the son-in-law and his kin to his home to partake of a feast. He tells his son-in-law that there is no need for him to respect his parents-in-law any more. The son-in-law will refuse to eat, however, till compelled to do so by the insistence of his father-in-law's kin and by his father-in-law's gift of a cow to his daughter's husband's brother. Henceforth he is allowed to eat with his parents-in-law and to appear naked before them.'[26]

'Later, the father-in-law visits the homestead of his daughter's husband's brother and will be given beer and meat. Before he can eat or drink he must be given a bull calf or sheep by the owner of the homestead.' The father of the bridegroom and the father of the bride have passed a similar ceremony shortly after the consummation of the marriage of their children. The rules of avoidance between them are very numerous. Nevertheless, it is customary for the father of the bridegroom and the father of the bride to give each other a spear or goat, 'to enable the two men to eat in one another's homes without shame'.[27]

We shall not here follow up all the remaining, very intricate, rules of behaviour between the in-laws, which include other avoidances but also a joking relationship, allowing foul language and horseplay in which there is a lifting up of the married woman's skirt.[28]

Finally there is still one information given by Miss Huffman in her description of the initiation ceremonies, which invites our attention. 'All male Nuer are initiated from boyhood to manhood by a severe operation (*gar*). Their brows are cut to the bone with a small knife, in six long cuts from ear to ear.'[29] After this operation the initiated boy is carefully guarded, as Huffman tells us, against the evil eye. It is for this reason that he wears 'a piece of sheepskin over his head, this piece of sheepskin being one part, the back section, of a married woman's garb which has been given for this purpose'.[30] I wonder if the goatskin cap which, according to Evans-Pritchard, the wife is wearing when she retires to a hut for the consummation of marriage, has this same protecting function (see above). Evans-Pritchard mentions a goatskin, while Miss Huffman speaks about a piece of sheepskin, but this will not be of importance since the former tells us that both, 'the skins of goats and sheeps are worn as loin garments by married women'.[31]

If we look over the information about the clothes of the Nuer, the functions of some of the articles of clothing are clear. The long grass skirt is a dancing-dress and has ornamental value. The leopard-skin is a badge. The cloth worn by women over the upper part of the body is a cover against the cold. If we accept Miss Huffman's explanation of the sheepskin cap worn by the Nuer boys after the cutting of the brows as reproducing *Nuer* opinion, this cap is a protection against the evil eye. It is clear that there is no reason whatever to assume an evolutionistic sequence of the different kinds of clothing. Why should one suppose that the need of protection is older than that of ornament or of wearing a badge? Why should one of the particular clothes mentioned be the original one, if all have such different functions?

But what to say about the function of the loincloth? It has unmistakably to do with sex and marriage. The obligation to cover the genitals has to do with marriage and not with sexual life as such, and it is felt towards both, the own and the other sex, though it seems to be more stringent towards the latter. Not wearing the loincloth at the proper time is felt as a misdemeanour and causes shame.

Has this covering of the pudenda its origin in a feeling of shame or is the reverse true? The answer seems simple. How may one conceive the feeling of shame to be the origin of clothing, while most of the people in most situations go stark naked? Still it is an intricate problem. When shame is not the original motive for wearing a loincloth, there must be another one and then fancies have free play, and everyone may choose his own, as we saw in the beginning.

Apart from unprofitable speculations, the Nuer material gives us one other possibility only. The initiated boys, after the operation, wear a sheepskin over their head, which is usually the back section of the married woman's garb, as a protection against the evil eye. It might be concluded that the woman's loincloth itself must have therefore the same function. Even then, however, nothing is said about the function of the loincloth of the men, neither about the question whether this protecting function of the married woman's garb is the original one.

Seeing what has been written about the wearing of Nuer loincloths and the eating tabus, it is hardly possible to maintain that its original function must have been that of protection against the evil eye. Accepting as an undeniable fact that the actual manifestations of shame are indeed caused by habit and convention, this does not exclude the possibility of the innate impulse of shame being a cause of some specific clothing.[32]

For there *is* an innate feeling of shame amply demonstrated by the behaviour of men and women all over the world, and accepted as such by all psychologists who, on the other hand, differ in many respects when writing about shame.

Psychologists may teach us that it is very difficult to say what shame really is. To differentiate the concept shame from such concepts as timidity, bashfulness, remorse, etc. is not easily done. The distinction between 'mental' and 'bodily' shame (*Geistes- und Leibesscham*) is a subject of much controversy. If such a distinction is to be made, what then is the relation between them? To Scheler,[33] whose exposition, although partly spoiled by a distinct 'Nazi' vision, is one of the best, bodily shame seems to be the original one, from which mental shame is to be deduced. Bollnow[34] in his remarkable study about '*die Ehrfurcht*' criticizes Scheler on this point, and Stern writes that children know mental shame long before bodily shame.[35]

How this may be, the behaviour of those who are ashamed is the same all over the world. When one is ashamed, one lowers one's eyes, since the contact with others is unbearable. All that one wants is not-to-be-there; to sink into the ground, and this wish may be so strong that suicide is the result.[36] If the feelings of shame are caused by the misbehaviour of another, he who is ashamed also looks away. So the sons of Noah did while covering their father's nakedness. So shame creates, so to say, a cover, even if it is not always a material one.

A most interesting picture of such a non-material covering is also given by Whiting.[37] Kwoma (New Guinea) men and women go stark naked but in their behaviour they show the wish to 'cover' the pudenda. A small boy already learns not to look at the private parts of his mother and sisters. Later on he learns that even staring at a girl's body in general is not allowed and so he keeps his eyes fixed on the ground or sits or stands with his back to a woman whenever he is in her presence. It is such an intricate behaviour that one is apt to think that it would have been easier to invent clothing. 'A properly modest Kwoma girl' sits in a special way and never will bend over in the presence of men lest they would see her pudenda. She may only do so when she is wearing her net bag hanging down her back. Evans-Pritchard wrote me: 'It is the same with Nuer girls. Though they are naked, they take care in the presence of men to sit with their thighs against each other. It would be wanton to sit with the legs wide apart.'

I think Scheler (p. 55) is right in saying that the special position of man in the long scale of beings, his situation between the divine and the animality, finds no feeling so clear, so keen and so direct an expression, as exactly in the feeling of shame. Shame arises when man acknowledges his own or others' deficiencies. Man feels ashamed when he becomes conscious of himself. It is this what is meant in Genesis (iii, 7), where it reads: 'And the eyes of them both were opened, and they knew that they were naked.' 'The shame which attends on this is not a sense of sin; it is a kind of knowledge, to which childhood could not attain.'[38] The same again we find expressed by Buytendijk saying: 'Shame is the feeling of existential unworthiness.'[39]

If under certain circumstances, normally in front of others, one's attention is drawn to one's own bodilyness, feelings of shame are roused. 'Bodilyness' must then be taken in a broad sense as Scheler means when he says that: 'in der Scham "Geist" und "Fleisch", Ewigkeit und Zeitlichkeit, Wesen und Existenz sich auf merkwürdige und dunkle Weise berühren'. Thus we may understand the parent-in-law tabus of the Nuer and so many other peoples and the attitude of the newly married towards each other. Until the first child is born, the marriage-bond, although being effected in public, is ignored by the parents of the young couple. The betrothed and the newly married husband and wife avoid any demonstration of sympathy in the presence of others, lest they should feel ashamed. Although since long before they may have had sexual intercourse, which fact was known by all, now that their relation is officially acknowledged it is felt to be of too personal a character.

Although sexual matters may be openly discussed and feelings of sin towards, or a condemnation of, all that regards sexuality and nakedness is unknown, shame arises when the situation becomes too personal. This is explicitly expressed by another Nilotic tribe, the Lango. The avoidance by a man of his mother-in-law and the reverence paid to her is said by them 'to be due to the idea that it would be unseemly for a woman to see the nakedness of a man who has had sexual relations with her daughter'.[40] Thus the necessity of 'covering' the pudenda in the presence of the in-laws could arise, although other solutions would have been possible. Very interesting is for instance the solution of the Dinka, a people culturally closely related to the Nuer. 'When a (Dinka) boy comes to the house of his betrothed the girl's mother pulls a skin over her eyes.'[41]

The feelings of shame roused by eating together, so strange to us, is nevertheless found in several peoples. Well known is what Karl von den Steinen tells us about the Bakaïri in South America. Sitting in a circle of naked men one of them offers him a piece of fish. Being hungry he begins to eat from it. All Bakaïri men turn their face away and it is clear that they feel ashamed. One of them, being more friendly with him, indicates von den Steinen to go into his hut. One does not eat in the presence of other people. He who wants to eat retires to his hut or eats behind a tree.

We may understand this if we compare it with the shame felt when seen defecating and urinating. Evans-Pritchard wrote me: 'The sexes go apart in different directions for the purpose. One should not see a person of the opposite sex performing these actions – but in the case of man and wife it would not matter – and, of course these things are of little importance so far as children are concerned.' The words here used by Evans-Pritchard could be exactly the same when recording the eating prohibitions of the Nuer. Eating and defecating both draw the attention to one's own body and may require therefore privacy, i.e. a covering. This need may be felt but is not always felt in the same way. With the Nuer it is especially felt in the presence of the in-laws, as long as their mutual bond is not yet accepted.

The feelings of shame, roused by the consciousness of one's bodilyness and 'existential unworthiness', always create some cover. Thus there is every reason to accept the loincloth of Nuer men and women as finding their origin in shame, 'an emotion,' as MacDougall calls it, 'second to none in the extent of its influence on social behaviour'.[42] This does not mean that we see in the emotion of shame *the* cause of *all* human, or of *all* Nuer clothing. In shame we see *one* of the manifold origins of (some specific) clothing, while at the same time many feelings of shame find their origin in the fact of clothing itself.

Notes

1. K. DUNLAP, 'The development and function of clothing', *Journal of General Psychology*, 1 (1928), 65.

2. W. SCHMIDT and W. KOPPERS, *Völker und Kulturen*, 1924, p. 435.

3. E. E. EVANS-PRITCHARD, *The Nuer*, Clarendon Press, Oxford, 1940, and *Kinship and Marriage among the Nuer*, Clarendon Press, Oxford, 1951.

4. 'Earlier field-work monographs were descriptive accounts of peoples: modern field-work monographs are analytical studies of sociological problems. The earlier books were about such-and-such a people and consisted of a succession of chapters each dealing with a different aspect of their life. Modern treatises, whatever their titles may be, are written to a sociological theme around a general problem in one of the social sciences' (E. E. Evans-Pritchard, *Social Anthropology; Inaugural Lecture*, 1948).

5. R. HUFFMAN, *Nuer Customs and Folklore*, Oxford University Press for International African Institute, London, 1931.

6. H. SCHURTZ (*Grundzüge einer Philosophie der Tracht (mit besonderer Berücksichtigung der Negertrachten)*, 1891, p. 7) writes that not a single people is totally devoided of clothes ... K. BIRKET-SMITH (*Geschichte der Kultur*, 1946, p. 197) declares that complete nakedness is only to be found with some peoples on the Upper Nile ... F. MÜLLER-LYER (*Phasen der Kultur*, 1915, pp. 122 et seq.) and others, mentioned by him, enumerate a long list of naked peoples ... CRAWLEY ('Dress', *Encyclopedia of Religion and Ethics*, vol. V, 1912, p. 43a. Reprinted in *Dress, Drinks and Drums*, Th. Bestermen, ed., 1931) says that 'the great majority of the lowest peoples known wear no clothes'. G. MONTANDON (*L'Ologenèse culturelle, Traité d'ethnologie culturelle*, 1934, p. 317) writes: '*Le nombre des tribus où les hommes sont tout à fait nus est trop grand pour qu'elles soient énumérées.*' Those tribes where women are also naked '*sont rares, mais existent néanmoins*' and he mentions eleven cases in which '*entre autres*' '*la nudité totale des femmes a été constatée*'.

7. CRAWLEY, loc. cit., p. 5.

8. HUFFMAN, loc. cit., p. 5.

9. *Kinship and Marriage among the Nuer*, p. 69.

10. See also EVANS-PRITCHARD, *The Nuer*, p. 30.

11. EVANS-PRITCHARD, *Kinship and Marriage among the Nuer*, p. 71.

12. op. cit., p. 8.

13. *Kinship and Marriage among the Nuer*, p. 68.

14. ibid., p. 101; HUFFMAN, op. cit.

15. EVANS-PRITCHARD, *Kinship and Marriage among the Nuer*, p. 101.

16. ibid., p. 60; see also HUFFMAN, op. cit., p. 37.

17. EVANS-PRITCHARD, *Kinship and Marriage among the Nuer*, p. 64.

18. ibid., p. 51; see also HUFFMAN, op. cit., p. 27.

19. EVANS-PRITCHARD, *Kinship and Marriage among the Nuer*, p. 55.

20. ibid., p. 99.

21. HUFFMAN, op. cit., p. 41; EVANS-PRITCHARD, *Kinship and Marriage among the Nuer*, p. 102.

22. EVANS-PRITCHARD, *Kinship and Marriage among the Nuer*, pp. 72, 73.

23. ibid., pp. 72, 99. There is some contradiction here between the first and second lines of paragraph V ('until a second child has been born' and 'after the birth of a first child').

24. ibid., p. 99.

25. ibid., p. 102.

26. ibid., pp. 99, 100.

27. ibid., pp. 100, 102.

28. EVANS-PRITCHARD, *The Nuer*, p. 249; *Kinship and Marriage among the Nuer*, p. 103; HUFFMAN, op. cit., p. 31.

29. EVANS-PRITCHARD, *The Nuer*, p. 249.

30. HUFFMAN, op. cit., p. 31.

31. EVANS-PRITCHARD, *The Nuer*, p. 30.

32. J. C. FLUGEL, 'The psychology of clothes', *International Psychoanalytical Library*, no. 18 (1950), p. 19.

33. M. SCHELER, *Über Scham und Schamgefühl: Zur Ethik und Erkenntnislehre, Schriften aus dem Nachlass*, vol. I, 1933.

34. O. F. BOLLNOW, *Die Ehrfurcht*, 1947.

35. W. STERN, *Psychology der Fruhen Kindheit*, 1927.

36. J. WISSE, *Selbstmord und Todesfurcht bei den Naturvölkern*, 1933, p. 490.

37. J. W. M. WHITING, *Becoming a Kwoma*, 1941.

38. J. DENNEY, 'Fall (Biblical)', *Encyclopedia of Religion and Ethics*, vol. V, 1912, p. 702a.

39. F. J. J. BUYTENDIJK, *Algemene Theorie der Menselijke Houding en Beweging*, 1948, p. 360.

40. J. H. DRIBERG, *The Lango, a Nilotic tribe of Uganda*, 1923, pp. 159, 160.

41. C. G. and B. Z. SELIGMANN, *Pagan Tribes of the Nilotic Sudan*, 1932, p. 155.

42. K. MCDOUGALL, *An Introduction to Social Psychology*, 1931, p. 127.

Jane Richardson and A. L. Kroeber:
'*Three centuries of women's dress fashions: A quantitative analysis*' (two graphs)

From *Anthropological Records*, 5, 2 (1940), University of California Press, Berkeley and Los Angeles.

A. L. Kroeber conducted a study of women's fashions which was published in 1919 as an article in the American Anthropologist *entitled* '*On the principle of order in civilization as exemplified by changes of fashion*' (*21* (*n.s.*), *235–63*). *In order to extend the scope of his data, Kroeber had Jane Richardson* (*then a student of his*) *measure, examine*

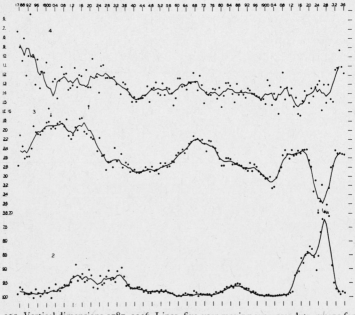

105. Vertical dimensions 1787–1936. Lines, five-year moving averages; dots, means for years. 2, length of skirt; 3, of waist; 4, of decolletage.

and statistically correlate parameters of women's evening-gown fashions from 1787 to 1936. Richardson measured three vertical dimensions and three horizontal dimensions of evening gowns and her data are summarized in the graphs below. Using this statistical information, Richardson and Kroeber then proceeded, in this extensive and unique study, to examine the relationship of variations in each dimension to variations in every other dimension, and to more general historical data. Because of the increased scope of the data, the authors were able to reveal the long-term cycles and trends of fashion design in a way which no other student of fashion and dress has to my knowledge been able to do. I regret that there is not room to print the entirety of this fascinating study in this volume. I have chosen to reproduce the graphs below in order to introduce the reader to this study and also because these graphs demonstrate very succinctly how rapidly the definitions of nudity, nakedness, dress and undress have changed within Western society.

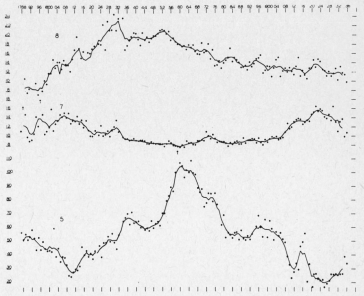

106. Horizontal dimensions, 1787–1936. Lines, five-year moving averages; dots, means for years. 5, width of skirt; 7, of waist; 8, of decolletage.

Ali Mazrui:

'The robes of rebellion: Sex, dress and politics in Africa'

From *Encounter*, XXXIV, 2 (February 1970), 19–30.

Fischer's article on the Nuer shows that definitions of nakedness and nudity are cross-culturally variable and unique to specific societies. Richardson and Kroeber's study of Western fashion statistically demonstrates the changes which have taken place in Western definitions of dress and undress. Combining, and in a way summarizing, these two, Ali Mazrui's article 'The robes of rebellion' shows what can happen when radically different and rapidly changing definitions of nakedness and dress are juxtaposed in the African urban context. Mazrui's article first serves to point out that tribal, traditional Africans and, on the other hand, Westernized Africans have radically different definitions of nakedness, nudity and proper dress; secondly, it suggests some of the economic, social and political implications of this pluralism; and thirdly, 'The robes of rebellion' shows how confusing to Westernized peoples can be the rapid fluctuations of fashion change (as portrayed in Richardson and Kroeber's graphs above). The rising hemlines of the mini-skirt bring Westernized and Christianized Africans too close to the tribal African definitions of dress and undress, and the long leg of the mini-skirt must be considered 'evil' if the tenuous distinctions between tribal and Westernized Africa are to be maintained. (See figure 104.)

> *Boston*
>
> Negro students at the city's 16 high schools changed their coats and ties for African dress yesterday. Principals of the schools agreed Wednesday to allow the students to wear African-style clothes, but another issue, whether Negro students would be allowed to form all-black student unions, was not decided.
>
> The dress issue precipitated racial disturbances last week in Boston public schools. Mayor Kevin H. White has formed a special high-school grievance committee to inquire into the racial troubles.

Algiers

Algeria considers herself one of the most revolutionary of Arab
or African countries. A visitor, however, is struck here as elsewhere in the developing world by the less-than-revolutionary.

A lot of women, for instance, even in 'European' Algiers, wear the
haik – the enveloping white robe that covers the head and the
whole body and is worn with a white lace veil, the size of a large
handkerchief, over the face. You ask around and you find that
many Algerian women feel the *haik* is part of the puritan image
created by President Houari Boumédienne. They say the image
encourages a traditional-minded father to keep his daughter at
home to keep house for the family until she marries the man the
family finds for her, rather than to put her through university or
let her take some other emancipated role in the developing society.

Old Algeria hands admit that the liberation of women has gone a
lot further in neighbouring Morocco and Tunisia than it has here,
that Boumédienne does not encourage the modern girls as deposed
President Ahmed Ben Bella did. They insist, however, that if you
measure progress by appropriately small units, the Algerian
woman has come a long way.

The mother may still wear the *haik*, but she does not hesitate to be
seen outdoors with her daughter or even her sister in Western
dress. And in more and more cases the *haik* is a *mini-haik*: the
white folds stop at, and reveal, a shapely calf, and the dress under-
neath is from Paris. On Sundays you see Algerian girls on the
beaches in bikinis – that never happened before independence.

Progress must be measured in small units because even in
revolutionary countries the desire for progress runs up against the
stone wall of tradition ... The visitor to Algiers may draw a wry
smile from the fact that nostalgia for the past is more easily sensed
than enthusiasm for the revolutionary future.

INTERNATIONAL HERALD TRIBUNE

Far away, many dust-laden miles away in Arusha some little man
in the administration, such as are to be found in all the govern-
ments the world over, in his little white shirt and collar and his
little Western tie, or in his national dress that gives him prickly
heat around his neck whenever the weather gets excessively hot
and humid, has decided that the Masai must wear clothes.[1]

This bitter lament against a new policy statement from Tanzania
early in 1968 formed part of the debate which was unleashed by the
declaration of that policy. The authorities in Tanzania had decided
that the Masai had been permitted naked indulgence for far too long;

that their withdrawal from normal attire constituted a withdrawal from the mainstream of progress in their countries. It had therefore been decreed that no Masai men or women were to be allowed into the Arusha metropolis wearing limited skin clothing or a loose blanket. The Masailand Area Commissioner, Mr Iddi Sungura, kept on issuing a number of warnings to the Masai threatening retribution if they clung to awkward clothing and soiled pigtailed hair.

From prominent Masai across the border in Kenya came protests. A Kenya Masai Member of Parliament holding a ministerial position, Mr Stanley Oloitipitip, asserted that Tanzania was denying the Masai the right to be themselves. Another Kenyan, Mr John Keen, threatened to turn up at Arusha, the new capital of the East African Community, dressed in his Masai attire and see what the authorities there would do to him. Tanzanian authorities in turn replied to this debate across the border by saying that such interference in the policies of Tanzania towards modernization and national integration was totally unacceptable. The Masai of Kenya could remain in their pristine traditionality, but the Masai of Tanzania were to be converted to the trappings of modernity.[2]

This whole controversy on the future apparel of the Masai has links with an important theme in the history of nationalism and of revolutionary fervour. My present concern is not with the Masai controversy as such; it is with this wider theme of the place of dress and nakedness in the history of thought. In its ramifications, this is a human phenomenon which has contacts with such important issues as, first, authenticity; secondly, identity; and thirdly, rebellion, both religious and political.

Nature uncovered

In order to understand some of the implications of the concept of authenticity we have to relate it to intellectual foils. What is authentic is often deemed to be that which is not artificial. That which is not artificial is often deemed to be that which is natural. Major intellectual movements in world history have romanticized nearness to nature and lamented the growth of civilization and industrialization because of the presumed concomitant growth of artificiality in man's life. The idea that expanding complexities of social organization maximize man's distance from the essence of things has been discerned in the works of political philosophers like Rousseau, and of poets like Wordsworth. The romanticization of the Noble Savage was at the heart of these critiques of developed life. Rousseau sometimes argues that civilized life enfeebles man and makes him too dependent on gadgets and artificial comforts. Equipped with all his artificial aids civilized man is indeed at a great advantage, but if you stripped him of these, and confronted him with bare nature, the effeminate ways of civilization will expose his lack of vigour. In Rousseau's own words (in *The Social Contract*):

> Give civilized man time to gather all his machines about him, and he will no doubt easily beat the savage; but if you were to see a still more unequal contest, set them together naked and unarmed, and you will soon see the advantage of having all our forces constantly at our disposal, of being always prepared for every event, and of carrying oneself, as it were, perpetually whole and entire about one.

Sometimes the Noble Savage was placed by philosophers and literary figures in the Americas. The Noble Savage was the Indian (in Alexander Pope's words)

> . . . whose untutor'd mind
> Sees God in clouds, or hears him in the wind;
> His soul proud Science never taught to stray
> Far as the solar walk, or milky-way;
> Yet simple Nature to his hope has giv'n,
> Behind the cloud-topt hill an humbler heav'n . . .
>
> (Essay on Man, 1732)

But with the greater interest in Africa which came with the great debates about the slave trade, the Noble Savage in the European imagination came to be located also in the African continent. The African came to be regarded as natural man *par excellence*. He might lack the capacity to blush, but commanded full ability to be bold. In the words of the poets Day and Bicknell (in 1773),

> What tho' no rosy tints adorn their face,
> No silken ringlets shine with flowing grace?
> Yet of etherial temper are their souls,
> And in their veins the tide of honour rolls;
> And valorous kindles there the hero's flame,
> Contempt of death, and thirst for martial fame.

In our own time the image of the African as a child of nature has been inherited by the movement of *Négritude*, of which the most distinguished spokesman on the African continent is Leopold Senghor, the poet-President of Senegal. Senghor defines *Négritude* as 'the sum total of the values of the civilization of the African world . . . More precisely, it was the communal warmth, the image-symbol and the cosmic rhythm which instead of dividing and sterilizing, unified and made fertile.'[3]

And Jean-Paul Sartre, the French philosopher, also draws attention to the 'proud claim of non-technicalness' which is at the heart of *Négritude*. The nearness to nature is persistent. In the words of Sartre, 'in concerning himself first with himself, the Negro proposes to gain nature in gaining himself'. Sartre then proceeds (in *Black Orpheus*) to cite the poet who said 'they abandon themselves, possessed to the essence of all things ignoring surfaces but possessed by the movement of all things,

> Needless, taking no account, but playing the game of the world,
> truly the elder sons of the world
> porous to every breath of the world
> flesh of the flesh of the world throbbing with the very
> movement of the world.'

The nearness to nature which is attributed to the Negro becomes associated with spontaneity; spontaneity finds expression sometimes in responsive sexuality; and sexuality connotes the nakedness of things. The entire life-style of the Negro is romanticized into one constant work of natural creation. To quote Sartre again,

> Techniques have contaminated the white worker, but the black remains the great male of the earth, the sperm of the world. His existence – it is the great vegetal patience; his work – it is the repetition from year to year of the sacred coitus. He creates and is fertile because he creates. The sexual pantheism of these poets is without doubt that which first strikes the reader. To labour, to plant, to eat, is to make love with nature . . .

> Behold yourself
> Erect and naked
> Shaft you are and you remember
> But you are in reality the child of this fecund shadow
> Which feeds of the milk of the moon
> Then you slowly shape yourself into a rod
> On this low wall entwined by the dreams of flowers
> And the perfume of the idle summer.

If the Negro is sometimes conceived as a symbol of masculinity, Africa is sometimes conceived in decidedly feminine terms. But in both conceptions the theme of nakedness is again recurrent. Leopold Senghor thinks of his part of Africa in such feminine terms. In the words of his famous poem,

Naked woman, black woman
Clothed with your colour which is life, with your form which is
beauty!
In your shadow I have grown up; the gentleness of your hands was
laid over my eyes . . .

Naked woman, black woman
I sing your beauty that passes, the form that I fix in the Eternal,
Before jealous Fate turn you to ashes to feed the roots of life.

The dress of identity

But it is not simply the issue of authenticity which is at stake in this
area of political argumentation; it is also the issue of identity. Identity is sometimes in regard to a particular individual and the kind of
quality and personality he has; and sometimes it is in regard to a
member of a particular community, nationality or religious affiliation
and the cultural traits exhibited by such a community. The identity
of the individual on his own may indeed include these traits inherited
from his cultural group, but in so far as they define his own distinctive personality, these traits are combined with other qualities.
Whether a man is temperamentally cheerful or moody, whether he is
warm-hearted or reserved, whether he is meticulous and formal in
his behaviour, or easy-going and jovial – all these are intensely personal characteristics which may not necessarily be derived from the
social group to which he belongs. The characteristics may sometimes
be accentuated or mitigated by cultural factors, but in general there
are personality factors in each individual which are distinctive to the
person and not typical of the community from which he springs.

Dress is related to this issue of the distinctive person. There has
been a school of thought which has assumed that you can indeed
judge a man by the way he dresses: 'For the apparel oft proclaims the
man' (Polonius). A man of good taste might therefore be judged by
the way he dresses. The class to which he belongs might be discernible by his general attire. In general etiquette, dress is sometimes
related to the particular occasion to which a man is called upon to
respond. A man turning up at a formal dinner in a bush shirt is
therefore dismissed in Western terms as bohemian. Some restaurants
in the more Westernized parts of Africa would insist on a tie (and
perhaps a jacket) for dinner, but not necessarily for lunch. The two
meals have been ritualized and permitted to demand distinctive attire
for those who participate in the ritual. In some British universities
the academic gown becomes important for some ceremonial occasions, and a less flamboyant gown becomes indispensable at high

table for some of the college dinners. The person who ignores these conventions is again judged to be inadequately attuned to the civilized values of the society.

But these very examples themselves illustrate how closely related are the *personal* aspects of dress to the *cultural*. The identity which is established by personal attire sometimes presupposes the tastes and norms of the society as a whole. The bohemian who turns up for dinner without a jacket or a tie is a bohemian by the canons of the society *within* which he is operating. But as *between* one society and another there may also be a place for dress as a distinctive differentiating characteristic. It was the late Frantz Fanon (the revolutionary thinker from Martinique and participant in the Algerian insurrection) who once said:

> The way people clothe themselves, together with the traditions of dress and finery that custom implies, constitutes the most distinctive form of a society's uniqueness, that is to say the one that is the most immediately perceptible. Within the general pattern of a given custom, there are of course always modifications of detail, innovations which in highly developed societies are the mark of fashion. But the effect as a whole remains homogeneous, and the great areas of civilization, immense cultural regions, can be grouped together on the basis of original, specific techniques of men's and women's dress.[4]

In the streets of Marrakesh and Algiers one therefore often knows that one is in a Muslim country. If one opened one's eyes in Bombay or New Delhi, the dress of many of the passers-by would be part of the revelation that one was in the midst of an Indian civilization. An exposure to Disneyland or other pleasure centres of California would soon familiarize the stranger to some of the dress manifestations of the American sub-culture.

In reality the idea of differentiating civilizations by the way their members dress is rapidly being antiquated by events. Perhaps the most successful cultural bequest from the West to the rest of the world has in fact been precisely Western dress. Mankind is getting rapidly homogenized by the sheer acquisition of the Western shirt and the Western trousers. The Japanese businessman, the Arab Minister, the Indian lawyer, the African civil servant have all found a common denominator in the Western suit.

To some extent this is what made the case of the Masai an elegant exercise in sheer cultural obstinacy. Here was a people who refused to climb on the bandwagon of Westernized apparel. The Area

Commissioner of Masailand in Tanzania was particularly frustrated to note that even those Masai who had been exposed to modern education continued their attachment to Masai modes of personal preparation. Area Commissioner Sungura admitted to being surprised to find among a group of 'bright-looking English-speaking secondary school-taught Masai youth' a young man called George Koyo who was complete with ochre-soiled clothing and hair, 'showing no sign whatsoever of his education which is better than mine'.

The whole Tanzanian policy of seeking to 'civilize the Masai' by getting them to wear trousers seemed to be a direct attack on the most distinguishing aspect of the cultural identity of the Masai. Surprise was widely expressed that Tanzania, 'which in many ways had stood for the African right to be distinctive, should at the same time have embarked on one of the most blatant acts of enforced deculturation since the great debate on female circumcision among the Kikuyu in Kenya half a century earlier. In fact one participant in the debate on the Masai, O. N. Njau, argued in a letter in the *East African Standard* (17 February 1968) the futility of enforced deculturation by citing the example of the circumcision debate.

> Far back in the early 1930s the missionaries saw the need of advising Kikuyu of the obvious fact that circumcision of girls was unnecessary. Despite the much-publicized campaign against this practice, even today more than 70 per cent of all Kikuyu girls are circumcised. The then Colonial Government attempted to carry out this advice and I remember that as late as 1957, circumcised girls were not admitted in the then intermediate schools. However, as we all know, there must have existed many loopholes as Kikuyu women are among the best educated in this part of Africa.

Njau also discussed the impact of Westernism on Indians and Pakistanis. To some extent he echoes the view of John Plamenatz, that the Indians are perhaps the most deeply 'Westernized' of all non-Western peoples.[5]

But Njau notes: 'Indians and Pakistanis have been acquainted with the Western civilization for centuries, yet they proudly use their traditional dress.'

A governmental policy that the Masai should become more Westernized in their dress, when pursued in a nationalistic country like Tanzania, had historical as well as cultural anomalies. President Nyerere himself had once complained that in a certain period of colonial rule Africans themselves regarded it as a compliment rather than an insult to be called 'Black Europeans' (Address to the Tanganyika National Assembly, 1962).

It is instructive to compare the Masai controversy with the agitation about mini-skirts in Tanzania. In October 1968 some girls wearing mini-skirts were manhandled by members of the TANU Youth League in Dar-es-Salaam. Riot police had to be called in to handle the youths. A resolution was proposed to ban mini-skirts, wigs and tight trousers from Tanzania with effect from January next year; but younger members of the ruling party thought January was too far away and embarked on measures to speed up the change. The Afro-Shirazi Youth League in Zanzibar soon endorsed the move by their fraternal organization on the mainland. In a resolution marking the close of a three-day seminar the Afro-Shirazi Youth League pledged that it would work resolutely to eliminate such remnants of foreign culture in the country. The whole tone of these resolutions was in the spirit of Kariakoo Market Place, where youthful gangs assaulted girls wearing mini-skirts and tight dresses, and riot police carrying guns and tear-gas dispersed huge Dar-es-Salaam crowds . . .[6]

Clearly, Tanzanian disapproval of the semi-nakedness of the Masai has a different basis from its disapproval of the semi-nakedness of mini-skirts. In the case of the mini-skirts part of the hostility stems from the allegation that this was 'a disreputable foreign intrusion into the dress culture of the country'. On the other hand, wasn't getting the Masai to wear trousers an imposition on them of a foreign mode of attire?

African poets have on occasion satirized the so-called black *évolué* or *assimilé* who had absorbed too readily the trappings of the conquering nation. In the lines of a Senegalese poet,

My brother you flash your teeth in response to every hypocrisy
My brother with gold-rimmed glasses
You give your master a blue-eyed faithful look
My poor brother in immaculate evening dress
Screaming and whispering and pleading in the parlours of
    condescension.[7]

But what ought to be borne in mind is that nakedness, while revealing the body of a man, may at the same time be disguising his identity. After all, when everyone strips they are reducing themselves to their basic commonality. If a Yoruba and a Muganda woman were both dressed in their national apparel you would have a basis for distinguishing the Nigerian from the Ugandan. But were the two women to strip themselves of their badge of nationality, reducing themselves to their essential femininity, a stranger seeing them would know more about their personal bodies but less about their personal identities. The price of nakedness in this case is national obscurity.

In this regard one might say that both complete nakedness and Western dress are having the same total effect on the problem of identity. The spread of Western dress and its acceptance by peoples vastly differing in cultural background and historical origins does itself have this consequence of blurring distinctions between peoples. A Nigerian man in a suit and a Ugandan man in a suit might be as difficult to differentiate nationally as the naked Yoruba and Muganda women. Identity as the ultimate basis of distinctiveness therefore stands to suffer whether Africa moves in the direction of total Westernization in dress or in the direction of total sartorial renunciation.

Yet the Masai retains a feature of distinctiveness by falling short of complete nakedness. The *shuka* with which he covers part of his body, and the ochre with which he colours his body, together constitute a persistent claim to cultural uniqueness. What is the acquisition of trousers by the Masai but a step away from this uniqueness?

Nudity and religious rebellion

In the course of the press debate on Tanzania's policy about clothing the Masai, the Masai elders in Kenya were reported to have asked the following question:

> If the Almighty God could stomach seeing the entire anatomies of Adam and Eve in their complete nudity, is it not a little prudish for an African government to have fits by merely viewing a casually exhibited Masai buttock?[8]

In reply a correspondent writing for an East African magazine said,

> It should be remembered that the Masai are not living before the fall of mankind as Adam and Eve did. When Adam and Eve disobeyed God, they were clothed by God before He drove them out of the Garden.

These remarks immediately dramatized the long-standing link between nakedness and certain forms of rebellion. The link does indeed go back to Adam and Eve and their own act of disobedience to God, which was itself connected with a prior act of rebellion by Satan. Milton in *Paradise Lost* begins by first presenting Satan and his followers as rebels against divine absolutism – believing as they did that it was 'better to reign in hell than serve in Heaven'. In Miltonic terms, this was the first political rebellion; but it was a rebellion of angels, who were then deported.

What could the fallen angels now do in revenge against God's punishment? The Miltonic version was that Satan and his followers decided to get their own back by perverting God's purposes for man. Satan makes the great journey towards the Garden of Eden intent on this ultimate subversion. Adam and Eve were striking pieces of creation, in whose very nakedness lay the glory of their innocence:

> Godlike erect, with native honour clad
> In naked majesty seemed lords of all,
> And worthy seemed, for in their looks divine
> The image of their glorious maker shone . . .
> Nor those mysterious parts were then concealed;
> Then was not guilty shame; dishonest shame
> Of nature's work, honour dishonourable,
> Sin-bred, how have ye troubled all mankind
> With shows instead, mere shows of seeming pure,
> And banished from man's life his happiest life,
> Simplicity and spotless innocence.   (Book IV, 288–318)

Obviously this was the time of human evolution when nakedness was not a symbol of sensuous desire, but of innocence:

> So passed they naked on, nor shunned the sight
> Of God or angel, for they thought no ill . . .

There are, of course, theological difficulties as to the nature of the Original Sin – was the Tree of Knowledge in fact carnal knowledge? Did Adam and Eve take a step towards sinfulness when they became conscious of their nakedness? Was it with Original Sin that death came to mankind?

If this interpretation is correct, if the forbidden fruit was indeed love-making, there is perhaps a touch of mystery that Christianity should regard this original capitulation to lust as the cause of all human death. In some sense it would seem to me more plausible to argue that the moment of lust between Adam and Eve was the guarantee of all human reproduction. It might even be argued that to a certain extent it is sin which makes us *human* – just as it is death which completes our definition as mortals. A human being who is not a mortal is a contradiction in terms. And it was Adam's sin which created human mortality.

But there are other social implications of sin. In political philosophy, government itself has sometimes been interpreted as the political equivalent of dress. There was once a political Garden ('paradise') where men lived happily in innocent abandon and naturalness. But this political Eden came to be lost in terms comparable to the loss of the personal Eden where Adam and Eve experienced a moment of intimacy. As Thomas Paine puts it, 'Government, like dress, is the badge of lost innocence . . .'

Sometimes political philosophy and theology have merged in this equation. To Augustine, the 'earthly city' (in the sense of secular government) became necessary when man proved his capacity for lawlessness by disobeying God himself. In a way the first godly city was the Garden of Eden – though it consisted of the most primary of all societies, man and mate. But Augustine carries the argument further. He not only says that it was sin which made government necessary. This is implied in the trend of his argument, but his more specific formulation is on the relationship between sin and servitude: 'Sin, therefore, is the mother of servitude, and first cause of man's subjection to man.'

The worst form of servitude, however, is servitude to sin itself. Augustine views subjection to evil as being worse than any form of slavery to man: 'It is a happier servitude to serve man than lust . . . He that is good is free, though he be a slave, and he that is evil, a slave though he be king' (*Civitas Dei*, IV).

With the coming of lust to human life nudity ceased to be a pure symbol of innocence and began to acquire all the connotations of bodily temptation. As that correspondent in an East African magazine put it: 'When Adam and Eve disobeyed God, they were clothed by God before he drove them out of the Garden . . .' The very concept of 'flesh' came to imply sensuousness; and the very idea of 'the flesh is weak' connoted the frailty of human discipline.

And yet Christian theology, while rejecting some of the more literal forms of body symbolism, nevertheless used a good deal of metaphor based on flesh as something sacred. The relationship between Christ and the Church is sometimes portrayed in decisively sensuous terms: 'Husbands, love your wives, as Christ loved the Church and gave Himself up for her' (Ephesians v, 25), or 'Husbands should love their wives as their own bodies. He who loves his wife loves himself. For no man ever hates his own flesh, but nourishes and cherishes it, as Christ does the Church, because we are members of his body' (Ephesians v, 28–30). Such notions of the body and the flesh as characteristic of Christ's relation to the Church are recurrent in the language of Paul. In condemning prostitution, for example, Paul said to the Corinthians,

Do you not know that your bodies are members of Christ? Shall I therefore take the members of Christ and make them members of a prostitute? Never! . . . Every other sin which a man commits is outside the body; but the immoral man sins against his own body. Do you not know that your body is a temple of the Holy Spirit within you, which you have from God? You are not your own; you were bought with a price. So glorify God in your body (I Corinthians vi, 15–20).

But it was not merely in its original theological formulation that Christianity managed to establish a link between rebellion and the body. There were also other ways, including the very notion of naked pain inflicted on the body as a form of divine passion. In the case of Jesus himself the martyrdom, though self-willed, was not self-embraced. Jesus did not *revel* in the sentence which awaited him. In his trial before Pontius Pilate Jesus behaved on the basis of the dictum that discretion was the better part of valour. He gave guarded or ambiguous answers to many of the crucial questions posed. He would not admit to his message or to his position in clear unequivocal terms, but shrouded them all in the shadows of multiple meanings. 'And Pilate asked him, saying, Art thou the King of the Jews? And he answered and said, Thou sayest it' (St Luke xxiii, 3).

To the extent then that Jesus was careful in what he said he was not rushing headlong towards his martyrdom. He seemed to be seeking a momentary defence behind a shield of ambiguity. And even when he was crucified there was still in him a sense of despair as he cried out, 'My God, my God, why hast Thou forsaken me?' Here again is a dignified reluctance to revel in affliction. But this dignity was not always present in the martyrdom of Christians later on. Some of the enthusiasm with which Christian martyrs later awaited their sentences of torture led to a spate of psychoanalytical speculation as to the ultimate motives for their behaviour.

As Theodore Reik has pointed out, the study of psychological and psychoanalytical literature suggests the widespread impression that religious martyrdom can be a form of sexual masochism. A host of references have been offered to prove that the sexual element may have unconsciously determined the psychic life of many Christian martyrs. Reik himself describes the equation as excessive. Such scholars were inadequately sensitized to an important difference. To dramatize this difference Reik presents two typical attitudes towards sexuality which have a common starting-point. He cites the case of a twenty-five-year-old man feeling a sexual excitement which he attempts to master. He does not succeed. Therefore he undresses, goes to his mirror, where he sees himself naked. He whips himself on his buttocks with a little dog whip until bloody weals appear – while constantly looking into the glass over his own shoulder. During this the sexual excitement increases until finally ejaculation occurs. The sight of his own blood is the signal for orgasm.

For his other example Reik cites a Catholic legend which illustrates the counterpart of this conduct. One of the kindest of all Christian saints passed many years of his manhood in sacred contemplation in the Chapel next to the Church of Santa Maria Maggiore in Assisi. One day he felt an intense and almost overpowering sexual desire. Reik continues:

It was winter at its hardest; Nature seemed asleep under the snow that covered the little garden of the monastery, but the Evil One was awake. When St Francis was tortured by this thorn in his flesh so that he was in danger of succumbing to the temptation, he rushed into the snow and rolled himself in a thorn bush of wild roses. And then and there a miracle happened and the dew of his blood made the green sprout and in the snow roses blossomed whose petals were sprinkled blood-red. Up to this day the nuns of Assisi sell pressed roses the white petals of which bear the stigmata of the Saint in memory of his victory over the impure spirit.[9]

This psychoanalyst then proceeds to draw the distinctive features of each of these two cases. In the experience of the twenty-five-year-old man in front of the mirror the pain constitutes an access to the otherwise forbidden satisfaction. In the experience of St Francis the pain served as defence against the sinful desire. In the first case it means a promotion of the sensual excitement, in the second its counterweight. Reik goes on to argue that both do approximately the same thing, but the meaning of each act is different as it is performed under different psychic conditions: 'In the first case the affliction of severe punishment brings forth the enjoyment, in the second the self-punishment has to prevent gratification.'

What matters from the point of view of analysis here is that both in masochism and in martyrdom the body provides the means to a higher plane of experience. Even the most spiritual of the martyrs needs the body as the foundation of his martyrdom. Would there have been a passion in the Crucifixion had Jesus not possessed a human body?

In Sunni Islam martyrdom is a peripheral phenomenon. There is little glorification of self-willed suffering, but in Shi'a Islam there is an important masochistic theme. For example, the murder of Hussein, the prophet's grandson, is celebrated every year by one Shi'ite School with wailing and a passionate beating of the chest. The

Ithnasharis sometimes go to the extent of making their chests bleed in ferocious sympathy with the martyrdom of Hussein. Here again the body of the believer is needed to provide access to physical suffering.

In some of the more simple religious movements the body is used not so much to provide access to pain as to provide access to ecstasy. The dance that leads on to a trance and to spiritual elevation becomes part of a total religious experience. R. R. Marett has even gone so far as to assert that primitive religion is 'not so much thought out as danced out'.[10]

African writers have often used the symbol of the African dance and the response to the drum as intimations of the ancestral spirit of Africa. In the words of David Diop:

> Negress my warm rumour of Africa
> My land of mystery and my fruit of reason
> You are the dance by the naked joy of your smile
> By the offering of your breasts and secret powers
> You are the dance by the golden tales of marriage nights
> By new tempos and more secular rhythms . . .
> You are the idea of All and the voice of the Ancient
> Gravely rocketed against our fears
> You are the Word which explodes
> In showers of light upon the shores of oblivion.

And Senghor has sometimes sung about 'the leader of the dance [making] fast his vigour to the prow of his sex'.

The half-naked body, bleeding in places, has at times symbolized the agony of martyrdom in Christian history. The half-naked body, sweating in places, has at times symbolized the ecstasy of a religious trance in the history of African rhythmic experience.

Nudity and political rebellion

It is not simply in the religious sphere that the issue of nakedness and dress has been interlinked with problems of rebellion and assertion. The realm of politics has, I have suggested, also sensed the relevance of apparel for human sensibilities.

1. Political rebellion can sometimes take the form simply of an obstinate refusal to change. To some extent this theme was discerned quite early in the attitude of the Masai when the new Tanzanian policy on their attire was proclaimed. One member of the tribe wrote an article to a Dar-es-Salaam newspaper pointing out that the policy was having the effect of forcing the tribe in the remoter places back into itself. The tribe had become more defensive than ever. The members that lived nearer the towns, and who had to establish contact with the towns, might feel the brunt of coercion and make concessions to it. But others who might at one time have been tempted to seek greater social intercourse with the urban areas might now be forced to reject those areas more completely.

These people have resolved to ignore any force that is out to destroy their traditional outlook whatever the cost might be ... Since they value their traditions more than all those things they can get from the so-called 'civilized' society they will do whatever they can to keep away from it (*Sunday News*, Dar-es-Salaam, 25 February 1968, p. 4).

If this then was the correct interpretation of the Masai response to the new policies in the days ahead, it constituted rebellion by withdrawal, a cultural assertion by a quiet defiance.

2. Another form of assertiveness is that of *residual* cultural distinctiveness. In this case a person may have been basically 'deculturated' away from his ancient civilization, and might have adopted a new way of life in many respects, but then decides to retain a residue of this former cultural identity. This is the case of a highly Westernized African or Asian whose main literary interest is in Shakespeare, whose favourite composer is Beethoven, who eats with a knife and fork at home, uses a flush lavatory and has the rest of his house furnished in exquisite Western standards, but who nevertheless then decides to dress himself not in a suit but in the African or Oriental national garment. Pandit Nehru sometimes symbolized this form of assertion by residual cultural distinctiveness – permitting himself to be Indian by dress and by general sympathy, yet Western by the totality of his intellectual and even domestic behaviour.

This form of assertion can sometimes invite ridicule from critics. Gandhi's determination to move around simply with a *dhoti*, naked from the waist upwards, even when he was having an audience with British Royalty, was a striking case of cultural assertiveness. But it did provoke from Winston Churchill the taunt that India could not be entrusted to 'a naked fakir'.

Yet Indians have often been admired by nationalists elsewhere for their determination to retain at least these residual trappings of their ancient culture. Even in the course of the controversy over the Masai early in 1968 in East Africa, that African correspondent whom I cited earlier had occasion to note the proud use of their traditional dress by Indians and Pakistanis although they had been familiar with Western civilization for centuries.

3. A third type of cultural assertion is that of ritualized rejection of a foreign dress that had already been adopted. This is somewhat different from the former case since in that former case the residual trapping may never have been adopted. Moreover, in the case of ritualized rejection of Western dress, for example, the rejection may be only on special occasions or in the course of political demonstrations. The rest of the time the nationalists might still go about in their neckties.

The ritualized rejection of Western dress of this kind has been known to happen in the history of Kenya's nationalism. Eliud Mathu, the first African member of the Kenya Legislative Council in the colonial period, once tore his jacket off at a public meeting in a dramatic gesture of rejecting Western civilization – if the price was the loss of land for the African. 'Take back your civilization – and give back my land!'

In the course of the Mau Mau rebellion there were similar moments of ritualized rejection of Western dress. Perhaps even more interesting was the utilization of nakedness as a method of adding solemnity to an oath. Josiah Kariuki tells us of the ritual which constituted the Mau Mau Batuni oath.

> We sat down and Biniathi then told us to take all our clothes off except our trousers, and we stood patiently waiting to be called by him. I was called second after Kanyoi and there was no disobeying the summons. I took off my trousers and squatted facing Biniathi. He told me to take the thorax of the goat which had been skinned, to put my penis through a hole that had been made in it and to hold the rest of it in my left hand in front of me.

This was part of the ritual which culminated in this undertaking:

> I speak the truth and vow before God
> And by this BATUNI oath of our movement
> Which is called the movement of fighting
> That if I am called on to kill for our soil,
> If I am called on to shed my blood for it,
> I shall obey . . .
> I speak the truth and vow before God
> That I shall never take away the woman of another man,
> That I shall never walk with prostitutes,
> That I shall never steal anything belonging to another
>   person in the movement,
> Nor shall I hate any other member for his actions,
> And if I do any of these things
> May this oath kill me . . .[11]

There was in this oath a commitment to fight the enemy, a commitment to collective solidarity among the Mau Mau fighters, and a commitment to frugality and self-denial, especially in the all too dangerous sensuous area of relations with women. But to give the whole Batuni oath the overpowering air of binding force, it was deemed necessary to strip the man who was taking it. Nudity in this case was the requisite atmosphere for ominous awe.

4. A fourth form of political assertiveness connected with dress is itself a form of imitation. In some of the previous cases what was being dramatized was the rejection of a blind imitation of Western ways, but under this other category there is an imitation not necessarily of Westerners, but of those who have already come to symbolize a prior anti-Westernism. The adoption of Chinese attire among revolutionaries in countries like Tanzania is one case of revolutionary imitativeness. The Chinese style of dress becomes a symbol of solidarity worthy of adoption by African radicals as well.

Perhaps even more dramatic was the case of Cuban styles of attire as manifested among revolutionaries on the island of Zanzibar. Soon after the revolution which overthrew the Sultan's regime in January 1964 there was a widely publicized report that Cuban militiamen were among the revolutionaries. But Michael Lofchie's theory about the source of the confusion is persuasive. It is probable that the Cuban rumour was due to the presence of several trade union leaders who had joined the revolutionaries early on the first day of the New Era. As Lofchie points out:

> Many members of these groups had adopted the Cuban style of dress and appearance, and even employed the Cuban cry *'Venceremos'* (We shall conquer) as a political symbol. Their Cuban type of uniform set them off clearly from the [Afro-Shirazi Youth League] members and was probably the basis of the report that the revolutionary army contained Cuban soldiers.[12]

In this case imitation of the dress of others, far from being a detraction from nationalism, was in fact an ally of it. 'For the apparel proclaims the man,' Polonius had said; and Zanzibaris in Cuban apparel proclaimed their revolutionary affiliations.

5. The fifth form of revolutionary assertion in politics, in so far as it is connected with the issue of dress and nakedness, comes as a response to the indignity of being compulsorily undressed or reclothed by a conquering power. The conqueror lays down the law about a new mode of dress or against an old item of attire. The nationalist then responds to this with the militancy of offended pride.

A striking example of this kind of phenomenon in revolutionary

Africa was the veil in Algeria. Frantz Fanon once tried to analyse the symbol of 'Algeria unveiled'. Fanon saw the veil of the Algerian woman both as a badge of identity and as a basis of solidarity:

> In the Arab Maghreb, the veil belongs to the clothing traditions of the Tunisian, Algerian, Moroccan and Libyan national societies. For the tourist and the foreigner, the veil demarcates both Algerian society and its feminine component . . . The woman seen in her white veil unifies the perception that one has of Algerian feminine society. Obviously what we have here is a uniform which tolerates no modification, nor variant.

Fanon goes on to discuss the policy of the French authorities in its attempt to eliminate the veil from Algerian society. The French formula was 'Let's win over the women, and the rest will follow.' It was assumed that beneath the patrilineal pattern of Algerian society there was a matrilineal essence.

The success of the French assimilation policy, therefore, depended in part on an adequate awareness of the importance of the Algerian mother, the Algerian grandmother, the aunt and the 'old woman'. The colonial administration was, according to Fanon, convinced of this doctrine:

> If we want to destroy the structure of the Algerian society, its capacity for resistance, we must first of all conquer the women; we must go and find them behind the veil where they hide themselves and in the houses where the men keep them out of sight.

But in the heat of the Algerian war, it was not simple propaganda that was used. The occupying forces resorted at times to the personal aggression of forceful unveiling of women in the streets. The situation got worse when Algerian women became more systematically committed to revolution. They were unveiled in the streets partly out of the French soldiers' desire to subject the Arab woman to indignity, but also at times out of suspicion that behind the veil was a stengun. Fanon discerned in European behaviour deeper psychological reasons as well. He had himself served as a medical psychoanalyst in Algeria and had treated both French soldiers and some prisoners of the Algerian War. Fanon notes: 'The rape of the Algerian woman in the dream of the European is always preceded by a rending of the veil.' The French soldiers were sometimes influenced by a rape complex at the subconscious level, if not in complete awareness.

> Unveiling this woman is revealing her beauty; it is baring her secret, breaking her resistance, making her available for adventure.

Hiding the face is also disguising a secret; it is also creating a world of mystery, of the hidden. In a confused way, the European experiences his relation with the Algerian woman at a highly complex level. There is in it the will to bring this woman within his reach, to make her a possible object of possession.

But in fact this was the time when the Algerian woman converted the veil more fully into a military camouflage. A technique was evolved of carrying a rather heavy object dangerous to handle under the veil, and still giving the impression of having one's hands free, of there being nothing under this *haik* except a poor woman or an insignificant young girl. It was not enough to be veiled. One had to look so much like a *fatma* that the soldier would be convinced that this woman was quite harmless. Fanon goes on to say that this technique was in fact extremely difficult.

Three metres ahead of you the police challenge a veiled woman who does not look particularly suspect. From the anguished expression of the unit leader you have guessed that she is carrying a bomb, or a sack of grenades, bound to her body by a whole system of strings and straps. For the hands must be free, exhibited bare, humbly and abjectly presented to the soldiers so that they will look no further.

But with the conversion of the veil into a military camouflage the enemy gradually became alerted.

In the streets one witnessed what became a commonplace spectacle of Algerian women glued to the wall, on whose bodies the famous magnetic detectors, the 'frying pans' would be passed. Every veiled woman, every Algerian woman became suspect. There was no discrimination. This was the period during which men, women, children, the whole Algerian people, experienced at one and the same time their national vocation and the recasting of the new Algerian society.

But the Algerian woman sometimes *abandoned* the veil as an exercise in military masquerade. There were occasions when it was important that the feminine Algerian soldier should walk the streets looking as Europeanized as possible. For some of these girls it took a lot to escape the sense of awkwardness which came with the act of walking in the street unveiled. A newly unveiled feminine revolutionary

has an impression of being improperly dressed, even of being naked. She experiences a sense of incompleteness with great intensity. She has the anxious feeling that something is unfinished, and along with this a frightful sensation of disintegrating ... The Algerian woman who walks stark naked in the European city re-learns her body, re-establishes it in a totally revolutionary fashion.

Fanon describes this as 'a new dialectic of the body and of the world'. The newly unveiled must overcome all timidity and awkwardness 'for she must pass for a European'.

In the case of the Zanzibari rebels in January 1964 the adoption of a foreign dress was an exercise in imitating admired revolutionaries elsewhere. The Zanzibaris embraced the Cuban style of attire. But in the case of the unveiled Algerian woman the idea was to embrace the French mode of attire and pass for a French woman. It will be seen that both exercises were in fact forms of revolutionary imitation. In the Zanzibari case it was an act of emulating comrades-in-arms on the international stage. In the case of the unveiled Algerian woman it was a case of imitating the enemy. Yet both remained acts of symbolic combat.

I have tried to suggest in this article that dress and nakedness are factors in human existence which have had important connections with diverse forms of assertiveness and rebellion. The Tanzanian government policy of trying to revolutionize the lives of the Masai by making them wear trousers falls into a long stream of human experience in which dress, culture and social transformation have been intimately linked. Sometimes the act can be the same but the meaning may be different. A French attempt to abolish the veil in Algeria and the campaign by Kemal Ataturk to abolish the fez in Turkey do, at one level, appear to be comparable types of phenomena. And yet Ataturk's quest to abolish the fez (and the veil) in Turkey following the disintegration of the Ottoman empire was in a large measure an act of cultural defensiveness. It was the quest for the kind of modernized status which would make the new Turkey survive. But the French attempt to unveil Algeria was by contrast an exercise in cultural aggression, compounded in the Algerian war by considerations of military precautions and tactical subterfuge.

The place of dress and nakedness in relation to rebellion goes back, as we know, at least to Adam and Eve. In Christian mythology one long-term consequence of the Original Sin was the evolution of the concept of 'private parts'. Until then these were not private; it was the consciousness of their role in sensuality, and the attempt to cover this up, which gave rise to the aura of intimacy. In short, private parts became private when God sentenced Adam and Eve to eternal clothing. In the words once again of that East African correspondent in Nairobi, 'It should be remembered that the Masai are not living before the fall of mankind . . . When Adam and Eve disobeyed God, they were clothed by God before he drove them out of the Garden.'

Nudity and dress have political as well as theological implications. In Africa the political implications have sometimes touched the whole movement of *Négritude* as a glorification of African naturalness. The emotive sensibilities of African culture, and the glistening response of the African body to rhythm and to the demands of the ancestral dance, have all become relevant.

But there have been other manifestations of the political meaning of dress and nudity in Africa's experience, ranging from the Mau Mau Batuni oath taken naked before the thorax of a goat, to the adoption of a Chinese style of dress in Tanzania as an act of identification with Mao Tse-tung.

If 'the apparel proclaims the man', so does the lack of apparel. The song of nationalism in Africa has sometimes included a vow of nudity; the trumpet of revolution has at other times awakened radicalism to its uniform; and the world of social issues has often had to touch the revealed parts of personal intimacy. The problem of the Masai in Tanzania today belongs to a whole universe of human experience. Here once again is one of the tense meeting-points between the garment of culture and the body of man in history.

Notes

1. RICHARD BROOKE-EDWARDS, 'A fourth freedom', *Transition*, 34 (1968), 39.

2. *Daily Nation*, Nairobi, 8 and 16 February 1968.

3. L. S. SENGHOR, *Prose and Poetry*, trans. Reed and Wake, Oxford University Press, 1965, p. 99.

4. FRANTZ FANON, *Studies in a Dying Colonialism*, trans. Chevalier, 1965, p. 35.

5. JOHN PLAMENATZ, *On Alien Rule and Self-Government*, Longman, 1960.

6. See *The Nationalist*, Dar-es-Salaam, and *East African Standard*, Nairobi, 8 and 9 October 1968. For a discussion of the politics of mini-skirts, see my article on 'Mini-skirts and political puritanism' in *African Report*, Washington, D.C., October 1968. A related instance of Tanzania's political puritanism is the country's decision to abolish the beauty contest for Miss Tanzania.

7. DAVID DIOP, 'The Renegade' in *Modern Poetry from Africa*, ed. Moore and Beier, 1963, p. 57.

8. *The Reporter*, Nairobi, 23 February 1968, p. 4.

9. THEODORE REIK, *Masochism in Sex and Society*, tr. Beigel and Kurth, 1962, pp. 349–50. For a discussion of related issues see Mazrui, 'Sacred suicide', *Transition*, 21 (1965).

10. R. R. MARETT, *Threshold of Religion*, 1909, p. xxxi. See also B. G. M. Sundkler, *Bantu Prophets in South Africa*, International African Institute, 1961, p. 198.

11. JOSIAH MWANGI KARIUKI, *'Mau Mau' Detainee*, 1963, pp. 29–30.

12. MICHAEL F. LOFCHIE, *Zanzibar: Background to Revolution*, Princeton University Press, Princeton, N.J., 1965, p. 276.

B. Body 'Language'

Then a tremendous slab snapped up in the middle of the ship and the first of the aliens stepped out in the complex tripodal gait that all humans were shortly to know and love so well. He wore a metallic garment to protect him from the effects of our atmospheric peculiarities, a garment of the opaque, loosely folded type that these, the first of our liberators, wore throughout their stay on Earth.

Speaking in language none could understand, but booming deafeningly through a huge mouth about half-way up his twenty-five feet of height, the alien discoursed for exactly one hour ... The men from U.N. would reply, each one hoping desperately to make up for the alien's lack of familiarity with his own tongue by such devices as hand-gestures and facial expressions. Much later, a commission of anthropologists and psychologists brilliantly pointed out the difficulties of such physical, gestural communication with creatures possessing – as these aliens did – five manual appendages and a single, unwinking compound eye of the type the insects rejoice in.

William Tenn, 'The liberation of Earth' in Brian Aldiss, ed., *The Penguin Science Fiction Omnibus*, Penguin Books, Harmondsworth, 1973, p. 304.

7. The 'Language' of Gesture

107. Kaethe Kollwitz, anti-war poster, 1924. From E. H. Gombrich, 'Ritualized gesture and expression in art', *Philosophical Transactions of the Royal Society*, B 251 (1966), plate 14„ figure 1.

A persistent theme throughout even the most diverse types of body expression research is the notion that body behaviour expresses and communicates, and therefore constitutes a type of 'language'. Even

Darwin admitted that *some* types of bodily expression are 'learnt like the words of a language', and therefore might be described as a 'language of the emotions' (*The Expression of the Emotions in Man and Animals*, pp. 352, 366). Darwin even explored the similarities and the relationship of what have now been called the verbal and non-verbal 'channels' of communication.

Charles Darwin:
The Expression of the Emotions in Man and Animals (excerpts)

First published in 1872; republished in 1965, ed. Francis Darwin, University of Chicago Press, Phoenix Books, Chicago, Ill. and London, pp. 354–5, 364.

The power of communication between the members of the same tribe by means of language has been of paramount importance in the development of man; and the force of language is much aided by the expressive movements of the face and body. We perceive this at once when we converse on an important subject with any person whose face is concealed. Nevertheless there are no grounds, as far as I can discover, for believing that any muscle has been developed or even modified exclusively for the sake of expression. The vocal and other sound-producing organs, by which various expressive noises are produced, seem to form a partial exception; but I have elsewhere attempted to show that these organs were first developed for sexual purposes, in order that one sex might call or charm the other. Nor can I discover grounds for believing that any inherited movement, which now serves as a means of expression, was at first voluntarily and consciously performed for this special purpose – like some of the gestures and the finger-language used by the deaf and dumb. On the contrary, every true or inherited movement of expression seems to have had some natural and independent origin. But when once acquired, such movements may be voluntarily and consciously employed as a means of communication.

The movements of expression in the face and body, whatever their origin may have been, are in themselves of much importance for our welfare. They serve as the first means of communication between the mother and her infant; she smiles approval, and thus encourages her child on the right path, or frowns disapproval. We readily perceive sympathy in others by their expression; our sufferings are thus mitigated and our pleasures increased; and mutual good feeling is thus strengthened. The movements of expression give vividness and energy to our spoken words. They reveal the thoughts and intentions of others more truly than do words, which may be falsified.

Although every specialized area of bodily expression research has, as I have said, been influenced [at least indirectly] by the idea that bodily expression = language, the two specialized sub-studies of gesture and bodily adornment and clothing have been especially intertwined with linguistic theory. It has often been assumed that gesture, for example, has a special affinity to verbal language. Whether this is the case or not seems to depend upon the current definition of 'gesture' and the current definition of 'language'.

The study of the linguistic characteristics of gesture goes back as far as Plato: in debating with Hermogenes in the Cratylus *about the nature of language, Socrates injects the problem of non-verbal gesture into the discussion.*

SOCRATES: . . . Answer me this question: If we had no voice or tongue, and wished to make things clear to one another, should we not try, as dumb people actually do, to make signs with our hands and head and person generally?

HERMOGENES: Yes, what other method is there, Socrates?

SOCRATES: If we wished to designate that which is above and is light, we should, I fancy, raise our hand towards heaven in imitation of the nature of the thing in question – but if the things to be designated were below or heavy, we should extend our hands towards the ground – and if we wished to mention a galloping horse or any other animal, we should, of course, make our bodily attitudes as much like theirs as possible.

HERMOGENES: I think you are quite right – there is no other way.

SOCRATES: For the expression of anything, I fancy, would be accomplished by bodily imitation of that which was to be expressed. (H. N. Fowler, *Plato*, with an English translation, Heinemann, 1926, vol. VI, p. 135)

The notion of the correlation of gesture and language emerges in more detail in Macdonald Critchley's aptly titled classic The Language of Gesture *(Arnold, 1939). There is, of course, a great stretch of time between the work of the Greek philosopher and the English neurologist, but they share a certain lack of clarity with regard to the definition of language. Critchley, for example, was particularly concerned with those gestures which have been described as 'sign languages':*

> In 1692 La Fin, one-time secretary to Cardinal Richelieu, advocated a 'silent language' executed by pointing towards various parts of the body. Thus the five vowels were to be indicated by touching the thumb to each finger-tip in turn, while the hollow of the hand stood for *y*. The remainder of the alphabet was signed as follows: *b*, brow, *c*, cheek, *d*, the deaf ear . . . (op. cit., pp. 33–4).

Robert Hertz in 'The pre-eminence of the right hand' (in Hertz, Death and the Right Hand, Cohen & West, 1960) also touched upon the subject of the language-like nature of signs made by gesturing with the hands:

> It is well known that many primitive peoples, particularly the Indians of North America, can converse without saying a word, simply by movements of the head and arms. In this language each hand acts in accordance with its nature. The right hand stands for *me*, the left for *not-me, others*. To express the idea of *high* the right hand is raised above the left, which is held horizontal and motionless – while the idea of *low* is expressed by lowering the 'inferior hand' below the right . . . These characteristic examples are enough to show that the contrast between right and left, and the relative positions of the hands, are of fundamental importance in 'sign-language' (pp. 103–4).

W. D. Brewer in 'Patterns of gesture among the Levantine Arabs' [American Anthropologist, 53 (1951), 232–7] maintains that 'At least from the time of Francis Bacon, authors have been concerned with the concept of gesture and its connection with language' (p. 232). And in this volume, Julia Kristeva's essay 'Gesture: Practice or communication?' (Chapter 9) re-evaluates the whole notion of gesture as non-verbal language and offers a new direction for exploration.

However, beyond theories about language and gesture and debates about theories of language and theories of gesture there is really very little in the way of concrete, ethnographic evidence. David Efron's study Gesture, Race and Culture, *however, stands out as a remarkable exception. Efron's study has been primarily remembered for its 'concrete proof' that gestural patterns change with cultural assimilation. This aspect of Efron's work was dealt with in Chapter 1 of this volume. Usually forgotten, however, is Efron's comparative material on Jewish and Italian traditional gestural systems and his demonstration that these differ in terms of 'linguistic' characteristics. Work such as Efron's helps us begin to appreciate that to say 'gesture is like language' is not nearly sufficient since although both Italian and Jewish gestural systems might be said to be 'language-like', they are, in fact, like very different types of language systems. As Kristeva suggests (Chapter 9), ethnographic research into the language of gesture may help point the way towards a new appreciation of language as well as of gesture and may further develop linguistic and socio-linguistic theories. (As Kristeva's essay deals with the subject of gesture it could be considered as part of the present chapter. However, as it uses the subject of gesture as an occasion for the discussion of semiotics and linguistics and because a major section of it deals with Birdwhistell's theories, it seemed important to include it within Chapter 9 which deals with linguistic and socio-linguistic theories of all aspects of bodily expression.)*

More recent and more sophisticated studies of gestural 'sign-language' have been carried out by Aaron Cicourel and the reader is referred to: Aaron V. Cicourel and Robert J. Boese, 'Sign language acquisition and the teaching of deaf children' in C. Cazden, D. Hymes and V. John, The Functions of Language in the Classroom, *Teacher's College Press, New York, 1972; Aaron V. Cicourel and Robert J. Boese, 'The acquisition of manual sign language and generative semantics',* Semiotica, *5 (1972), 225–56; Aaron V. Cicourel, 'Gestural sign language and the study of non-verbal communication' in J. Benthall and T. Polhemus, eds.,* The Body as a Medium of Expression, *Allen Lane; Dutton, New York, 1975; and Aaron V. Cicourel, 'Cross-modal communication: The representational context of sociolinguistic information processing' in A. Cicourel,* Cognitive Sociology: Language and Meaning in Social Interaction, *Penguin Books, Harmondsworth, 1972.*

David Efron:

Gesture, Race and Culture: A tentative study of some of the spatio-temporal and 'linguistic' aspects of the gestural behaviour of Eastern Jews and Southern Italians in New York City, living under similar as well as different environmental conditions (excerpts)

Mouton, The Hague, 1972, pp. 94–107, 121–30.

In 1941 David Efron (then a postgraduate student studying under Franz Boas) published a shortened version of the doctoral thesis which he had prepared at Columbia University. This work, now entitled Gesture, Race and Culture, *takes as its subject the gestural communication of Jewish and Italian immigrants living in New York City. The work is divided into various parts: one offers a descriptive and pictorial comparison of traditional Jewish and Italian gestures and another then compares the gestures of assimilated Jews and Italians. We have already considered these aspects of Efron's research in Chapter 1. Another important aspect of Efron's study is his comparison of the 'linguistic' characteristics of Jewish and Italian (traditional and assimilated) gestural systems. He argues that traditional Jewish gestural communication is 'ideographic' in that it refers to the structure of discourse, unlike the gestural communication of traditional Italians which he describes as 'physiographic' in that it refers to the content of the discourse rather than to the discourse itself. Efron's research can serve to remind us that there are different types of gestural, non-verbal 'language' just as there are different types of verbal language. As socio-linguists such as Basil Bernstein have begun to explore the sociological roots of certain types of verbal communication, it would seem that the time is now ripe for a return to Efron's research and for a consideration of what social conditions permit or generate different types of non-verbal discourse. (See B. Bernstein, ed.,* Codes and Control: Applied Studies Towards a Sociology of Language, *Routledge & Kegan Paul, London and Boston, 1973, and B. Bernstein, 'A socio-linguistic approach – social learning' in Julius Gould, ed.,* Penguin Survey of the Social Sciences, *Penguin Books, Harmondsworth, 1965, pp. 144–68.)*

Tendencies in the Gestural Behaviour of 'Traditional' Eastern Jews in New York City

'Linguistic' Aspects: Ideographic versus Physiographic Gesture

A notion that was in vogue among early investigators of 'sign-language', during the second half of the nineteenth century, which still seems to enjoy some credit with certain students of gestural 'expression' of our own times, is that which sees in manual gesture a kind of natural *hieroglyphic* writing in the air. As far as we know this notion was first advanced by Francis Bacon.

> For there seems to be other Traditive Emanations besides Words and Letters . . . For we see Nations of different Language to trade with one the other, well enough to serve their turne, by Gestures. Nay in the Practice of many that have bin dumbe and deafe their birth, and otherwise very ingenious, we have seen strange Dialogues held between them and their friends who have learn'd their Gestures . . . Notes therefore of things, which without the helpe and mediation of Words signifie Things, are of two sorts; whereof the first sort is significant of Congruitie, the other *ad placitum*. Of the former sort are Hieroglyphiques and Gestures; of the latter are those which we call Characters Reall . . . As for Gestures they are, as it were, Transitory Hieroglyphiques. For as words pronounced vanish, writings remaine, so Hieroglyphiques expressed by Gestures are transient, but Painted, permanent . . . This in the meane is plain, that Hieroglyphiques and Gestures ever have some similitude with the thing signified, and are kind of Emblemes; wherefore we have named them the Notes of things from Congruitie.[1]

The same notion has repeatedly been set forth since by psychologists and philosophers. It has also tempted from time to time the imagination of the anthropologist. To give here a single example, Tylor claimed that both 'gesture-language and picture-writing may be mostly explained without the aid of history', for they are 'direct products of the human mind', in contrast to speech and alphabetic writing, which 'must be investigated historically, depending as they do in so great measure on the words and characters which were current in the world thousands of years ago'. Again, both the picture-words and the gesture-words, or 'pictures in the air', 'belong to similar conditions of the human mind', namely, 'the imitation of visible qualities as a means of expressing ideas'.[2] The restricted scope of this monograph does not permit a detailed discussion of this theory here.[3] With reference to the empirical material that will be described in the present section, it is pertinent, however, to point out two of the fallacies underlying such a conception. This conception gratuitously assumes (a) that pictorial (of 'things') gesture is a congenital mode of communication, (b) that *all* gesture is pictorial in nature. The first of these assumptions is refuted by the fact that pictorial bodily movement, whether gestural or graphic, *presupposes* visual and/or tactile experience. The second ignores the even more obvious fact that *non-pictorial* gesture plays a predominant role in almost any type of colloquial (non-ritualized) gesticulation.[4] The results of our comparative study indicate rather that the presence of pictorialism in the gestural movements of an individual depends largely on his 'history', or cultural descent. They show, on the other hand, that non-pictorial gesture may discharge a 'linguistic' function as important as that of the pictorial one. A few classificatory considerations will pave the way for a presentation of these results.

A gestural movement may be 'meaningful' by (a) the emphasis it lends to the content of the verbal and vocal behaviour it accompanies, (b) the connotation (whether deictic, pictorial or symbolic) it possesses independently from the speech of which it may, or may not, be an adjunct. In the first case its 'meaning' is of a *logical* or *discursive* character, the movement being, as it were, a kind of gestural portrayal, not of the object of reference, or 'thought', but of the course of the ideational process itself (i.e., a bodily re-enactment of the logical pauses, intensities, inflections, etc. of the corresponding speech sequence). This type of gesture may in turn be (a) simply *baton-like*, representing a sort of 'timing out' with the hand the successive stages of the referential activity, (b) *ideographic*, in the sense that it traces or sketches out in the air the 'paths' and 'directions' of the thought-pattern. The latter variety might also be called *logico-topographic* or *logico-pictorial*. In the second case the 'meaning' of the gesture is 'objective', and the movement may be (a) *deictic*, referring by means of a sign to a visually present object (actual pointing), (b) *physiographic*, depicting either the form of a visual object or a spatial relationship (*iconographic* gesture), or that of a bodily action (*kinetographic* gesture), (c) *symbolic* or *emblematic*, representing either a visual or a logical object by means of a pictorial or a non-pictorial form which has no morphological relationship to the thing represented.[5] From a more general standpoint, the logico-topographic movement has not escaped the attention of certain students of gesture. Thus, Karl Bühler in his *Ausdruckstheorie* (Verlag G. Fischer, Jena, 1933, p. 45), calls it a gestural 'mirroring' (*Spiegelung*) of the associative processes of thought, a 'spatial symbolization of logical nuances and directions' ('. . . logische

Scheidungen räumlich symbolisiert, logische Wendungen durch räumliche angedeudet . . .'). Bühler fails, however, to distinguish the logico-pictorial gesture from what he calls the '*Deixis am Phantasma*', that is to say, a gestural pointing at a logical *object*. Engel's classical example, quoted by Bühler, is very fitting. 'Wenn Hamlet die Ursache entdeckt hat, warum der Selbstmord ein so bedenklicher Schritt sey, so ruft er aus: "Ach da liegt der Knoten!", und in demselben Augenblicke bewegt er den Finger vor sich hin, als ob er äusserlich mit dem Auge gefunden hatte, was er doch innerlich mit dem Scharfsinne fand' (Engel, *Ideen zu einer Mimik*, Berlin, 1875, pp. 130–31). Although this type of gestural motion is basically akin to the ideographic one, in the sense that they both have logical (as distinguished from visual) referents, there still exists, however, an important difference between them, from the standpoint of the specific contentual nature of the referent in each case. In effect, the '*Deixis am Phantasma*', or logical pointing, relates to a mental *object* ('Ach da liegt *der Knoten!*'), whereas the ideographic gesture refers to a mental *process*, i.e., it delineates the 'curve' of the referential activity itself. The specific difference in content existing between the logical 'deixis' and the logical 'pictura' has been overlooked in all the treatises on gestures we are acquainted with. The more general difference between the ideographic and the physiographic gestures has been clearly pointed out, on the other hand, by several students of gestural behaviour. Among these Cicero was, as far as we know, the first to draw such a distinction. Although the concept on which he bases it is, as in the case of Bühler, a mentalistic one, the distinction *per se* is correct. For Cicero the real gesture is that kind of movement which expresses the internal *workings* of the mind; an external, *natural* sign of the '*affectionum animi*', in contrast to the pictorial one which expresses merely the *objects* of thought; the latter he calls '*gestus scenicus*', proper of an actor but unfitting to an orator ('Omnes autem hos motus subsequi debet gestus, non hic verba exprimens, scenicus, sed universam rem et sententiam, non demonstratione, sed significatione declarans.' *De Oratore*, Lib. III, c. 59). Cicero's '*significatio*' coincides with our concept of ideographic or logico-pictorial gesture, while his '*demonstratio*' refers to what we call physiographic gesture. Similarly, Engel distinguishes between 'expressive' (*ausdrückende*) and 'pictorial' (*malende*) gestures ('Malerey ist mir . . . jede sinnliche Darstellung der Sache selbst welche die Seele denkt; Ausdrück jede sinnliche Darstellung der Fassung, der Gesinnung womit sie sie denkt; des ganzen Zustandes, worinn sie durch ihr Denken versetzt wird.' Engel, op. cit., Bd I, p. 79). Among the 'expressive' movements, Engel distinguishes again three types:

the purely 'physiological' (involuntary), the 'voluntary' and the 'analogical'. The first two do not concern us now. The third has something to do with our ideographic movement. It pictures, says Engel, 'nicht das Objekt des Denkens, aber die Fassung, die Wirkungen, die Veränderungen der Seele' (ibid., Bd I, p. 97). This description embraces, however, more than what is implied in our own, for it includes also the gestures depicting a logical *attitude*, such as the turning motion of the head, or the rejective movement of the hand, as a 'pantomime' of the logical rejection of an idea. It does not refer specifically to the gestural portrayal of a logical *process*. There are, however, two short remarks in Engel's treatise which would seem to indicate that he was not entirely unaware of the specific nature of the logico-pictorial gesture. These are when he speaks of the way in which the changes in the 'speed' and 'direction' of our ideational processes sometimes reflect themselves in changes in the speed and direction of our walking motions, as well as of our gestural movements (cf. ibid., Bd I, pp. 125–6). The author who came nearest to our notion of logico-pictorial or ideographic gesture is Gratiolet, who describes this type of movement as a variety of what he calls the 'symbolic' one (any movement referring to an imaginary object or situation). 'Si l'idée est fort configurée,' he says, 'en même temps que l'esprit en sent tous les détours, le regard et le doigt élevé semblent suivre le fil conducteur de quelque méandre très compliqué' (*De la Physionomie et des Mouvements d'Expression*, Hetzel, Paris, 1865, p. 322). Gratiolet's 'meandering' gesture is very similar to what we have ourselves called a gestural 'embroidery' re-enacting the logical zig-zags and undulations of a complex thought-pattern.

Now, notwithstanding the large amount of gestural movement involved in his colloquial behaviour, the 'traditional' Eastern Jew very seldom displays physiographic or symbolic gestures.[6] In contrast to the 'traditional' Southern Italian who, it will be shown below, is inclined to *illustrate* gesturally the 'objects' of his thinking activity (the 'referents'), the ghetto Jew is more likely to give a *gestural notation* of the 'process' of that activity, a gestural description of the 'physiognomy', so to say, of his discourse (the 'reference'). To use an analogy, the 'traditional' Jew very rarely employs his arm in the guise of a pencil, to depict the 'things' he is referring to, but uses it often as a pointer, to link one proposition to another, or to trace the itinerary of a logical journey; or else as a baton, to beat the tempo of his mental locomotion. One might say that his gestural movements are related more to the 'how' than to the 'what' of the ideas they re-enact. The popular notion that 'he talks with the hands' can be taken in a metaphorical sense only. *Per se* his gestures as a rule 'say' little or nothing. They 'speak' only to a person who understands the accompanying words, particularly if he is familiar with the 'meanings' of certain more or less stereotyped intonational forms characteristic of ghetto-Yiddish.[7] When such condition is present, the 'logical' significance of these 'baton' – and 'pointer' – gestures is unmistakable. It is then perfectly clear that almost each turn or twist in the movement corresponds to a change in the 'direction' or in the 'altitude' (logical emphasis) of the 'curve' of thought. These shifts in logical direction and level result in the complex embroideries and zigzags described above, which in a sense are something like gestural charts of the 'heights' and 'lows', 'detours' and 'crossroads' of the ideational route.

The 'logical' nature of this type of gesture becomes strikingly apparent in those cases in which the movement presents a quasi-'syllogistic' form, its zigzags or sinuous inflections corresponding to the two premises and the conclusion of a thought-configuration. Examples of these logico-topographical or 'propositional' gestures will be found in Figures 108 and 109.[8]

108. Ghetto Jews: logico-topographical gestures (gestures = syllogisms).

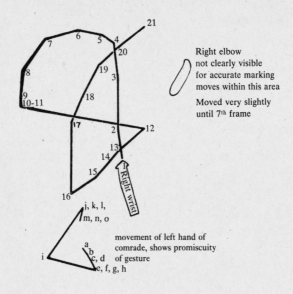

Right elbow
not clearly visible
for accurate marking
moves within this area

Moved very slightly
until 7th frame

movement of left hand of
comrade, shows promiscuity
of gesture

109. (a) Ghetto Jew: gestural embroidery.

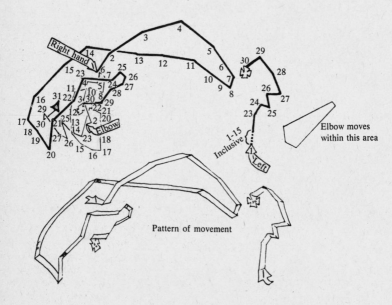

Elbow moves
within this area

Pattern of movement

(b) Ghetto Jew: gestural embroidery.

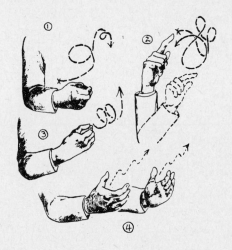

(c) Ghetto Jew: sinuous gesture.

... The statement regarding the relative paucity of physiographic and pictorially symbolic elements in the gestural movements of the 'traditional' Jew is based upon an observation of approximately 450 cases of verbo-gestural behaviour, in most of which a great deal of manual motion was present, and the verbal part of which contained a good number of words or groups of words referring to spatial objects and relationships, and to bodily actions. With only a few exceptions, no disposition was detected in the speakers to pictorialize gesturally these words. In the great majority of cases the 'thing'-word or the 'action'-word was found to be accompanied instead either by a 'baton'-movement or by a strictly ideographic one. This phenomenon stands out in sharp contrast when compared to that observed in the case of the 'traditional' Italian (cf. below).

Fifty-five of the cases above mentioned are included in the following table. In the first column appear, out of context,[9] the 'thing'-words (symbolizing visuo-spatial forms, situations or relationships) and the 'action'-words (symbolizing bodily activities) contained in the verbal behaviour of the subjects observed. In the second, a reproduction is given of the movements performed by the gesturer while he was uttering these words.[10]

TABLE I

*Ideographic versus Physiographic Gesture
('Traditional' Eastern Jew)*

Case	'Thing'- and 'action'-words	Accompanying movements	
1	two halves	*(gesture)*	
2	turning around	*(gesture)*	
3	and fell down	*(gesture)*	short outward -movement, palms up
4	in between	*(gesture)*	
5	walking fast	*(gesture)*	repeated several times
6	hit him on the head	*(gesture)*	
7	set apart	*(gesture)*	
8	his thinking twists[11]	*(gesture)*	
9	going backwards	*(gesture)*	repeated several times
10	one against the other	*(gesture)*	
11	a tremendous explosion	*(gesture)*	descriptive gesture
12	thumbing through the book	*(gesture)*	
13	he drags himself along[12]	*(gesture)*	
14	he climbs to the roof[13]	*(gesture)*	
15	broken into pieces	*(gesture)*	
16	cracked his head open	*(gesture)*	repeated several times
17	under the wheels	*(gesture)*	
18	too low	*(gesture)*	
19	a huge pile of junk	*(gesture)*	repeated several times
20	and stopped all of a sudden	*(gesture)*	
21	lashing back and forth in the water	*(gesture)*	repeated several times
22	stroking the book	*(gesture)*	

Case	'Thing'- and 'action'-words	Accompanying movements	
23	straining himself to lift it up from the ground		
24	pushing him away		repeated several times
25	I looked around		
26	whipping the poor little boy		repeated several times
27	propping him up		repeated several times
28	and finally turned the pushcart over		repeated several times
29	threw herself overboard		
30	running against each other		
31	I hammered it into his head		
32	one on the top of the other		
33	just in the middle		
34	jumped across		
35	on the edge		
36	rolling down the hill		repeated several times
37	the walls were shaking		repeated several times
38	from the top of Mount Sinai		with edge of palm
39	a very long beard		
40	crushed ('*zupletscht*')		palm down, in forceful movement. *Descriptive gesture*
41	a tight knot		repeated several times
42	a long row		
43	playing the harp		palm out and upward
44	split in two		
45	standing in front of you		repeated several times
46	right and left		repeated several times

Case	'Thing'- and 'action'-words	Accompanying movements	
47	a sharp inclination		
48	and pierced it through		
49	he cast the cane on the ground		
50	an oval shape		repeated several times
51	the door wide open		
52	upside down		
53	shooing the children away		
54	and they collided		
55	one after the other		repeated several times

Although the ideographic movement is a phenomenon frequently observed among 'traditional' Jews of Lithuanian and Polish origin in general it appears to be particularly characteristic of a certain sub-group within the ghetto population, namely, the Lithuanian 'Yeshiva'-type[14] of Jew, used to argumentative and syllogistic reasoning. During the two-year period of our inquiry we enjoyed the opportunity of frequenting the company of a good number of these Yeshiva Jews in New York City (teachers and students of the *Yeshiva Rabbi Itzjak Elhanan*, speakers at orthodox Lithuanian Jewish learned societies, etc.), and of watching closely their gestures. Our observations would seem to indicate that the greater prevalence of logico-pictorial motions in the gestural behaviour of this type of Jew is due to the nature of his educational training. A quantitative test of the frequency of this kind of gesture in twenty-five Yeshiva Jews and twenty-five non-Yeshiva Jews yielded the following results:

	Number of subjects[15]	Time of gestural movement	Number of ideographic gestures[16]
Yeshiva Jews	25	170 minutes	718
Non-Yeshiva Jews	25	151 minutes	355

Gestural Emphasis: With the exception perhaps of purely symbolic gesture, most conversational bodily motions carry some emphatic weight, in the sense that they tend to reinforce the value of social stimulation of the verbal behaviour they accompany. Generally speaking, a gestural movement may be emphatic in two different ways: (a) by its *force* and/or *sweep*, (b) by its *form*. In the first case the speaker strives to impose his thoughts upon the interlocutor *bodily*, so to say, trying to give, by means of a violent and ample movement, an appearance of *fait accompli* to his words. In the second case the speaker strives to persuade more with the 'idea' than with the hand. The movement is neat, sometimes punctilious, as if intended to italicize, or bring into relief certain parts or stages of the ideational process. One might call the first kind of gestural emphasis a *dogmatic* one, the second a *logical* one.

The type of emphasis found more frequently in the gestural movement of the ghetto Jew is the logical one. Even in situations of great excitement his gestures are very seldom violent and far-flung. In spite of the fact that he gesticulates so much and so often, he rarely 'lets his gesture go'. There seems to be a lack of substantial power behind it. The motions give more an effect of nervous energy than of 'animal' force. This becomes strikingly apparent when contrasted with the gestures of the 'traditional' Southern Italian who is sometimes actually carried away by the robustness and amplitude of his own movements. It has been our repeated observation that even under the grip of an emotion ghetto Jews seldom exhibit forceful and expansive gestures. In fact, we have witnessed a good number of cases in which their gestures in such a situation became even more confined in area and more punctilious in form than they usually are. It is interesting to point out in this connection that the opposite case, that is to say, the use of grandiose gestures in the manifestation of ideational or affective processes of a purely conversational character, appears to be rather characteristic of the 'traditional' Italian.

As a rule the 'logical' emphasis in the gestures of the ghetto Jew involves a change in the speed and/or the direction of the movement, the latter being, as it were, a kind of gestural 'catapulting'[17] of the corresponding segment of discourse. This is exemplified by a good number of the gestural zigzags contained in our collection of graphs. The phenomenon just described calls for a careful, specific inquiry.

Symbolic Gesture: Unlike the physiographic movement, which exhibits an entire, or partial, direct morphological relationship to the bodily attribute or action it represents, and may therefore be understood by individuals belonging to markedly different cultures, the symbolic one, whether pictorial or non-pictorial in form, has, as a rule, a purely emblematic character, that is to say, the 'referee' of the thought-gesture activity (i.e., the gestural symbol) shows no morphological analogy with its 'referent' (i.e., the thing, bodily action or logical object referred to).

As in the case of iconographic and kinetographic movement, the gestural behaviour of the ghetto Jew betrays a scarcity of symbolic

110. Ghetto Jews: symbolic gestures.

(a) Thumb-digging movement; digging out of an idea.

(b) Poking with index on palm; impossibility. 'This will happen when grass will grow on this' (the palm). Also the hammering in of an idea.

(c) Palm on cheek or behind ear; astonishment, bewilderment, rejecting.

(d) Turning palms up; 'What can I do? I do not know.' Physiognomic expression determines meaning.

(e) Plucking of beard or stroking of chin; thoughtfulness, deliberation, doubt, etc.

elements. During the long period of our inquiry, we came across only six movements in the gestural behaviour of this group which might be classified under the category of the symbolic. Strictly speaking, only two of these are distinctly emblematic. The others, on the contrary, may be found to signify more than one specific object or concept, depending on the linguistic content they accompany. When they are used as an exclusive means of communication, their 'meanings' are more or less vague, and may be interpreted differently by two different spectators. Moreover, they may recur under entirely different psychological situations. (Cf. Figures 110 a–e.)

Pantomime: Since the gestural movements of the 'traditional' Eastern Jew are seldom physiographic or symbolic (of objects), they rarely function as an exclusive means of linguistic interaction, in contrast to the 'traditional' Southern Italian who, as will be shown below, is perfectly able to carry on conversation without the aid of the spoken word. In our study of so-called pantomimic gesticulation, we were fortunate to secure the assistance of several prominent Italian and Jewish actors in New York City.[18] The former showed no difficulty whatsoever in enacting a series of 'dumb-shows', which are entirely meaningful to any person acquainted with the system of gestural pictures and symbols used by their group. The latter, on the contrary, were unable to create any specifically significant pantomime based on 'Jewish' gestures.

Using the quasi-meaningful pictorial movements of the ghetto Jew, together with some of the so-called 'universal' descriptive motions, Mr Van Veen drew up an artificial pantomime which was shown to several 'traditional' Jews. Their interpretations of the pictorial 'story' differed a great deal, showing that the few illustrative 'Jewish' gestures have no standardized meaning. This was particularly evident in two of such cases in which the same subject ascribed different meanings to the same pictorial 'Jewish' gestures because these were found to function in different gestural contexts.

A similar attempt was made by the author on several occasions with ideographic movements (of both the 'baton'- and the 'pointer'-types), punctuating and delineating tempo of the logical process, ideational pause, shift in logical direction, etc. The results here were somewhat different. In most cases the subjects knew that 'the gestures had something to do with the order of your ideas', as one of them put it, or, in the words of another subject, that I was 'tracing a line of thought'. Only the investigator was aware, however, of what that 'order' and that 'line' concretely 'meant'.

Tendencies in the Gestural Behaviour of 'Traditional' Southern Italians in New York City

'Linguistic' Aspects: Ideographic versus Physiographic Gesture

In contrast to the gestural movements of the 'traditional' Eastern Jew, which, it has been shown, are predominantly of a logical character (whether of the 'baton'- or the 'pointer'-type), being relatively poor in descriptive (of 'things') elements, those of the 'traditional' Southern Italian contain a rather fair number of *physiographic* forms, and betray, on the other hand, a relatively marked scarcity in *ideographic* ones. The gestures of the Italian appear to be related more to the objective content of discourse than to its logical trajectory. The popular dictum that 'he talks with the hands' is as literally true in the case of the Italian as it was metaphorically in that of the Jew. To be sure, the gestural motions of the former are far from being always, or even predominantly, pictorial of things or activities. As far as quantity of movement is concerned, many of them are in fact simply 'expository' in nature, marking the paces and strides of the corresponding speech sequence. From this standpoint the gestural behaviour of the Italian does not differ a great deal from that of the Jew. Apart from this common characteristic, however (which is probably present in any type of non-ritualized colloquial gesticulation), the gestural behaviour of the two groups is strikingly different in that the physiographic movement (gestural onomatopoeia) as well as the symbolic one (gestural emblem) are phenomena as frequent in the case of the Italian as rare in that of the Jew; and, conversely, in that the strictly ideographic gesture (delineating the course of a meander of thought), typical of the latter, is almost entirely absent in the former. During the whole period of our inquiry we came across only two instances of gestural movement among Italians which might be classified under the category of the ideographic. If the movements of the 'traditional' Jew have been likened to gestural 'charts', outlining the logical itineraries of the corresponding ideational processes, those of the 'traditional' Italian may be said to be something like gestural 'slides', illustrating the very things referred to by the accompanying words. In this sense the gestural behaviour of the Italian appears to be more 'substantival' than that of the Jew, for it contains a much larger number of visuo-spatial replicas of the 'referents' of thought. This method of *'demonstratio ad oculos'* in gesture proves to be highly instrumental in increasing the stimulus value of the verbal aspect of discourse. Moreover, unlike the scheme propounded to the people of Laputa by the professors of the Grand Academy of Lagado,[19] this procedure of talking by gestural 'things' may be conveniently used as the exclusive means of communication. From the data collected in the Italian quarter during the first stage of our inquiry (i.e., direct inspection of gestural behaviour, and ensuing interrogation of subjects), we have been able to draw a more or less exhaustive inventory of the 'bundle of pictures' that a 'traditional' Southern Italian usually carries in his hands. This gestural vocabulary comprehends no less than 151 manual 'words', implying more or less definite meaningful associations. Some of these formalized movements are found also in the gestural behaviour of other, 'civilized' as well as 'primitive', groups. The others are local in character and their meanings are clear only to a member of a 'traditional' Southern Italian community, or to any person who is familiar with the system of gestural pictures and symbols used by the Southern Italian. Five of these are shown in Figure 111 a–e.

111. Traditional Italians: symbolic gestures.
(a) 'Good', 'sweet', 'pretty'. The origin of this is in the fact that many Neapolitans had large curling moustaches. When they approved of anything they would ostentatiously curl the tip.
(b) 'To eat'. The origin is found in the fact that spaghetti was first eaten by hand, lifted up in the air and trickled into the mouth. This gesture pantomimes the act of so doing.
(c) 'I'm broke', or 'I'm hungry'.
(d) 'What do you want?'
(e) 'To drink'.

It is possible to trace the historical continuity of many of the gestures included in our chart. Some of these go as far back as ancient Greece and Rome. This may be ascertained by a comparison of our chart with the descriptions or the pictorial reproductions of Greek and Roman gestures found in Karl Sittl's fully documented book, *Die Gebärden der Griechen und Römer* (Verlag Teubner, Leipzig, 1890), as well as in Andrea di Jorio's *Mimica degli Antichi Investigata nel Gestire Napoletano* (Stamperia del Fibreno, Naples, 1832). In Quintilian's descriptions of Roman oratorical gestures we recognize several of the movements included in our collection. Several of these movements, used by 'traditional' Southern Italians in New York City, were parts of the 'sign-languages' of Anglo-Saxon and German monks in the eleventh, fifteenth and sixteenth centuries. Three of the gesture-'dictionaries' of these monks will be found in F. Klüge's *Zur Geschichte der Zeichensprache, Angelsächsische Indicia Monasterialia* (Techmer's 'Internationale Zeitschrift für Allgemeine Sprachwissenschaft', J. Ambrosius Barth, Leipzig, 1885, II Band, 1 Hälfte, p. 116) and Leibniz's *Collectanea Etymologica* (Nicolai Foerster, Hanover, 1717).

In general there is little difference between the gestural lexicon of the 'traditional' Neapolitan in New York City and that of his ancestor in Europe one century ago, as recorded by di Jorio in his book above mentioned. This also holds true for the dictionary of Sicilian gestures published in the latter half of the nineteenth century by Pitre (cf. 'I Gesti' in his *Biblioteca delle Tradizioni Popolari Siciliane*, vol. 15, Pedone Lauriel, Palermo, 1889).

As to the contemporary Southern Italian in the Old World, the similarity between his gestural vocabulary and that of the unassimilated Southern Italian here can easily be grasped from a comparison of the gestures of our chart with those of an analogous collection of drawings made from life a few years ago in Italy by the Italian artist, Leone Augusto Rosa (*Espressione e Mimica*, Hoepli, Milan, 1929).

Our own chart contains chiefly gestural pictures and symbols referring to the following categories of objects: (a) bodily functions (including sensory and motor activity, as well as sexual behaviour), (b) moral qualities, values and attitudes, (c) logical and affective states, and (d) superstitious motives. With a few exceptions it does not include the many iconographic gestures (depicting shapes, structures or positions of material objects) frequently performed by the 'traditional' Italian. These were omitted owing to the fact that, unlike the others, they have no standardized form. The frequency with which these 'thing-' gestures make themselves apparent in the 'traditional' Italian may be grasped from Table No. 2 containing forty-eight cases of verbo-gestural behaviour, the verbal aspect of which included a considerable number of words referring to forms or positions of material objects.

TABLE 2

Ideographic versus Physiographic Gesture
('Traditional' Southern Italian)

Case	'Thing'- and 'Action'-words	Accompanying movements
1	overseas	
2	a big crowd	
3	to bring his family over	
4	on the top of the building	
5	flat ground	horizontal movement, with palm parallel to ground
6	so I finally wrote to him	index finger of one hand used with writing movement upon other
7	a tiny piece of meat	thumb and index finger of one hand holding index finger of other hand in such a way as to indicate a small measurement
8	for the next couple of weeks	
9	in the open	as in No. 2
10	and dived into the pool	
11	trying to take them apart	
12	turn around the next corner	
13	put it down!	
14	they came to an understanding	
15	but could not avoid the clash	
16	he run upstairs	
17	not a single window in the room	
18	water on both sides	
19	pulling it down slowly	
20	and they jailed him	fingers held in position of vertical bars in front of face

Case	'Thing'- and 'Action'-words	Accompanying movements
21	Imagine, an old fellow like he riding on the merry-go-round!	circular movement repeated several times
22	shoved me aside	swift movement of arm away from body, palm thrust forward
23	planting the flagpole in the ground	
24	I am sending her to commercial school to learn typing	fluttering movement of fingers in imitation of typing process
25	You better make a hook with the wire	forefinger bent in hooked shape
26	first up and then down	
27	stirring the soup with a stick	
28	they stood them flat against the wall	frontal thrust of arm, palm forward
29	in a funny, round bathtub	
30	cut off his beard	scissors movement of first two fingers on right hand
31	over the rope	
32	half of it	a slicing movement with the edge of the palm
33	a large plate	
34	they are both alike	like in No. 32, but with both hands
35	under the bridge	
36	I haven't got the money	see No. 42
37	going from one extreme to the other	
38	Right now!	using 'here' for 'now'
39	he used to be very fat	
40	you better use the ladder	

Case	'Thing'- and 'Action'-words		Accompanying movements
41	piling up the hay	⌒⌒	repeated several times
42	I do not want to hear about it		transversal brushing movement with edge of one hand on palm of other held supine (meaning apparently rejection)
43	stumbled and fell	↓ℎ⌢⌢	downward motion of hand, continued with scalloping movements
44	it went straight up in the air	⸲ₒ↑	talking about fireworks
45	going back and forth		talking about a rocking horse; palm vertical, thumb pointed in direction of 'back' followed by forward movement of remaining fingers
46	a deep gash	↓	
47	he has a screw loose	↻	
48	water running all over the place	⌢⌢⌢⌢	

The results of this tabulation stand out in sharp contrast when compared with those obtained in the case of the ghetto Jew. Such comparison will convey a vivid representation of what was meant when we spoke analogically of the gestural 'slides' of the Italian versus the gestural 'maps' of the Jew. One might describe also the difference by saying that the latter is more apt to give a gestural *notation* of the logical features of discourse, while the former is more likely to give an *illustration* of its predicative aspects.

The contrast between the 'traditional' Jew and the 'traditional' Italian becomes even more striking when one considers the cases in which the latter not only pictorializes the 'thing' or 'action' referents of his thinking activity, but also uses graphic or plastic movement to portray or model gesturally the process of the logical activity itself, e.g., when he performs a round motion with curved palms, as if he were bringing a material object into shape. These '*modelling gestures*' correspond, from the point of view of 'content' or 'reference', to the ideographic (of the 'pointer'-type) movements of the ghetto Jew.

1. *Gestural Emphasis*

In contrast to the ghetto Jew, who is likely to string out a whole series of jerky little climaxes in his gestural movements *along* the path of the accompanying speech, the 'traditional' Italian usually saves his gestural accents and exclamations for energetic conclusions of discourse. Again, in contrast to the Jew, who is prone to accentuate his words by means of a change in the direction and the speed of the gesture, the Italian is more apt to do it by an increase in its radius and/or its force. His gestural emphasis falls chiefly under the category of the 'dogmatic'.

When gesturing with one arm only, and if he needs to emphasize a point, the Italian is very likely to underline gesturally the corresponding words by bringing the idle arm into play for a moment with a replica of the same movement. The Italian may also italicize the content of a part of his discourse by means of a special symbolic movement carrying the more or less specific 'meaning' of emphasis.

As far as our observation goes, the *ideographically emphatic* gesture, so typical of the ghetto Jew, is almost entirely absent in the 'traditional' Italian.

2. *Pantomime*

The standardized 'gesture-words' mentioned before, as well as the less stereotyped gestural pictures described above, enable the 'traditional' Italian of New York City to carry on conversation independent of spoken language. This procedure is usually resorted to as a means of intra-group secretiveness, or when distance prevents or hinders verbal intercourse.

In the course of our exploration of the streets of 'Little Italy' we came across several interesting instances of pantomimic behaviour among Southern Italians. They are similar in character to the series of 'dumbshows' which at a later stage of our inquiry were enacted for us by three prominent Italian actors of this city. Several of the gestural pictures and symbols used by the actors are found in the Neapolitan pantomimes of di Jorio, published over a century ago. A reproduction of one of these is found opposite.

112. Pantomimic gesticulation. From Andrea di Jorio's *La Mimica degli Antichi Investigata nel Gestire Napoletano.*

Notes

1. *Of the Advancement and Proficience of Learning*, 1640 edn, Young & Forrest, Oxford Book VI, pp. 258–9. (The reason why people gifted with the instrument of speech must 'learn' the allegedly innate gestural signs of the deaf-mutes, before they are in a position of conversing with them gesturally, is not given.)

2. cf. *Researches into the Early History of Mankind*, John Murray, 1870, introduction, p. 3; also pp. 17, 84.

3. This will be done in a separate essay, now in preparation, dealing exclusively with theories of gestural movement.

4. A variety of the hieroglyphic theory of gesture tries to obviate this criticism by injecting the additional and unproved assumption that every non-pictorial gesture stems from a pictorial archetype.

5. Needless to say, the difference between the pictorially and the non-pictorially symbolic movements is purely formal. Referentially they are identical, for the pictorialism of the former has nothing to do with the pictorial qualities of the object it represents. There exist, however, certain cases in which the symbolic gesture possesses a partial descriptive relationship to the thing represented. These 'hybrid' (referentially speaking) movements are rather hard to classify, for they fall under two different categories.

6. One might wonder to what extent this phenomenon may have been culturally conditioned by the biblical prohibition to make images of what is in the heavens, the earth and the waters (Exodus XX, 4).

7. As, for example, the peculiar vocal inflection of the word 'Nu', which often goes together with a kind of 'question-mark' or 'exploratory' sinuous little gesture.

8. No such phenomenon was observed in the case of the 'traditional' Italian. Neither was it found to be present in the gestural behaviour of the 'assimilated' Italian or Jew.

9. It was practically impossible to take down in writing the entire speech sequences, without losing track of what was going on on the gestural side of the phenomenon under observation. Indeed, only a recording machine could keep pace with the gestures and words of a ghetto Jew or a 'traditional' Italian. In fact, in some cases the investigator found it extremely difficult to register quickly enough the isolated words he was hunting for, together with their accompanying movements. Fortunately, a record of the linguistic contexts *in toto* was not essential for our purpose in this case. The isolated words contained in the table are close translations of the corresponding Yiddish terms.

10. Strictly speaking, in most cases the movements corresponded not to the isolated words given but to full sentences of which these words were integrating parts. This does not invalidate our analysis, however, for the point we wish to make is that when the 'thing'- or 'action'-words were uttered no physiographic motion was present.

11. The Yiddish expression was: 'Er ot zu fiel dreidlaj', i.e., 'his thinking, or conduct, has too many circles or twists' (is too circuitous); perhaps the closest translation would be 'he does not think [or act] straight'.

12. Yiddish expression: 'Er shlept zij.'

13. Yiddish expression: 'Er kletert zij af'n daj.' Used figuratively to denote a person who instead of approaching a problem or a situation directly, 'on the ground', takes an unusual and difficult route, such as 'climbing a wall'.

14. An orthodox religious Jewish institution of higher learning, consecrated to the training of rabbis and teachers for the Eastern-Jewish communities. The emphasis in the curriculum is on the study of the logical structure and dialectical subtleties of Talmudic law.

15. The educational background of each subject was determined either by direct interrogation of the individual concerned, or by information obtained from people who knew him well. The gesturers were unaware of the fact that their gestures were being observed.

16. Including the 'baton'- as well as the 'pointer'-type movements. The strictly ideographic motions (pointer-type) were the minority in most cases.

17. The term is used here in a purely analogical way. It is *not* meant to imply a dichotomy of 'inner' thought and 'outer' gestural 'expression' of that thought. We conceive of gestural behaviour as an intrinsic part of the thinking process, and have no use for the skin-fetishism of the mentalist.

18. Signorina Baldi, Signor Sterni and Signor Migliaccio (Italian); and Messrs Buloff and Ben-Ami (Jewish). The writer again takes occasion to acknowledge his indebtedness to each of these actors.

19. Swift's amusing story is worth quoting: '[It] was a Scheme for entirely abolishing all Words whatsoever; and this was urged as a great Advantage in point of Health as well as Brevity. For it is plain that every Word we speak is in some Degree a Diminution of our Lungs by Corrosion, and consequently contributes to the shortening of our Lives. An expedient was therefore offered that, since Words are only Names for *Things*, it would be more convenient for all Men to carry about them such *Things* as were necessary to express the particular Business they are to discourse on. And this Invention would certainly have taken Place, to the great Ease as well as Health of the Subject, if the Women, in conjunction with the Vulgar and Illiterate, had not threatened to raise a Rebellion, unless they might be allowed the Liberty to speak with their Tongues after the Manner of their Ancestors; such constant irreconcilable Enemies of Science are the common People. However, many of the most Learned and Wise adhere to the new Scheme of expressing themselves by *Things*, which hath only this Inconvenience attending it, that if a Man's Business be very great, and of various kinds, he must be obliged in Proportion to carry a great Bundle of

Things upon his Back, unless he can afford one or two strong Servants to attend him. I have often beheld two of those Sages almost sinking under the Weight of their Packs, like Peddlers among us, who when they meet in the Streets would lay down their Loads, open their Saddles, and hold Conversation for an hour together; then put up their Implements, help each other to resume their Burdens, and take their Leave. But for short Conversations a Man may carry Implements in his Pockets and under his Arms, enough to supply him, and in his House he cannot be at loss; therefore the Room where Company meet who practise this Art is full of all *Things* ready at Hand, requisite to furnish Matter of this kind of artificial Converse.' (*Gulliver's Travels*, Part III.)

8. The Language of Dress and Adornment

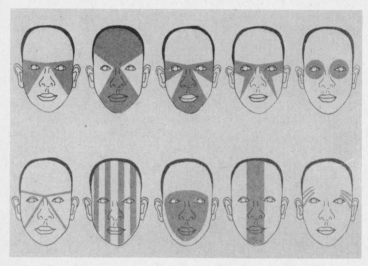

113. Representative Nuba facial designs. From James C. Faris, *Nuba Personal Art*, Duckworth, 1972.

As with the study of gesture, the study of adornment and clothing has often been conducted within a linguistic framework. And as with the linguistic study of gesture, the linguistic study of clothing and adornment has been hampered by confusion with regard to the nature of 'language'. For example, two recent works which deal with the language-like characteristics of body painting and adornment – Terence Turner's 'Tchikrin: A Central Brazilian tribe and its symbolic language of bodily adornment' (*Natural History*, 78 (October 1969), 50–59, 70) and James Faris's *Nuba Personal Art* (Duckworth, 1972) – use the term 'language' in radically different ways. Turner is very vague about the term and seems to assume that it is perfectly clear what 'language' is, while Faris, although more precise, plunges into a linguistic analysis of Nuba body painting based upon a Chomskyian generative grammar that may leave the reader somewhat confused with regard to what Chomsky means by 'language'. Simon Messing's 'The non-verbal language of the Ethiopian toga' (see below) uses the term 'language' in yet another way. Different societies, different specialized subjects, different linguistic models and different concepts and definitions of 'language' have produced a literature on the language of the body and its aids of dress and adornment which consistently fails to integrate into any meaningful whole.

To resolve this situation it is important that students select *one* linguistic theory and one that is broad enough to be applicable to verbal and non-verbal communication simultaneously. One good candidate for this job would be the semiotic theory of Ferdinand de Saussure, which sets out a framework for the study of not only language as it normally occurs in our verbal discourse, but also non-linguistic sign systems. (See T. Polhemus, 'Social bodies' in J. Benthall and T. Polhemus, eds., *The Body as a Medium of Expression*, Allen Lane; Dutton, New York, 1975.) Two studies of clothing which utilize a semiotic framework appear in this present chapter: Barthes's 'The garment system' and Bogatyrev's 'Costume as a sign'. However, we can surmise from Kristeva's criticisms of semiotics (see Chapter 9) that before the social scientist can use semiotics as an accepted framework for the study of the social aspects of the human body, the in-group debates between semioticians must be at least partially resolved.

Roland Barthes:
'*The garment system*'

From *Elements of Semiology*, trans. Annette Lavers and Colin Smith, Jonathan Cape, 1967, pp. 25–7.

For the layman, Roland Barthes's Elements of Semiology can serve as an introduction to the subject of semiotics. We are fortunate, therefore, that Barthes chose as one of his examples the subject of clothing and 'The garment system'. This illustration comes as part of Barthes's discussion of the semiotic distinction between language and speech. The distinction is more complex than might at first be assumed and the reader may find it helpful to read all of the first section of Barthes's book. Briefly, the distinction might be explained this way: language:code::speech:message. It may also be helpful to consider the illustration which Barthes offers later on in his book: If we consider a restaurant menu, a horizontal reading of the entrées might be considered a system or code – a language system. A vertical reading of the same menu, however (what we do when we order a meal) produces a syntagmatic chain, a message – speech. In dealing with the garment system, Barthes argues that costume:*language*::clothing:*speech.*

The reader may also want to refer to Barthes's larger work on the subject of clothing: Système de la mode (*Seuil, Paris, 1967*).

We shall keep the terms *language* and *speech*, even when they are applied to communications whose substance is not verbal . . . We saw that the separation between the language and speech represented the essential feature of linguistic analysis; it would therefore be futile to propose to apply this separation straightaway to systems of objects, images or behaviour patterns which have not yet been studied from a semantic point of view. We can merely, in the case of some of these hypothetical systems, foresee that certain classes of facts will belong to the category of the *language* and others to that of *speech*, and make it immediately clear that in the course of its application to semiology, Saussure's distinction is likely to undergo modifications which it will be precisely our task to note.

Let us take the garment system for instance; it is probably necessary to subdivide it into three different systems, according to which substance is used for communication.

In clothes as *written* about, that is to say described in a fashion magazine by means of articulated language, there is practically no 'speech': the garment which is described never corresponds to an individual handling of the rules of fashion, it is a systematized set of signs and rules: it is a language in its pure state. According to the Saussurean schema, a language without speech would be impossible; what makes the fact acceptable here is, on the one hand, that the language of fashion does not emanate from the 'speaking mass' but from a group which makes the decisions and deliberately elaborates the code, and on the other hand that the abstraction inherent in any language is here materialized as written language: fashion clothes (as written about) are the language at the level of vestimentary communication and speech at the level of verbal communication.

In clothes as *photographed* (if we suppose, to simplify matters, that there is no duplication by verbal description) the language still issues from the fashion group, but it is no longer given in a wholly abstract form, for a photographed garment is always worn by an individual woman. What is given by the fashion photograph is a semi-formalized state of the garment system: for on the one hand, the language of fashion must here be inferred from a pseudo-real garment, and on the other, the wearer of the garment (the photographed model) is, so to speak, a normative individual, chosen for her canonic generality, and who consequently represents a 'speech' which is fixed and devoid of all combinative freedom.

Finally in clothes as *worn* (or real clothes), as Trubetzkoy had suggested,[1] we again find the classic distinction between language and speech. The language, in the garment system, is made (i) by the oppositions of pieces, parts of garment and 'details', the variation of which entails a change in meaning (to wear a beret or a bowler hat does not have the same meaning); (ii) by the rules which govern the association of the pieces among themselves, either on the length of the body or in depth. Speech, in the garment system, comprises all the phenomena of anomic fabrication (few are still left in our society) or of individual way of wearing (size of the garment, degree of cleanliness or wear, personal quirks, free association of pieces). As for the dialectic which unites here costume (the language) and clothing (speech), it does not resemble that of verbal language; true, clothing always draws on costume (except in the case of eccentricity, which, by the way, also has its signs), but costume, at least today, *precedes* clothing, since it comes from the ready-made industry, that is, from a minority group (although more anonymous than that of Haute Couture).

Note
  1. *Principes de Phonologie*, trans. by J. Cantineau, 1957 edn, p. 19.

Simon D. Messing:
'*The non-verbal language of the Ethiopian toga*'
From *Anthropos*, 55, 3–4 (1960), 558–60.

It has been assumed by some students of semiotics (see Barthes, Elements of Semiology, 1967, pp. 23–5) that language-codes (e.g. costume) are social in nature, while speech-messages are individual and idiosyncratic. Barthes refers this argument back to de Saussure and de Saussure's interest in Durkheim's sociological theories. The sociologist, however, may want to question such a neat dichotomy between what is social and what is psychological and individual. If Durkheim had responded to de Saussure on this matter it is my guess that he would have argued that even 'individual' variations of style can carry and derive meaning from a social context. Simon Messing in his short article 'The non-verbal language of the Ethiopian toga' demonstrates that for the Ethiopian, subtle, 'idiosyncratic' variations of the way in which an item of clothing is worn (= 'speech') can have communicative meanings which are intersubjective and socially defined. I see no reason why this should be unique to the Ethiopians; buttoning the collar buttons on men's shirts, rolling up the sleeves, letting the shirt hang outside the trousers, are all 'stylistic features' which in given social contexts may convey precise social messages.

Students of symbolic human behaviour have observed, in widely separated parts of the globe, that several cultures have developed remarkable outlets for expression that are non-verbal.[1]

For example, there are fine but unmistakable patterns of gesture among Levantine Arabs,[2] the twenty-inch distance maintained by U.S. males[3] and the non-verbal 'language of the buffalo robe' of American Plains Indians,[4] to name just a few of the best-known culture traits.

In Ethiopia, where formality in interhuman relations is considered essential among the dominant Amhara people, non-verbal communication is achieved by the way one drapes one's toga, collectively known as *shamma*. This has the advantage of being able to communicate at a distance, beyond the sound of speech, what mood one is in, whether or not one wishes to maintain social distance, what status one has and what role one wishes to assume, what type of function one is about to attend. One might say that the Ethiopians have long ago cracked the 'sound barrier' of human communication, by means of their *shamma*.

This garment, worn by both sexes and on all social levels of the Amhara people, is made from cotton spun at home and fashioned by a weaver. It is untailored, but draped with care.

The term *shamma* is rarely used, for there are a number of different textures of the material for different purposes, and these are indicated by specific terms. There is the heavier double *shamma* (*kutta*) for warmth and longer wear; the half *shamma* (*nätäla*) for wear during the hot daytime, basically less expensive and thus proverbial for poverty, but sometimes finely embroidered along one edge and thus prestigeful.

Complicating matters further are the six specifications which vary between rural and urban, and between regions. A full-size rural *shamma* may measure five by ten feet and is the most common garment of the peasant during the work week in the dry season, day and night. Usually it has a simple, narrow, dyed border, which however is colourfast in cold water only. The roughest, coarsest and most durable workaday *shamma* has no border and is called *goda*.

Sometimes the 'sack dress' (*qämis*) of the peasant woman is made of this material. In the old days, freehold farmers distinguished themselves from peasant serfs (*gabbar*) by dyeing a foot-wide red border. But this visible distinction has fallen into disuse during the reign of the present Emperor, and is encountered only in the more remote rural landholding families.

The *kutta* may not be quite as coarse but is larger, up to six by fifteen feet, and is worn at night, in the rainy season and by travellers. Even in the centre of the capital, Addis Ababa, one may see peasants at night curled up head to foot in this large *kutta*, resembling a motionless sack which begins to stir only when the warm rays of the morning sun strike it.

The *näṭäla* is more loosely woven, like muslin, and about half the size of the *kutta*. Since recent years it is produced in a factory in the city of Dire Dawa, and has assumed an urban role. It is now finely embroidered along the border where the dyed strip used to be. In urban areas one finds this type merged with the former toga of royalty (*jano*, or *jano kutta*), of fine material, with embroidery in purple, gold and silk, and arabesque designs along the border (*ṭebäb*, or *derb jano*). In recent years, nationalism is expressed by urban women who buy the garment with embroidery in the national colours of modern Ethiopia, green, yellow and red.

But the traditional, expressive fashion of draping the *shamma* is little changed. One can distinguish the following symbolic expressions and corresponding meanings:

Symbolic Expression 1: The *shamma* is draped about the upper body and thrown back over the shoulders, leaving a turtleneck effect in the centre.

Meaning: A) If the wearer is a young man, it indicates that he considers himself a 'gay blade' going into town in debonair, expansive mood, open to friendly human relations.

B) If the wearer is an 'elder' (any man over forty may be referred to as *shemagalye*, and is usually bearded) he is a sober, respectable person, open to address in a self-assured, optimistic mood. (Term: *tälabbäsä*.)

Symbolic Expression 2: The *shamma* is not draped but permitted to hang full length, one corner trailing in the dust, the other thrown across the other shoulder. The body is thus cloaked from the neck down, and the eyes are downcast. (Term: *ashnäffäṭä*.)

Meaning: Depressed mood, sadness; overcome with the serious sadness of life; grief; unhappiness. This evokes passive sympathy on the part of strangers, but active sympathy on the part of kinfolk and friends.

Symbolic Expression 3:

A) The 'turtleneck' section of the *shamma* is lifted so as to cover the mouth. (Term: *qenṭeb täkänannobä*.)

Meaning: Reserve; wearer feels himself superior in his surroundings, or among strangers, one of whom might possess *buda* (evil eye sickness) that would otherwise penetrate through the mouth. Sometimes the expression simply means pride.

B) The 'turtleneck' section is lifted even higher, so as to cover the nostrils also. (Term: *kofännänä*.)

Meaning: Extreme pride, so that a man who expresses this too often without possessing very high rank is criticized as *abba kofenanye* (lit. father of overbearing pride). Women who avail themselves of this at any time are even mocked as mentally unbalanced, unless they walk with their husbands who are equally draped. (Term: *täshkäräkkärä*, lit. veiled.) But this fashion provides more protection from the buda spirit that might enter via the nostrils. The eyes are not vulnerable, for they are considered offensive rather than defensive weapons. Protection is implied by the term (*tägonaṭṭäfa*). Both varieties of protective draping signal 'keep your distance', 'don't touch me'.

Symbolic Expression 4: The *shamma* is draped to leave the upper part of the body bare, or at least not covered by the *shamma*. The corner flaps are tucked in like a belt, but in one position the flaps rest on raised forearms, sometimes accompanying the begging gesture of outstretched palms. (Term: *awwärärrädä*.)

Meaning: To express an attitude of self-abasement before a feudal lord in the recent past, among some rustics still today. (Recently, women, particularly women dancers-singers (*azmari*), have taken over this fashion, for it combines respect with utility: the garment is tucked in while the flaps can be used to sway in the rhythm of the musical accompaniment.)

Symbolic Expression 5: The *shamma* is draped as in expression 4, but in such a way as to leave the left flap as large as possible.

Meaning: Preparation for pleading one's case in litigation before a judge (*bädanya fit*). The loose left flap is grasped by the right hand so that it can be shaken towards the face of the adversary when giving testimony, accusation or complaint. It may even be shaken in the face of the judge, if one dares, to indicate outraged justice and abandoned despair, while praying loudly that heaven may 'give light' to the judge and make him see the truth.

Symbolic Expression 6: The flaps of the *shamma* are draped across the chest, so as to form the sign of the cross; accompanied by low bow.

Meaning: Preparation for going to church (*beta kristyan*), passing a church, or encountering a 'great man' (feudal noble, etc.), when the flaps can easily be dropped on one's forearms.

Symbolic Expression 7: The *shamma* is draped so that the lower part covers the lower part of the body like a skirt-apron (*sherret*) (resembling that of the ancient Egyptians). Only women use this fashion.

Meaning: This is the most common feminine drape, the equivalent of expression 1 of males. When at work, the top flaps can be readily slung over the chest, leaving both arms free (*asharräṭä*).

Symbolic Expression 8: While the lower *shamma* is tucked in a skirt-apron effect like in expression 7, the upper part is held straight and horizontal above the shoulders, like huge wings.

Meaning: This fashion is used to dramatize mourning (*lekso*) during the funeral dance of women, while they utter lamentations and eulogies. Men hold up a spear or rifle in like fashion during the boasting (*fukkara*) that dramatizes the family at weddings.

There are also a number of utilitarian, non-symbolic ways of draping the toga, which must not be confused with the symbolic ones. For example, labourers knot the toga across the chest to keep arms free; policemen sometimes knot the *shamma* of the prisoner to themselves, much like creditors used to chain debtors; to prevent sunstroke, a light *nätäla* may be wrapped around the skull, much like priests wrap the muslin around their caps (*mätamtamiya*).

The *shamma* has proved resistant to change even in the capital city, where even educated Amhara still like their wives to wear at least a light one over their modern dress. However, as indicated

114. Expressions of the Ethiopian Toga. Top, left to right: debonair assurance; sadness; reserve; self-abasement. Centre, left to right: preparing for litigation; during litigation; the low bow; respect. Bottom, left to right: greeting the church by kissing outer wall; debonair woman (here impersonated by a man); in the funeral dance of women (here impersonated by a man); utilitarian protection from sun, rain, heat, cold.

above, a few new fashions are beginning to develop largely due to adoption by women of former symbolic expressions that have fallen into disuse among men due to the gradual disintegration of the old feudal system at the present time.

Notes

1. LA PIERE and FARNSWORTH (*Social Psychology*, New York, 1949, p. 86) divide all *overt symbolic behaviour* into that which involves speech and that which does not. Cf. also SIMON D. MESSING, 'Changing Ethiopia', *The Middle East Journal* 9 (1955), 413–32, SIMON D. MESSING, 'The Highland-Plateau Amhara of Ethiopia', Ph.D. dissertation, Philadelphia, 1957.

2. W. D. BREWER, 'Patterns of gesture among the Levantine Arabs', *American Anthropologist*, 53 (1951), 232–7.

3. EDWARD T. HALL, 'The anthropology of manners', *Scientific American* (1955), 84–9.

4. CARLETON S. COON, *Measuring Ethiopia and Flight into Arabia*, Boston, 1935, p. 116.

Petr Bogatyrev:
'*Costume as a sign*'

From *The Functions of Folk Costume in Moravian Slovakia*, Mouton, The Hague and Paris, 1971, pp. 80–85.

Petr Bogatyrev was a linguist in the tradition of the Prague school of semiotics. His study of folk costume in Moravian Slovakia constitutes one of the richest ethnographic reports that we have on the linguistic aspects of dress and costume. The real value of Bogatyrev's work is that it comes beautifully close to creating an area of common discourse between linguists and social scientists (especially ethnographers). This book has recently been translated and republished (see title above) and for this reason I have constrained myself and present only one chapter here. The reader may also want to refer to Chapters 18, 19 and 20 — if not the entire work. [An introductory paragraph has been removed from the text for the sake of clarity.]

Costume is sometimes an object, sometimes a sign. Let us dwell, at this point, on the concepts of *object* and *sign*.[1]

'Studying the reality about us,' says V. N. Vološinov,

we observe two kinds of *things*. Some things, such as natural phenomena, implements of production, household articles, etc., have no ideological meaning. We can use them, admire them, study their construction, thoroughly understand how they are made and how they are used in production – but, try as we may, we cannot consider such a thing as a tank or a steam hammer, for example, as a 'sign' referring to some other object or event.

It's quite a different matter, however, if we take a stone, paint it with lime and place it on the boundary between two farms. That stone will take on a certain 'meaning'. It will no longer simply be itself – a stone, a part of nature – it will have acquired another, new meaning. It will refer to something that is *beyond* itself. It will become a *signal*, a *sign* of definite and constant meaning; i.e., of the boundary between two portions of land.

Another example: if we were to see a picture of a steam hammer being used to wreck a tank, we wouldn't derive any 'deeper meaning' from it. However, if we make a May Day poster of the drawing, place the Soviet hammer-and-sickle emblem on the steam hammer, draw a two-headed eagle on the tank, add a group of workers operating the steam hammer, and sketch in a group of frightened generals jumping out of the tank – then this picture becomes 'allegorical', with a meaning instantly clear to us: the dictatorship of the proletariat has destroyed the counter-revolution.

In this case the steam hammer is a *sign*, a 'symbol' of the joint strength and indomitability of the proletarian dictatorship, while the battered tank is the symbol of the shambles of White Guardist plots. By the same token, the hammer and sickle are more than mere depictions of tools – they are symbols of the proletarian state. The two-headed eagle is the symbol of Tsarist Russia.

But just what has taken place? A phenomenon of material reality has become a phenomenon of ideological reality: a *thing* has become a *sign* (a concrete, material sign, to be sure). The steam hammer and the tank depicted in the drawing are a manifestation of something actually occurring in reality which is *beyond* the drawing, *beyond* the piece of paper bearing the pencilled marks.

We can also *partially* endow material things with symbolic meaning. For example, implements of production may be ideologically embellished, as in the case of the stone implements of primitive man, which bore drawings or decorations, i.e., *signs*. The implement itself, of course, did not become a sign.

It is possible to give a tool an *artistically perfect form*, as long as that artistic form is in harmony with the production role of the tool. In such a case we might say we achieve the greatest possible rapprochement, a near fusion, of the sign with the implement.

But here, too, we observe a certain boundary of meaning: the tool as such does not become a sign and the sign as such does not become a tool. Even an item of consumer goods can become an ideological sign. For example, bread and wine become religious symbols in the Christian rite of communion. However, consumer items, just like tools, can be fused with ideological signs only as long as the boundary of meaning between them is preserved. Thus, bread is baked in a certain shape, but that shape is not determined solely by the practical consumer role of the bread. It may also possess certain (albeit primitive) *signs*, with ideological meaning (e.g., the case of specially shaped pastries and breads for holidays, etc.).

Thus individual material things are also signs, and, as we have seen, any thing in nature, in technology or consumer use can become a sign, acquiring meaning which goes beyond the boundaries of its individual being (as a thing of nature) or its precise purpose (fulfilling some production or consumer role).[2]

Such are the concrete examples which Vološinov uses to clarify the differences between object and sign. Sometimes an item is, in its pure form, an object at one time and a sign at another. Costume, having a number of functions, is usually simultaneously an object and a sign. Close structural associations of object and sign in one item are often found outside the realm of costume as well. Let us take for example the well-known legend of Theseus. Theseus agreed that if he lived, his ship would return with white sails, and if he died, it would return with black ones. In both cases the sails remain objects; they must have all the properties of sails: quality, thickness and firmness of material, specific shape, etc., but at the same time the sail becomes a sign indicating whether Theseus is living or dead. In the legend the sail's role as a sign (one involving life and death) was more important than that which it played as an object. But while it was a sign, it was still an object as well. This is the case with costume: costume always plays a practical role, but is always a sign and an object at the same time. Cases where a costume is a sign only are quite rare. A theatrical paper Chinese costume, for example, has as its function to show that the wearer is playing the role of a Chinese; however, it serves as an object as well, in so far as it covers the actor's body. When we study the individual functions of costume, we see that the individual functions of the costume relate to it sometimes as to an object and other times as to a sign. Of all the functions we have analysed so far, only the practical function and, to some extent, the aesthetic function, relate to the costume itself (the object).[3] A whole group of other functions simultaneously relate to the costume as object and to aspects of life which the costume symbolizes. Thus the holiday function focuses closely on the costume itself: the costume must be made of costlier material, must be beautiful, and there are a large number of stipulations, including costly material, which not only have bearing on the physical costume but serve to demonstrate *through* the costume that 'today is not just *any* day, but a holiday'. This is true also of the status-distinction function. The fact that a garment is of costlier material such as worn by the rich not only has bearing on it *as clothing*, but also indicates the status of its wearer. And here, I repeat, the dress also changes as an object. In the village of Vajnory near Bratislava, wealthy peasants formerly embroidered their sleeves with gold, while the poorer used only silk. If we were to take two costumes, one a rich woman's and the other a poor woman's, and send them both to town to an appraiser, he, unaware that they served as status symbols, would still appraise the sleeves as things: the rich woman's embroidered in gold, and the poor woman's embroidered merely in silk. There are, on the other hand, some special conditions under which a costume indicating the social position of the wearer may be a pure sign. For example, on a military uniform there are many signs which indicate the wearer's rights and privileges with regard to those beneath him in rank. A soldier sees an officer and knows that he is obliged to obey his commands at the front; the quality, aesthetic value, etc., of the officer's uniform are irrelevant. If we take the uniform of a wealthy soldier, made of the same material as the officer's uniform, and send it to an appraiser who disregards distinctions in military uniforms, he may assign a higher value to that of the soldier than to that of the officer, or he may make no distinction since the material is the same; in the army, however, there is a vast difference between the officer's and the ordinary soldier's uniform.

In order to grasp the social function of costumes we must learn to read them as signs in the same way we learn to read and understand different languages.

Darker colours in some cases indicate nationality, as in Slovakia, where the Germans wear darker colours than the Slovaks; in other instances they indicate difference in religion, as in the case of Protestants and Catholics; in still other cases, as we have shown earlier, they signify difference in age.

Just as drivers learn to recognize signals, and as soldiers learn to recognize various uniform signs, so from childhood, members of a given community learn to distinguish the costume of the unmarried from that of the married woman. Many of the costume functions studied by us refer almost exclusively to other aspects of social life. When an unwed mother is forced to wear parts of the married woman's costume, everyone's attention is focused on the fact that she is wearing *them* instead of those appropriate to the dress of the unmarried maiden; no one is interested in quality of material or whether the wearer looks pretty or unattractive in the costume.

Here, too, one must know how to read the signs, since a particular item which in one community is the sign of the unwed mother may, in other communities, be worn by virgins.

Similarly, the regionalistic function aims toward making the costume distinct from that of another region, even in cases where that other region's costume may be more practical or more beautiful.

To give another example: a costume having a social-sexual function may indicate that a woman is married. Though a married woman might consider the unmarried maiden's costume, as an object, more sensible than her own, she still does not dare wear it.

Thus, in studying the individual functions of costume we see that some of its functions, though referring to aspects of reality outside the costume, nonetheless have a bearing on the costume itself. There are, however, very few functions which relate only to the costume as an object, whereas there are many which refer only to aspects of outside reality symbolized by the costume.

As I have already mentioned, a costume has a whole structure of functions, and usually (as in the case of the sails on Theseus's boat) besides the functions related to the costume as an object (the practical function, for example), there are many functions related to outside reality. That functional structure always renders the costume both *object* and *sign* at the same time.

Language, too, involves several functions simultaneously. Let us take an example. We ask a passer-by for the way to the station. He tells us. His statement, as a sign, is an indication of the way. On the other hand, when we listen to his directions, we observe that the speaker uses dialectical expressions; we detect his dialect and with it we detect his social position (Jakobson).

But everyone, when speaking with others, adapts himself to those with whom he is speaking. An example: one asks a villager how to get to the station. If the inquirer is an eight-year-old boy, the villager, adapting himself to the child's language, will tell him in a certain way. If some other villager like himself asks, he will answer in terms different from those he used with the eight-year-old. If the inquirer should be, let us say, a minister, the villager will express his directions in an entirely different way. In Gogol there is a beautiful description of how the hero of *Dead Souls*, Čičikov, continually changes his behaviour as he moves among different social spheres, meeting people of diverse socio-economical and cultural milieux. Something analogous occurs with costume. Every costume has a number of functions. Sometimes uncontrolled by the will of the wearer himself, his costume may tell us his social position, his cultural level, his taste. Indeed, costume (like speech) not only satisfies the practical needs and personal taste of the wearer, but serves to indicate his environment, and to satisfy the norms of that environment. And everyone, in his speech and in his costume, adapts to his milieu. It is a fact well-known to ethnographers that when villagers return from the city to their native village they discard urban clothes which they have been wearing up to then and don the village costume so as not to differ in dress from the rest of the community – so as not to be 'white crows'.

Notes

1. We take the word *sign* in its broadest sense. Within the concept of 'sign' we could distinguish the SIGN itself, SYMBOL and SIGNAL. Concerning SIGN and SYMBOL see D. Čiževskij, 'Ètika i logika', *Naučnye trudy Russkogo Narodnogo Universiteta v Prage* ['Ethics and Logic', *Scientific Works of the Russian People's University in Prague*], 4 (1931), 231–2, 234–5. For definitions of *sign*, see the works of Professor Bühler.

2. V. N. Vološinov, 'Slovo i jego social'naja funkcija', *Literaturnaja učeba*, Žurnal pod redakciej M. Gor'kogo ['The word and its social function', *Training in Literature*, a journal edited by M. Gorkij], 5 (1930), 45–6.

3. Here we disagree with Vološinov, who attributes the aesthetic function to the sign. Compare the above-quoted words concerning decoration of tools by primitive man. It must be admitted, however, that the question of whether the aesthetic function is to be attributed to the object or the sign is not completely clear; we shall therefore leave it open.

---

9. Linguistic and Socio-linguistic Theories of Bodily Expression

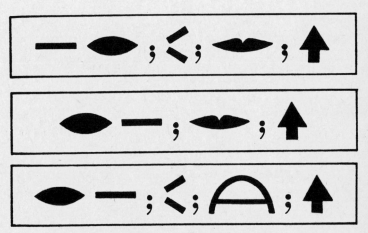

115. Symbols used by Ray Birdwhistell for establishing experimentally which changes in facial expression are communicatively significant. From Ray L. Birdwhistell, 'Kinesics and communication' in M. McLuhan and E. Carpenter, eds., *Explorations in Communication*, Beacon Press, Boston, 1970.

While we are waiting for linguistics and semiotics to come up with some unifying perspectives, we can put the time to advantage by underlining that any linguistic theory which would be helpful to the study of the social aspects of the body would have to be a *socio-linguistic* theory. It is ironic that those social scientists so eager to do battle with the ghost of Darwin and/or the ghost of Freud, in defence of a territory of bodily expression marked 'social', have often allowed themselves to fall into non-sociological debates about the nature of language. Some like Ray Birdwhistell have, however, attempted to move the study of non-verbal, bodily communication back into a social context (see, for example, Birdwhistell's publication, *Kinesics and Context: Essays on Body-Motion Communication*, Allen Lane The Penguin Press, 1971). Others such as Edward Hall have clung to theoretical, non-sociologically oriented linguistic theories as if language and communication fell somewhere outside the bounds of society and culture. But the most insistently sociological theories of bodily communication and symbolism have come from Mary Douglas, who maintains not only that bodily, non-verbal communication operates within a social context, but also that the messages conveyed by bodily expression are about the society itself.

In this chapter I present selections which represent various approaches or perspectives to the problem of the language-like characteristics of bodily expression. The first selection represents a linguistic tradition which falls within the scope of 'semiotics' – the science of signs. Two of the articles in the last chapter (Barthes's and Bogatyrev's) which dealt with the language-like characteristics of clothing are also representatives of this particular tradition. As a comparison of these three articles quickly reveals, there is much disagreement between semioticians and it is therefore difficult to summarize this tradition. One comment, however, would seem to be in order. Semiotics offers a special opportunity for the study of the cross-cultural nature of bodily expression since it has consistently attempted to exceed the limitations of linguistic traditions which would seek to explain language *as we know it* and not language as it might be, could be or even *is* – if we are prepared to recognize the communicative–linguistic capacities of all types of sign systems in all parts of the world.

Julia Kristeva:
'Gesture: Practice or communication?'

From *Semioticé: Recherches pour une sémanalyse: Essai*, Seuil, Paris, 1969, pp. 90–112. English translation copyright © Jonathan Benthall, 1973.

A note on 'Gesture: Practice or communication?' contributed by the translator, Jonathan Benthall.

Anglo-American readers may find this text of Julia Kristeva's hard to follow in parts, since it is often elliptical and allusive, drawing on intellectual traditions such as Husserl's phenomenology which have never appealed widely to the Anglo-American intellectual world. Translation into English has not been easy. However, her essay combines a full command of the relevant socio-linguistic material with access to much wider perspectives on the subject of the body and gesture, and will repay close study.

Part II of Mme Kristeva's essay is more straightforward, since it is essentially a summary of the work of Ray Birdwhistell, preceded by some introductory remarks on the work of other American anthropologists and linguists. While saluting Birdwhistell's enterprise, because it represents an attempt to free the study of gesture from a verbal–linguistic approach, she considers that it does not go far enough, since it is still locked into assumptions about communication, the *message,* the *human* subject, *etc. All these assumptions (she argues) are socially conditioned, being the product of a society based on exchange values.* Marx's concept of production *eludes this limitation of Western thought and opens the way to new ways of understanding not only gesture but all 'signifying practice' of any kind. Most of Part I of her essay is devoted to speculation about this idea, which is certainly extremely challenging and radical.*

If you are shut off from our language and do not understand our reasoning, speak to us in barbarous gestures instead of the voice.

Aeschylus, *Agamemnon*

Through gesture man remains within the limits of the species, and so of the phenomenal world, but through sound he resolves the phenomenal world into its first unity . . . in general every gesture has a sound parallel to it; the most intimate and frequent alliance of a sort of symbolic mime and sound constitutes language.

Nietzsche, *The Dionysiac Conception of the World* (1870)

For beside culture through words there is culture through gestures. There are other languages than our western language, which has opted for privation, for the desiccation of ideas, and where ideas are presented to us in the inert state without setting off in their passage a whole system of natural analogies, as happens in oriental languages.

Artaud, *Letters on language*, 1 (15 September 1931)

1. From the Sign to Anaphora

If we choose these reflections as epigraphs, it is not only to indicate the interest that 'anti-normative' thought has always taken in gesturality, and more than ever after the epistemological break of the nineteenth and twentieth centuries, when – through Marx, Nietzsche, Freud and certain 'poetic' texts (Lautréamont, Mallarmé, Roussel) – such thought has tended to steal away from the grids of 'logocentric' rationality ('subject', discourse, communication). It is rather to accentuate the *contradiction*[1] among the three epigraphs, or, better, their *complementarity*, which linguistics is confronting today before renewing itself. In fact, at the moment when our culture is seizing itself in what constitutes it – the word, the concept, speech – it is trying *also* to leave behind these foundations so as to adopt *another* point of view, situated outside its own system. In this movement of modern thought on semiotic systems, two tendencies seem to sketch themselves.

On the one hand – starting from the principles of Greek thought which valued the *sound* as accomplice of the idea and so as the principal means of intellection – literature, philosophy and science (including their least Platonic manifestations, as is proved by the quotations from Aeschylus and Nietzsche) have opted for the primacy of verbal discourse considered as a *voice*-instrument for expressing a 'phenomenal world', a 'will' or an 'idea' (a meaning). In the field of meaning and communication thus demarcated, the notion of semiotic *practice* is excluded. And it is thus that all *gesturality* is presented as mechanical, redundant in relation to the voice, the illustration or duplication of speech, and so visibility more than action, what Nietzsche called 'accessory representation' rather than process. The thought of Marx escaped this Western presupposition which consists of reducing all *praxis* (gesturality) to a representation (vision, audition). Marx studied as *productivity* – work plus permutation of products – a process which presents itself as communication (the system of exchange). He analyses the capitalist system as a 'machine' through the concept of *Darstellung*, that is to say, a self-regulating *mise en scène*: not spectacle, but impersonal and permuting gesturality which, having no author (subject), has no spectator (receiver) nor actors, for everyone is his own 'action-taker' who destroys himself as such, being at once his own scene and his own gesture.[2] Thus we find, at a crucial moment in Western thought which affirms itself in the process of contesting itself, an attempt to get away from significance (subject, representation, discourse, sense) and replace it by something other than significance: production as gesture, and thus not teleological because destructive of 'verbalism'. (We designate by the term 'verbalism' the fixation of a sense and/or a structure as cultural enclosure of our civilization.) But semiotics has not yet drawn from the Marxist enterprise those conclusions which would recast it.

On the other hand, a tendency is establishing itself more and more clearly towards tackling semiotic practices *other* than those of verbal languages. This tendency goes together with the interest in extra-European civilizations irreducible to the schemata of our civilization,[3] in the semiotic practices of animals (usually of an analogue kind whereas in human language part of communication is coded digitally[4]) and in non-phonetic semiotic practices (script, graphics, behaviour, etiquette).

Several researchers who are working on different aspects of gesturality have established and tried to formalize the irreducibility of gesture to verbal language. 'Mime language is not only language but also action and participation in action and even in things.' So writes the great specialist of gesturality Pierre Oléron, having demonstrated that grammatical, syntactic or logical categories are inapplicable to gesturality because they operate with discrete divisions.[5] Recent studies recognize the necessity of the linguistic model for an initial approach to these practices, but are trying to free themselves from the basic schemata of linguistics, to elaborate new models on new *corpora*, and to enlarge, *a posteriori*, the power of the linguistic procedure itself; and thus to revise the very notion of language, understood no more as communication but as production.

It is at this precise point that, for us, the interest of a study of gesturality lies; a philosophical and methodological interest of the first importance for the constitution of a general semiotics, because such a study allows one to override in two fundamental points those grids, elaborated on a verbal corpus, which linguistics imposes on semiotics today and which are often pointed out among the inevitable defects of structuralism.[6]

Gesturality, more than phonetic discourse or the visual image, can be studied as an activity in the sense of a *spending*, of a productivity anterior to the product, and so anterior to *representation* as a phenomenon of significance in the circuit of communication. It is thus possible to study gesturality not as a representation which is (in Nietzsche's words) 'a motive of action, but touches in no way the nature of the action', but as an activity anterior to the represented and representable message.

Evidently, gesture transmits a message in the context of a group and is only 'language' in this sense; but more than this message already there, it is – and it can make conceivable – the *elaboration* of the message, the *work* which precedes the constitution of the sign (of the meaning) in communication. From this starting-point – the *practical* character of gesturality – a semiotics of gesture should have as its *raison d'être* the crossing of the structures of code–message–communication, and the introduction of a mode of thought whose consequences are hard to foresee.

Gesturality – reduced to extreme poverty in the field of our verbal civilization – blossoms in cultures exterior to the Greco-Judaeo-Christian enclosure.[7] The study of this gesturality, with the help of models taken from the same civilizations where it is manifested, will give us in return new ways of thinking out our own culture. Hence the necessity for a close collaboration between anthropologists, historians of culture, philosophers, writers and semioticians towards this 'way out from speech'.

In such a perspective we shall confine ourselves here to two reversals that the understanding of gesturality as *practice* introduces into semiotic systems:

(a) the definition of the basic *function* (we shall not say basic 'unit') of the gesture;

(b) the differentiation between practice–productivity and communication–significance.

We shall take some examples from anthropology, not by way of clinching evidence, but as material for the argument. Anthropological studies of the semiotic systems of so-called 'primitive' tribes always start, to the best of our knowledge, from the current philosophical principle (a Platonic one) that these semiotic practices are the expression of an idea or concept anterior to their signifying manifestation. Modern linguistics, modelled on the same principle (we are thinking of the dichotomy of the linguistic sign into signifier and signified), co-opts such a notion immediately into the circuit of Information Theory.

Another reading seems possible to us of the data cited by the anthropologists: that is, of 'primitive' explanations concerning the functioning of semiotic systems. We shall content ourselves here with a few examples:

'Things have been *designated* and named *silently* before existing and have been called into being by their name and their sign' (our italics).

'When (things) were situated and potentially designated another element detached itself from *glā* and placed itself on them so as to *know* them; this was the foot of man (or "foot seed"), symbol of the human consciousness.'[8]

Again:

'According to the Dogon's theory of speech, the fact of saying the precise name of a being or of an object is equivalent to *showing* it symbolically' (our italics).[9]

The latter author, recalling the symbolism of the hairpin as 'evidence of the creation of the world by Amma' according to the Dogon, recalls the 'association of the object's shape with an elongated finger', and interprets it as an 'index-finger elongated to *show* something'; whence 'the finger of Amma creating the world in *showing* it' (our italics).[10]

On the other hand, certain studies of non-phonetic, scriptural, semiotic systems have insisted on the complementarity of two principles of semiotization: *representation* and *indication*. For instance, there are the six Lieou-Chou principles of handwriting (403–247 B.C.):

1. figurative *representation* of objects;
2. *indication of action;*
3. combination of ideas;
4. composition of figurative and phonetic elements;
5. displacement of sense;
6. borrowing.

Also there is the division of Chinese characters into *wen* (figures with a *descriptive* tendency) and *tsen* (characters composed with an *indicative* tendency).[11]

If all these reflections suppose the synchronic anteriority of the semiotic system with regard to 'segmented reality', it is striking that this anteriority, contrary to the explanations of ethnologists, is not that of a concept in relation to a voice (signified–signifier), but that of a gesture of *demonstration*, of *designation*, of *indication of action* in relation to 'consciousness' and idea. Before the sign – this 'before' is a spatial and not a temporal anteriority – and before any problematics of *significance*[12] (and so signifying structure), it has been possible to think out a practice of *designation*, a *gesture* which shows not to signify, but to *englobe* in one and the same space (without the dichotomies of idea–word, signified–signifier), let us say in one and the same *semiotic text*, 'subject' and 'object' and practice. This procedure makes impossible these notions of 'subject', 'object' and practice as entities in themselves, but includes them in an *empty relation* (with gesture equated to showing) of an *indicative* but not signifying type, which signifies only in an 'afterwards' – that of the phonetic word and its structures.

It is well known that modern linguistics has constituted itself as a science from phonology and semantics; but it is time perhaps to leave these phonological and semantic models – that is, to leave *structure* – and try to reach what is not structure, what is not reducible to structure or what escapes it completely. Evidently, the approach to this other-than-structure, this other than the phonetico-syntactic, is only possible through this structure itself. So the name we shall give to this basic function – indicative, relational, empty – of the general semiotic text is *anaphora*. Both the meaning of this term in structural linguistics[13] and its etymology will be recalled. The *anaphoric* – and so relational – function is transgressive in relation to the verbal structure through which we necessarily study it. It connotes an *opening*, an *extension* – of the sign system which is 'posterior' to it but through which it is necessarily thought, as a kind of afterthought. This opening or extension is indeed confirmed by the data of the ethnographers. For the Dogon, Amma, who creates the world in showing it, means 'opening', 'extension', 'bursting of a fruit'.

On the other hand, the *anaphoric* function (we can from now on employ this term as a synonym of 'gestural') of the general semiotic text constitutes the ground − or the stratum − on which a process unfolds: that semiotic production which is perceptible, as fixed and represented significance, only at two points, speech and writing. Before and behind *voice* and *script* there is *anaphora*: the gesture which *indicates*, establishes *relations* and eliminates entities. The relationships between hieroglyphic writing and gesturality have been demonstrated.[14] The semiotic system of the Dogon, which finally seems to be a semantic scriptural system rather than a verbal system, relies also on *indication*: for them learning to speak is learning to indicate by tracing. The extent to which the role of *indication* is primordial in the semiotics of this people is proved by the fact that each 'spoken word' is duplicated by something other which designates it but does not represent it. This *anaphoric* is alternatively a graphic support, or a natural or fabricated object, or a gesturality which indicates the four stages of elaboration of the semiotic system according to the belief of the Dogon (for instance, 'the speech of men in rules'[15]).

To accept gesturality as anaphoric *practice* places in parentheses the study of gesture with the aid of the model of the sign − and so also with the aid of grammatical, syntactic and logical categories. It suggests the possibility of approaching it through mathematical categories of functions.

These considerations on *anaphora* recall Husserl's reflections on the nature of the sign. In fact, when he defines the 'double meaning of the term sign', Husserl distinguishes *sign-expressions*, those which mean and have meaning (*Bedeutung*), from *indices* (*Anzeichen*) which 'express nothing' and so are deprived of meaning.

This distinction, which Derrida has analysed (see *La Voix et le Phénomène*) seems to mark an opening in the Husserlian system − which is quickly closed up − where significance in the sense of meaning (*Bedeutung*) has no currency: the edge of *indication*.

Motivation establishes a *descriptive unity* between, on the one hand, acts of judgement in which are constituted for the thinking being states of things that have the property of indicating, and, on the other hand, those states that are indicated. This *descriptive unity* must not be conceived as a 'structural quality' (*Gestaltqualität*), founded in acts of judgement; it is in this unity that the essence of indication resides.

(Logische Untersuchungen, 1900–1901, vol. 2)

Besides this *non-structurality*, Husserl emphasizes the non-evidence of the index. However, he poses the indicative relationship as being a *motivation* whose objective correlate would be a 'because', which is none other than the perception of *causality*.

So, the breach in the *expressive signified* sees itself quickly welded by *causality*, which underlies the Husserlian index and invests it with meaning (*Bedeutung*).

Husserl accentuates however the difference between the two modes of signifying, and sees *indication* as realizing itself, even 'originating', in the 'association of ideas' (where 'a relation of coexistence forms a relation of appurtenance'). As for the category of *expressions*, it must englobe 'all discourse and every part of discourse'.

Now from indices as well as expressions 'we exclude the play of physiognomies and gestures'. For ' "expressions" of this kind have not, *strictly speaking, significance*'; and if a second person attributes significance to them, this is only to the extent to which he *interprets* them; but even in this case 'they have no significance in the pregnant sense of the linguistic sign, but only in the sense of indices'.

Thus, the Husserlian distinction between index and expression leaves intact the space where the gesture is produced, even if gestural *interpretation* belongs to the category of index. Without meaning (*Bedeutung*) and without *motivating a cause*, neither expression nor index, the gesture surrounds the vacant space where operates what can be considered as index and/or expression. There – in this elsewhere – index as well as expression are the outer limits which, finally, become one limit only: that where the sign springs up. What the gesture lets us glimpse is thus excluded from expression no less than from indication (for its production leaves behind the surface where signs are systematized).

Here a caveat is called for. We are far from defending the thesis – current in certain studies on gesture – that would see in gesture the origin of language. If we insist on *anaphoricity* as the basic function of the semiotic text, we do not propose it as *original*, and we do not consider gesture as diachronically anterior to voice or script. It is simply a matter of defining – starting from the gesture's *irreducibility to voice* (thus to significance, to communication) – a general *particularity of the semiotic text* as a correlational, permutational and annihilating praxis. This particularity is left in the shade by communicative theories of language.

From here on, it is a matter of suggesting the necessity of a close collaboration between general semiotics on the one hand, and on the other hand the theory of production and certain postulates about the unconscious and the dislocation of the subject. It is not impossible that the study of gesturality may be the territory for such a collaboration.

Anterior to significance, the anaphoric function of the semiotic text necessarily introduces into the field of reflection that this function traces, some concepts that we see emerge in all civilizations that have reached a high semiotization of gesturality.

First, the concept of *interval*: an emptiness, a jump, which does not oppose 'matter' (that is, acoustic or visual representation) but is identical to it. The interval is a non-interpretable articulation, necessary to the permutation of the general semiotic text and approachable through a notation of an algebraic type, but external to the space of the information.

Second, the concept of *negativity*,[16] of annihilation of the different terms of the semiotic practice (considered in the light of its anaphoricity), which is a process of incessant production, but which destroys itself and can only be stopped or immobilized *a posteriori*, by a superposition of words. Gesture is the epitome of an incessant production of death.[17] In its field, the individual cannot constitute himself; gesture is an *impersonal* mode because it is a mode of productivity without production. It is spatial – it leaves behind the 'circuit' and the 'surface' (because such is the topological zone of 'communication') and requires a new formalization of a spatial type. Being anaphoric, the semiotic text does not necessarily demand a structural (logical) connection with an example-type. It is a constant possibility of aberration, incoherence, tearing away, and so the creation of other semiotic texts. Thence it may be that a study of gesturality as production is a possible preparation for the study of all subversive and 'deviant' practices in a given society.

In other words, the problem of significance is secondary in a study of gesturality as practice. This comes back to saying that a science of gesture aiming at a general semiotics need not necessarily conform to linguistic models, but might cross them, enlarge them, beginning by considering the 'sense' as *indication*, the 'sign' as *anaphora*.

All these remarks on the character of the gestural function only aim at suggesting a possible approach to gesturality as being irreducible to 'signifying' communication. It is clear that our remarks call in question the philosophical bases of contemporary linguistics and can only find their means in an axiomatized methodology. Our aim has been merely to recall that if linguistics – as Jakobson remarked – has long striven to 'annex the *sounds* of speech . . . and incorporate linguistic *significances*' (our italics),[18] then possibly the time has come for us to annex *gestures* and incorporate productivity into the science of semiotics.

The present state of the science of gesturality, as it presents itself in its most elaborated form – in American kinesics – is far from such an agreement on aims. It interests us to the extent that it tends to be independent of the schemata of verbal linguistics. But it is not a decisive initiative towards the construction of a general semiotics.

2. American Kinesics

'Kinesics as a methodology,' writes the American researcher Ray Birdwhistell, whose work we shall refer to, 'deals with the communicative aspects of the learnt and structural behaviour of the body in movement.'[19]

His definition suggests the characteristics, and the limits, of this recent science, situating it on the margin of communication theory and behaviourism. We shall revert later to the ideological effect that such a dependence imposes on kinesics. First, though, we shall recall its history as well as the general features of its equipment and its procedures.

The birth of kinesics

Darwin is called by kinesicists the source of the 'communicative' study of body movements. His *Expression of the Emotions in Man and Animals* (1872) is often cited as the seminal work for present-day kinesics, though reservations are made about the lack of 'communicative' or sociological perspective in the Darwinian study of gesturality.

Then the work of Franz Boas marks the birth of American kinesics. This ethnologist was interested in the body behaviour of the tribes of the north-west coast; he encouraged the research of Efron on the contrasts between the body behaviours of Italians and East European Jews.[20] But it is chiefly the anthropologico-linguistic initiative of Edward Sapir, and in particular his thesis that corporal gesture is a code which must be *learnt* with a view to a successful communication,[21] that suggest the tendencies of kinesics today. The researches of American psychiatrists and psychoanalysts have since emphasized the relativity of gestural behaviour. Weston LaBarre illustrates Malinowski's concept of 'phatic' communication and provides documents on the 'pseudo-languages' that precede verbal discourse.[22]

It seems too that 'micro-cultural analysis' – exemplified particularly in the writings of Margaret Mead[23] – with the use of cameras and emphasis on the cultural determinants of behaviour, has particularly stimulated the development of kinesics.

So, towards the 1950s, the combined efforts of American anthropologists, psychoanalysts and psychologists had already sketched out a new sphere of research: body behaviour as a particular code. Then the necessity was seen for a specialized science which could interpret and understand this new code as a new sector of communication. It is in the American linguistics of Bloomfield,[24] but still more that of Sapir,[25] Trager and Smith[26] that the new science of gesturality looked for its models to constitute itself as a *structural* science. Thus, by the route which we have just described, there appears in 1952 Ray Birdwhistell's *Introduction to Kinesics* which marks the beginning of a *structural* study of body behaviour. The psychological and empirically sociological view of language in the theories of Sapir is well known. He distinguished between a 'personality' in itself and an environing 'culture' which influences it. This involves a mechanistic and vague differentiation between a 'social point of view' and an 'individual point of view' in the approach to the 'linguistic fact', with a preference towards the 'personal' point of view.[27] This thesis would be hard to sustain today, after the pulverization by Freud, and by psychoanalysis in general, of the 'person' as a subject equated to an 'interactional entity'. But it is what determined the kinesic initiative. Above all, it determined the postulate of Sapir that discourse can be studied as a series of separately analysable 'levels' permitting us to put our finger on the precise place in the discursive complex that brings us to make such and such a personal judgement.[28] It is Sapir too who recognizes the importance of body behaviour in communication and who notices its close *relationship* with certain levels of discourse. This thesis, as we shall see, will provide one of the major preoccupations of kinesics.

In the same 'personalist' current of American linguistics treating problems of *vocabulary* (Sapir: 'Personality is largely reflected in the choice of words') and *style* (Sapir: 'There is always an individual method, however poorly developed, of arranging words in groups and remodelling them into larger units'), Zellig Harris has studied the structure of discourse as a field of intersubjective behaviour.[29] But his distributionist models have the advantage of having allowed kinesicists to by-pass the sacralized units and groupings of traditional linguistics.

To these linguistic origins of kinesics we should add the psycholinguistic researches of Whorf[30] and Osgood.[31] These, analysing language as the model of thought and practice, have oriented kinesic studies towards the problem of 'the relationship between communication and other cultural systems as carriers of cultural character and of personality'.

Kinesics was thus born at the crossroads of several disciplines and is dominated by behaviourist and communicative schemata. Clearly it has difficulty in identifying its object and its method. It sideslips easily towards collateral disciplines where rigour of documentation goes together with a cumbersome technicism and a philosophical naïveté in interpretation. Enlarging the sphere of its investigations, American kinesics has collided with the problem of the *meaning* of gestural behaviour. It has tried to find solutions by leaning on the ethnology of gesturality[32] and on research into the specialized gestures of different groups.[33] These studies join kinesics indirectly in offering it a *corpus* for its specialized research.

Another branch of behaviourism has a similar relationship to kinesics: this is 'contextual analysis', which offers rich sociological, anthropological and psychoanalytical data with a view to a 'systematic ulterior description of the structural logic of interpersonal activity in a precise social milieu'.[34]

Let us also notice a new extension, over the last few years, of the behaviourist study of gesturality: *proxemics*. Proxemics is concerned with the way in which the gesticulating subject organizes *his space* as a coded system in the process of communication.[35]

All these variants – whether tentative or important – on the study of body behaviour as a message (communication) are inscribed in the stock of fundamental data that kinesics, specialized as a linguistic anthropology, aims to structure and to interpret as a specific *code*.

Two principal problems face kinesics in the course of its constituting itself as a science:

1. the use it will make of linguistic models,
2. the definition of its own basic units and their articulation.

Kinesics and linguistics

Let us recall that the first studies of gestural language were far from subordinating it to communication and still less to verbal language. Thus it has been possible to defend the principle that all varieties of non-verbal language – premonitory signs, divination, diverse symbolisms, mimicry and gesticulation, etc. – are more universal than verbal language, which is stratified into a diversity of languages. A distribution has been proposed of the signs belonging to gestural language, in three categories:

1. communication without intention to communicate and without exchange of ideas,

2. communication with intention to communicate but without exchange of ideas,

3. communication with intention to communicate *and* exchange of ideas.[36]

This gestural semiology, naïve as it may be, pointed to the perspective (thereafter forgotten) of studying body behaviour as a practice without necessarily trying to impose on it the structures of communication. Certain analyses of the relationship between verbal and gestural language defend the autonomy of the gestural as regards speech, and demonstrate that gestural language translates quite well *modalities* of discourse (such as order, doubt, prayer) but only imperfectly the categories of grammar (such as nouns, verbs, adjectives). Also that the gestural sign is imprecise and polysemic; that the 'normal' syntactic order – subject–object–predicate – can vary without loss of meaning for the participants; that gestural language is related to the language of children (as in both cases there is emphasis on the concrete and the present, there is antithesis, and there is a final position for negation and interrogation) and also related to 'primitive' languages.[37] Gestural language has even been considered as the 'true' means of expression capable of providing the laws of a general linguistics where verbal language is only a late and limited manifestation within the gestural. Phylogenetically, 'miming' would have been transformed slowly into verbal language, at the same time as mimographism was transformed into phonographism. Language depends on *mimism* – the repercussion, in the composition of an individual's gestures, of ocular *mimemes* – which takes two forms: phonomimism and cinemimism. The child's gesturality is a form of cinemimism, with a preponderance of manual mimism (*'manuelage'*). This organizes itself later on, at the ludic or game stage of development, when the child becomes a 'mimodramatist'; ending finally with the 'propositional gesture' of the conscious adult.[38]

Very different is the aim of kinesics. Starting from an empirical psychologism, the *communication* which the gestural code obeys in American kinesics is considered as a 'multichannel structure'. 'Communication is a system of interdependent codes transmittable through influenceable channels with a sensory base.'[39] In such a structure, spoken language is not *the* communicative system, but only *one* of the infra-communicative levels. The point of departure for study of the gestural code is thus the recognition of the *autonomy* of body behaviour within the communicative system, and the possibility of describing it *without* employing the grids of phonetic behaviour. It is after this basic postulate that the co-operation between linguistics and kinesic data intervenes, to the extent to which linguistics is more advanced as regards the structuring of its *corpus*. It is clear from now on – and we shall see this still better in what follows – that the relationship between linguistics and kinesics thus conceived, even if it reserves a certain independence for kinesics as regards *phonetic* linguistics, obliges it on the other hand to obey the fundamental presuppositions of linguistics in general: the presupposition of a communication that values the individual while placing him in a circuit of exchange (going so far as to envisage a dichotomy between 'emotive' and 'cognitive' behaviour). Thus kinesics – far from introducing a rupture into phonetic models – only provides some variations which confirm the rule.

Kinesics, like anthropological linguistics, sets itself the task of studying the 'repetitive elements' in the current of communication, abstracting them and testing their structural significance. It is a question first of isolating the *minimal* signifying element in position or movement, and of establishing with the aid of an oppositional analysis its relations with elements of a larger structure; then, repeating this procedure, of constructing a code with hierarchic segments. At this level of research, *sense* is defined as the 'structural significance of an element in a structural context'.[40] The hypothesis is even advanced that the structural elements of the gestural code have in general the same variability of semantic function as words.[41]

The gestural code. The analogy between speech and gesture, as the basis of kinesics, imposes first the need to isolate different *levels* of the gestural code: whether the levels corresponding to those admitted by the linguistics of language, or those levels which allow the study of the interdependency between language and gesturality.

In the first direction, Voegelin has succeeded in finding in gestural language – with the help of a system of notation inspired by choreography – a quantity of distinctive signs approximately equal to the quantity of phonemes in a language. Voegelin concludes from this fact that language by gesture can be analysed on two levels analogous to the phonemic and morphemic levels of languages.[42] Another gestural taxonomy has been proposed by Stokoe,[43] who calls the basic gestural elements 'cheremes'. Each gestural morpheme, the smallest unit that bears a meaning, is composed of three cheremes: structural points of position, configuration and movement, called respectively tabula (tab), designatum (dez), signation (sig). Stokoe assumes three levels in his study of gesturality:

(a) cherology – the analysis of cheremes,

(b) morphocheremics – the analysis of combinations between cheremes,

(c) morphemics – morphology and syntax.

For other researchers, by contrast, gestural language contains no unit corresponding to phoneme; analysis stops at the level of units corresponding to the morpheme.[44]

In the second direction, we must pause to review the theses of Ray Birdwhistell, whose theory is the most elaborated of American kinesics. For him, if gesturality is a redundancy, and so a duplication of the verbal message, it is not only that. It has its particularities which give to communication its polyvalent aspect. Hence the analogies and the differences between the two levels, language and gesturality. Birdwhistell stresses as follows his reservations about pressing too far the parallel between gesturality and phonetic language: 'It is very possible that we may be forcing the data of body movement into a pseudo-linguistic grid.'[45]

If he accepts the parallel, it is more for reasons of utility (of an ideological kind) than through any conviction in the final validity of such a parallel. In his terminology, the *minimal unit* of the gestural code, which would correspond to the level of phone/phoneme in verbal language, bears the name of *kine* and *kineme*. The *kine* is the smallest element perceptible in body behaviour, such as for example the raising or lowering of the eyebrows (bb $\wedge$ $\vee$); this same movement, repeated in a single signal before stopping at the position o (initial position), forms a kineme. Kinemes combine with each other, while joining up with other kinesic forms which function as prefixes, suffixes, infixes and transfixes, and thus they form units of a superior order: *kinemorphs* and *kinemorphemes*. The *kine* 'eyebrow-movement' (bb $\wedge$) can be *allokinic* with the kines 'head-shake' (h $\wedge$), 'hand-movement' (/ $\wedge$) or with *accents*, etc., thus forming kinemorphs. In their turn, kinemorphemes combine in *complex kine-morphic constructions.*[46] Thus the structure of the gestural code is comparable to the structure of discourse into 'sounds', 'words', 'propositions', 'sentences' and even 'paragraphs' (movements of the eyebrows can denote doubt, question, demand, etc.).[47]

Where does the difference between verbal language and gesturality begin?

Two classes of phenomena seemed to emerge first, for Birdwhistell, within the kinesic circuit.

The first class of phenomena appears in communication *with* or *without* speech and these are called macro-kinesic data. So macro-kinesics deals with the structural elements of *complex* kinemorphic constructions, that is to say forms of gestural code which are comparable to words, propositions, sentences and paragraphs.

The second class is exclusively linked to the stream of speech and these are called *supra-segmental* kinemorphemes. Light head-movements, eye-blinking, pursing of the lips, quivering of the chin or shoulders or hands, and so forth – these phenomena are held to belong to a 'quadripartite kinesic stress system'. The supra-segmental kinemorphemes of this stress system have a syntactic type of function. They mark special combinations of adjectives and nouns, adverbs and 'action words', and even participate in the organization of propositions, or else connect propositions within syntactically complicated sentences. The four accents that the supra-segmented kinemorphemes connote are as follows: principal accent, secondary accent, non-accentuation and disaccentuation.[48]

A third type of phenomenon has been noticed in the course of later analyses. These phenomena do not possess the structural properties of macro-kinesic or supra-segmental elements and moreover are bound to the *particular* classes of particular *lexical items*. The elements of this third level of gestural code, called *kinesic markers*, must not be confused with what is generally called 'a gesture'. Bird-whistell makes clear that the 'gesture' is a 'bound morph', meaning that gestures are forms incapable of autonomy, that they require a kinesic behaviour – infixal, suffixal, prefixal or transfixal – to obtain an identity. Gestures are a kind of 'transfix' because they are inseparable from verbal communication.[49] Similarly, *kinesic markers* only obtain meaning when bound to certain *audible syntactic items*, except for the difference that kinesic markers – unlike gestures – are, as it were, subject to a *particular* phonetic context. Thus, as Birdwhistell rightly remarks, the introduction of the notion of 'kinesic marker' into the gestural code is a compromise between one position – which would have defined such a behaviour as macro-kinesic – and another which would ascribe it a supra-linguistic or supra-kinesic status in the semiotic system. The classification of kinesic markers is made according to the classes of lexical units they are associated with, which gives priority once again to linguistic structures in the construction of the gestural code. Kinesic markers have four general particularities:

1. their articulatory properties can be presented in *oppositional* classes.

2. kinesic markers appear in a *distinct* syntactic environment (the lexemes that they are associated with belong to distinct syntactic classes).

3. there are situational articulatory oppositions (which allow the confusion of signals to be reduced).

4. if the distinction of units is impossible in their articulation, it will be dependent on the surrounding syntactic oppositions.

Thus the kinesic marker can be defined as an *oppositional* series of behaviours in a particular environment.[50] Several varieties of kinesic markers are analysed. For instance, the *pronominal* kinesic markers (K^P) associated with, or replacing, pronouns – structures which depend on the opposition between distance and proximity: *he, she, it, those, they, that, then, there, any, some/I, me, us, we, this, here, now*. The same gesture, enlarged, pluralizes the pronominal kinesic marker; thus are obtained the *markers of pluralization* (K^{PP}) which denote: *we, we's, we'uns, they, these, those, them, our, you* (plural), *you all, you'uns, youse, their*. *Verboid* markers are also distinguished, associated with the K^P without interruption of movement; among them, markers of time (K^t) play an important role. Let us also note markers of *area* (K^a) denoting: *on, over, under, by, through, behind, in front of*, and accompanying verbs of action; and markers of *manner* (K^m) associated with phrases like '*a short time*', '*a long time*' or '*slowly*', '*swiftly*'. One debatable category is that which represents the markers of *demonstration* (K^d).

It is necessary to insist on the importance of this level of kinesic analysis. Even if kinesic markers seem, in the gestural code, to be analogous to adjectives and adverbs, pronouns and verbs, they are not considered as *derivatives* of spoken language. They constitute a first endeavour to study the gestural code as a system autonomous from speech, though approachable through speech. It is significant that this effort to escape from phoneticism involves necessarily a terminology that is no longer 'vocal' but 'scriptural'. Birdwhistell speaks of *marker* as others have spoken of 'trace' and 'gramme'. The gesture seen as a marker, or perhaps the marker seen as a gesture: those are the philosophical premises which remain to be developed in order to relaunch kinesics as a semiotic science that is not exclusively linguistic, and to bring to light the fact that the methodology of linguistics is elaborated on systems of verbal communication and is but *one possible* approach, neither exhaustive nor essential, to this *general text* which englobes, besides the voice, different types of *production* such as *gesture, writing, economics*. American kinesicists seem to be aware of this opening promised by a study of gesturality not subordinated to linguistic schemata: 'Kinesic and linguistic markers can be alloform, that is to say, structural variants of each other, at another level of the analysis.'[51] This orientation tends to make the notion of communication more supple (Birdwhistell considers that 'The revaluation of the theory of communication has the same importance as has been seen in the recognition of the fact that neutral, circular or even metabolic processes are intra-psychological systems'[52]), but does not manage to get out of this framework.

To this stratification of kinesics we must add an excrescence. This is the study of *parakinesics* associated generally with the macro-kinesic level of analysis. Parakinesics is presented as the gestural parallel of the paralinguistics (as advocated by Sapir) which studies accessory phenomena of vocalization and in general the articulation of discourse.[53] Parakinesic effects particularize individual behaviour in the social process which kinesics distinguishes in gestural communication; and conversely these effects make possible the description of the socially determined elements of an individual system of expression. These effects only appear once macro-kinesic elements have been identified, and so they lay bare whatever crosses, modifies and gives a social colouring to the kinesic circuit. This 'parakinesic material' incorporates the following: *movement qualifiers* which modify small sequences of kinic or kinemorphic phenomena; *activity modifiers* which describe the entire movement of the body or the structure of movement of participants in an interaction; and finally, *set-quality activity*,[54] a pluridimensional gesturality whose study remains to be done and which would analyse behaviour in games, charades, dances, theatrical productions, etc.

But Birdwhistell, in common with other authors, shares the opinion that an analogy or even a substitution is possible between kinesic and paralinguistic phenomena. Each individual is held to choose, according to his idiosyncratic determinants (which it is up to the psychologist to study), vocal or kinesic displays to accompany his discourse.

Thus kinesics is tending to make phonetic structuralism more supple, while remaining methodologically blocked by psychology, by empiricist sociology and its accomplice the theory of communication, and also by linguistic models.

Kinesics is dominated by the prejudices of a positivist sociologism. It operates through terms which the very development of linguistics[55] is in the process of sweeping away, as is psychoanalysis and the semiotics of 'secondary modelling systems':[56] the terms 'subject', 'perception', 'sensorial' equality or difference, the 'human being', the 'truth' of a message, society as intersubjectivity, etc. Such an ideology depends on the society of exchange and on its 'communicative' structure; it imposes *one* possible interpretation of semiotic practices ('semiotic practices are communications') and obscures the actual process of elaboration of these practices.

To seize this elaboration would amount to getting out of the ideology of *exchange* and so out of the philosophy of communication. The goal would be to axiomatize gesturality as a semiotic text in process of production, and so not blocked by the closed structures of language. This *translinguistics* – to whose formation kinesics could contribute – requires, before its equipment is built up, a revision of the basic models of phonetic linguistics. American kinesics, despite its effort to free itself from linguistics, proves that such work has not yet begun. But without such work it is impossible to break what Artaud called 'the intellectual domination of language' and give the meaning of 'a new and deeper intellectuality that is hidden beneath gestures'. And not only beneath gestures, but beneath every semiotic practice.

Notes

1. The author has commented that the 'contradiction' referred to is between Aeschylus and Nietzsche on the one hand (for whom gestures correspond to sounds) and Artaud on the other (for whom gestures do not express what phonic languages say). *Translator.*

2. cf. the interpretation of this concept by L. Althusser in *Lire Le Capital*, vol. II, pp. 170–71.

3. cf. the work of the Soviet semiologists, *Trudy po znakovyn sistemam*, Tartu, 1965.

4. We come back here to the important work of T. A. Sebeok, and particularly to 'Coding in the evolution of signalling behavior', *Behavioral Science*, 7, 4 (1962), 430–42.

5. PIERRE OLERON, 'Études sur le langage mimique des sourds-muets', *Année psychologique*, 52 (1952), 47–81. Against the reducibility of gesturality to speech: R. KLEINPAUL, *Sprache ohne Worte, Idee einer allgemeinen Wissenschaft der Sprache*, Verlag von Wilhelm Friedrich, Leipzig, 1884, p. 456; A. LEROI-GOURHAN, *Le Geste et la parole*, Albin Michel, Paris.

6. JEAN DUBOIS has shown how, blocked by the schemata of communication, structural linguistics can envisage the problem of the *production of language* only by reintroducing – a regressive gesture in the context of modern thought – the intuition of the speaking subject. (Cf. 'Structuralisme et linguistique', *La Pensée* (October 1967), 19–28.)

7. cf. M. GRANET, *La Pensée Chinoise*, chs. 2 and 3, Paris, 1934; 'La droite et la gauche en Chine', *Études Sociologiques sur la Chine*, Presses Universitaires de France, Paris, 1953; the texts of Artaud on the Tarahumaras (*La Danse du Peyotl*) or his commentaries on Balinese theatre; ZÉAMI, *La tradition secrète du Nô*, translated with commentary by René Sieffert, Gallimard, Paris, 1967; the Indian tradition of Kathakali theatre (*Cahiers Renaud-Barrault*, May–June 1967), etc.

8. G. DIETERLEN, 'Signe d'écriture bambara', quoted by Geneviève Calame-Griaule, *Ethnologie et langage: la parole chez les Dogons*, Gallimard, Paris, 1965, pp. 514, 516.

9. CALAME-GRIAULE, op. cit., p. 363.

10. ibid., p. 506.

11. TCHANG TCHENG-MING, *L'Écriture chinoise et le geste humain*, doctorate in letters, Paris, 1937.

12. R. JAKOBSON correctly objects that 'showing with the finger' denotes no *precise* 'significance'. But this objection by no means eliminates the interest of the conception of *indication* and *orientation* (or *anaphora* as we shall call it later) for a revision of semantic theory. Such seems to be the trend of the communication by Harris and Voegelin at the Conference of Anthropologists and Linguists held at the University of Indiana in 1952. (Cf. results of this Conference in *Supplement to International Journal of American Linguistics*, 19, 2 (April 1953), mem. 18, 1953.)

13. cf. L. TESNIÈRE, *Esquisse d'une syntaxe structurale*, P. Klincksieck, 1953.

14. TCHANG, op. cit.

15. CALAME-GRIAULE, op. cit., p. 237.

16. L. MÄHL speaks of 'zerology' – the reduction to zero of the denotata, and even of the signs which represent them, in a given semiotic system. Cf. *Tel Quel*, 32.

17. The author has commented, 'Death alludes to the non-symbolized destructive drive which marks itself in the gesture and which implies the dissolution of the subject as entity.' *Translator*.

18. R. JAKOBSON, *Essais de linguistique générale*, Éditions de Minuit, Paris, 1963, p. 42.

19. 'Paralanguage: 25 Years after Sapir' in HENRY W. BROSIN, ed., *Lectures in Experimental Psychiatry*, University of Pittsburgh Press, Pittsburgh, Pa., 1959.

20. DAVID EFRON, *Gesture and Environment*, King's Crown Press, Morningside Heights, N.Y., 1941.

21. E. SAPIR, *Selected Writings of Edward Sapir*, ed. David G. Mandelbaum, University of California Press, Berkeley and Los Angeles, 1949.

22. W. LABARRE, 'The cultural basis of emotions and gestures', *Journal of Personality*, 16 (September 1947), 49–68; *The Human Animal*, University of Chicago Press, Chicago, Ill., 1954.

23. M. MEAD, 'Personal character and the cultural milieu' in D.. HARRING, ed., *On the Implications for Anthropology of the Geselling approach to Maturation*, Syracuse University Press, Syracuse, N.Y., 1956. Also G. BATESON and M. MEAD, *Balinese Character: A Photographic Analysis*, Special Publications of the New York Academy of Sciences, vol. II, 1942; M. MEAD and FRANCES COOKE MACGREGOR, *Growth and Culture: A Photographic Study of Balinese Childhood*, G. P. Putnam's Sons, New York, 1951.

24. LEONARD BLOOMFIELD, *Language* (1933), Holt, Rinehart, New York, 1951.

25. E. SAPIR, *Language: An Introduction to the Study of Speech*, Harcourt, Brace, New York, 1939.

26. GEORGE L. TRAGER and HARRY LEE SMITH Jr, *An Outline of English Structure* (1951), American Council of Learned Societies, Washington, D.C., 1963.

27. E. SAPIR, *Selected Writings of Edward Sapir*, pp. 533–43, 544–59.

28. ibid., p. 534, quoted by R. Birdwhistell in 'Paralanguage: 25 years after Sapir'.

29. ZELLIG HARRIS, *Methods in Structural Linguistics*, University of Chicago Press, Chicago, Ill., 1951.

30. BENJAMIN LEE WHORF, *Language, Thought and Reality*, Massachusetts Institute of Technology Press, Boston, Mass., 1956.

31. E. OSGOOD, 'Psycholinguistics: A survey of theory and research problems', *Supplement to the International Journal of American Linguistics*, 20, 4 (October 1954), mem. 10, Waverly Press, Baltimore, Md, 1954.

32. GORDON HEWES, 'World distribution of certain postural habits', *American Anthropologist*, 57 (n.s.), 2 (1955), includes a detailed list of body positions in different cultures.

33. ROBERT L. SAITZ and EDWARD J. CERVENKA, *Colombian and North American Gestures: A Contrastive Inventory*, Centro Colombo Americano, Bogotá, 1962, pp. 23–49.

34. ibid.

35. EDWARD T. HALL, 'A system for the notation of proxemic behavior', *American Anthropologist*, 65 (n.s.), 5 (1963).

36. KLEINPAUL, op. cit.

37. O. WHITE, 'Untersuchungen über die Gebärdensprache. Beiträge zur Psychologie der Sprache', *Zeitschrift für Psychologie*, 116 (1930), 225–309.

38. M. JOUSSE, 'Le mimisme humain et l'anthropologie du langage', *Revue anthropologique* (July–September 1936), 101–225.

39. R. BIRDWHISTELL, *Conceptual Bases and Applications of the Communicational Sciences*, University of California, Berkeley and Los Angeles, April 1965.

40. ibid., p. 15.

41. R. BIRDWHISTELL, 'Body behaviour and communication', *International*

Encyclopedia of the Social Sciences, Collier-Macmillan, 1972; Macmillan, New York and Free Press, Glencoe, 1964.

42. C. F. VOEGELIN, 'Sign language analysis: One level or two?', *International Journal of American Linguistics*, 24 (1958), 71–6.

43. W. C. STOKOE, 'Sign language structure: An outline of the visual communication system of the American deaf', *Studies in Linguistics: Occasional Papers*, Department of Anthropology and Linguistics, University of Buffalo, no. 8, 1960, p. 78. Summarized by Herbert Landar in *Language*, 37 (1961), 269–71.

44. A. L. KROEBER, 'Sign language inquiry', *International Journal of American Linguistics*, 24 (1958), 1–19 (studies of Indian gestures).

45. BIRDWHISTELL, *Conceptual Bases and Applications of the Communicational Sciences.*

46. BIRDWHISTELL, *Introduction to Kinesics*, University of Louisville Press, Louisville, Ky, 1952, and 'Some body motion elements accompanying spoken American English', *Communication: Concepts and Perspectives*, ed. Lee Trager, Spartan Books, Washington, D.C., 1967.

47. ibid.

48. R. BIRDWHISTELL, 'Communication without words', unpublished manuscript, 1965. At this level of analysis, two *interior* kinesic 'junctures' are also mentioned: the 'plus juncture' (+) which appears so as to change the position of the principal kinesic accent, and the 'hold juncture' which binds together two or several principal accents, or else one principal and one secondary.

49. ibid.

50. R. BIRDWHISTELL, 'Some body motion elements accompanying spoken American English'.

51. ibid., p. 38.

52. ibid.

53. GEORGE L. TRAGER, 'Paralanguage: A first approximation', *Studies in Linguistics*, 13, 1–2 (1958), 1–13.

54. BIRDWHISTELL, 'Paralanguage: 25 years after Sapir'.

55. F. MAHL, G. SCHUZE, 'Psychological research in the extralinguistic area', pp. 51–124, in T. A. Sebeok, A. S. Hayes, M. C. Bateson, eds., *Approaches to Semiotics: Cultural Anthropology, Education, Linguistics, Psychiatry, Psychology. Transactions of the Indiana Conference on Paralinguistics and Kinesics*, Mouton, The Hague, 1964.

56. 'Secondary modelling systems' is a term borrowed from Soviet semiology. *Translator.*

Ray Birdwhistell:
'*Kinesics*'

From *International Encyclopedia of the Social Sciences*, ed. David Sills, vol. VIII, Collier-Macmillan, 1972; Macmillan, New York and Free Press, Glencoe, 1968, pp. 379–85.

I will let the second half of Julia Kristeva's article serve to introduce the work of Ray Birdwhistell. Of Birdwhistell's many writings I have chosen the article which he wrote for the International Encyclopedia of the Social Sciences *entitled simply '*Kinesics*'. The reader will also want to* *refer to Birdwhistell's 'Kinesics and communication' which appears in E. Carpenter and M. McLuhan, eds.,* Explorations in Communication *(Beacon Press, Boston, 1960, pp. 54–64) and, of course, to Birdwhistell's newly edited collection of works entitled* Kinesics and Context: Essays on Body-Motion Communication *(Allen Lane The Penguin Press, 1971). An essay by Birdwhistell also appears in J. Benthall and T. Polhemus, eds.,* The Body as a Medium of Expression *(Allen Lane; Dutton, New York, 1975).*

Kinesics is the science of body behavioural communication. Any person who has 'learned how to behave in public' and is at all aware of his response to the awkward or inappropriate behaviour of others recognizes the importance of body motion behaviour to social interaction. It is more difficult to conceive that body motion and facial expression belong to a learned, coded system and that there is a 'language' of movement comparable to spoken language, both in its structure and in its contribution to a systematically ordered *communicative system*.

Communication is a term used to describe the structured dynamic processes relating to the interconnectedness of living systems. As such, it has much of the indefiniteness and usefulness of terms like 'gravity', 'electromagnetic field' or, perhaps, 'metabolism' in their respective phenomenological contexts. While communication studies must investigate certain biological, social and cultural processes, communication is an essential *aspect* of, not a master category for, such processes. Communication is a multi-channel system emergent from, and regulative of, the influenceable multi-sensory activity of living systems. The spoken and the body motion languages thus are *infra*communicational systems that are *interdependently merged* with each other and with other comparable codes that utilize other channels; they are operationally communicative. Emphasis upon communication as a multi-channel system stresses the difficulty of final objective appraisal of the relative or specific importance of spoken language to communication before we know more about communication. It is unproductively tautological to argue from the fact that language is characteristic of humans to the position that language is the central or the most important communicative code utilized by humans. All infracommunicational channels are equally necessary to the whole of which they are dependent sub-systems. To attempt to weigh their relative importance to cultural continuity without more evidence than is now available is somewhat like arguing whether sex or food is more important to speciational continuity.

Communication is a continuous interactive process made up of multi-levelled, overlapping, discontinuous segments of behaviour. The interaction of communication does not cease when interactants lapse into silence, to begin again with the onset of phonation; other channels continue communicative operations even when the auditory–aural channel is not in use. Humans move in relatively orderly fashion while they vocalize and when they are silent; they can perceive the regularity in the visible movement of others (or at least become aware when it is irregular) and proprioceptively in themselves. They can smell, taste, touch and otherwise register perception of themselves and their surroundings. When regularities appear, they are not simply mechanical, 'automatic' or happenstantial. Research with visible body motion is convincing us that this behaviour is as ordered and coded as is audible phonation. Like language, infracommunicational body motion behaviour is a structured system that varies from society to society and must be learned by the membership of a society if it is to interact successfully.

It is as yet unclear how taste, smell, touch, heat and cold, to speak only of the sensory potential of the more obvious communicative channels, are structured and utilized. However, as we gain control of the theory and the methodology (including the technology) prerequisite to their isolation and description, these should prove to have decipherable codes. Body behavioural communication has been the subject of extensive research and major theoretical formulations contributed by descriptive and structural linguists. Yet much of the structural analysis of body motion behaviour had to await the development of the movie camera and the slow-motion projector before elements of kinesic structure could be isolated and demonstrated as significant. Comparably, even the preliminary investigation of the relationships between linguistic and kinesic structure discussed below could not be tested and demonstrated until the linguist and the kinesicist gained control of the sound movie, the tape recorder, the slow-motion projector and the speech stretcher. Engineers are confident that the technology for recording the behaviour of other sensory channels is now within the range of possibility. However, such developments are not likely until there is sufficient sophistication about the essential nature of these channels so that the investigator is not drowned in an ocean of insignificant data. Just as linguistic research laid bare data for kinesic investigation, linguistics and kinesics, as they exhaust their respective behavioural fields, should point the way for definitive research in the other communicative channels.

It is within this conceptual framework that some of the results of communicational body motion research are sketched below. The scientific investigation of human body motion communication is a recent development. While a bibliography of thousands of items could be developed which attest to the fact that the graphic artist, the writer, the story-teller, the dancer and the ethnographer have long noted the fact that men gesture, posture, move and grimace in interesting, significant and unusual fashions, it does not seem that anyone prior to the twentieth century suspected the structured, language-like nature of human body behaviour.

Contemporary study

Darwin is often seen as the father of modern communicative studies of body motion. Yet neither in his *Expression of the Emotions in Man and Animals*[1] nor anywhere else does he seem to have made the qualitative jump between his brilliant observations of animal and human body motion and expression and these as related to ordered communicative systems. Franz Boas is said by his students to have laid the groundwork for Sapir's brilliant intuition that body motion was coded and that this code had to be learned for successful communication.[2] Efron,[3] another of Boas's students, conclusively demonstrated the culture-bound nature of the south-eastern European, Jewish and Italian gestural complexes. From these insights and from others provided through psychoanalysis and psychiatry, LaBarre[4] reviewed the literature to discuss 'phatic' communication and the 'pseudo languages' that preceded and surrounded vocal language. However, the beginning of the scientific investigation of the *structured* nature of body motion communication was marked by the publication of the *Introduction to Kinesics*.[5]

More directly relevant to the development of kinesics was the theoretical and methodological progress of the modern descriptive linguists, who in their penetrating and exhaustive analysis of human vocalic behaviour presented a model that could be used for the investigation of other kinds of behaviour.[6] One stimulus to investigate the meaningful variability of human body behaviour came from the culture shock induced by the difference between Kutenai and American gestural and expressional patterning. Body motion research gained maturity and discipline under responsible linguistic tutelage. The recognition that a bilingual Kutenai moved in a consistently and regularly different manner when speaking Kutenai than when speaking English could not be understood until systematic analysis of the structure of American kinesics was undertaken.

Context and meaning. From the outset of kinesic research, investigators have been distracted by the temptation to pursue the phantom of 'meaning'. Each new form or segment of structure isolated during investigations provoked the question, 'What does it mean?'

Even linguists, long since chastened by the relative sterility of their own explorations into the semantics of speech forms, seemed to cherish the hope that the kinesicist might present them with an 'expressionary' or a kinecography that would list specific gestural, expressional or movement complexes, together with their exclusive meanings. It is true that when informants are questioned they may give the investigator an extensive listing of such forms and a range of meaning for each. Cross-cultural comparison quickly reveals that an Arab from Beirut, a Chinese from Taiwan and a Harlem Negro respond quite differently to apparently identical body behaviours. It can be easily established that these differences in response are cultural rather than idiosyncratic; different cultures exploit the potential for body motion in differing ways. Data are accumulating in the literature; particularly worthy of note is the work of Gordon Hewes,[7] who has compiled an extensive cross-cultural listing of body posture. However, like other studies of the specialized gestures of particular groups,[8] these belong more properly in the province of ethnographic studies than in the area of kinesics or communication studies. Such lists often have the same relationship to kinesic anthropology that dictionaries do to linguistic anthropology – they are suggestive, but of indirect relevance.

Structural analysis of even the apparently most discrete facial expression (the 'smile' or the 'frown'), the apparently most explicit gesture (the 'nod' or the 'head shake'), or the apparently most indicative posture ('military uprightness' or 'sag') show reports of such behaviour to be impressionistic summaries of quite complex and systematically varying particles of activity that are, more importantly, always dependent upon other behaviours. The assemblage of component body behaviours that is reported by informants cannot stand alone any more than the phoneme can stand alone in functional speech behaviour. Furthermore, while some informants may have quick responses as to the 'meaning' of such behaviours and others may be goaded into choosing more likely 'meanings' from a dichotomous battery, when these body behaviours are studied in a natural social setting they prove to depend upon the range of stimuli available in the larger contexts of interactive behaviour in which they appear. It appears that these non-lexical forms have the same variability of semantic function as do 'words'. Whatever it is we mean by 'meaning', it is a term which covers the relationship between an isolated event and its appropriate spectrum of surrounds.

Research into the nature of body motion communication over the past decade has proceeded in two differing but intimately related directions. An attempt has been made to isolate the significant forms of communicative body motion behaviour and, in separate research operations, to gain perspective upon the nature of the levels of context in which these forms function. These latter operations, ultimately concerned with meaning, have been termed *context analysis*. While research in this area remains exploratory, it is promising. In differing ways, the studies of Goffman,[9] that of Hall,[10] and that of Ruesch[11] have been pioneering. Their work points towards the rich data that await the investigator who would systematically describe the structural logic of interpersonal activity in precise social settings. More cogent to context analysis is the work of Scheflen.[12] He and others who have followed his lead report the isolation of interactional units characteristic of the psychotherapeutic situation. Such studies give promise that minutes-long sequences of communicative behaviour may be as structurally marked as are syntactic sentences ($\frac{1}{2}$ to 4 or 5 seconds in duration) or the kinesic constructions that are contained within triple-cross kinesic junctures (ranging between 5 seconds and 2 or $2\frac{1}{2}$ minutes). These larger regular shapes of behavioural sequences increase the possibility of objectively measuring the function of particular communicative elements in contextual contrasts. Discovering the structural aspects of the interactive process is necessary to the objective definition of the 'meaning' of the integral units, the messages carried by the communicative system. From the point of view of context analysis, *meaning* is the behavioural difference occasioned by the presence or the absence of a particular cue at a particular level of context. The range of meaning of a particular cue is governed by the range of contexts in which the cue can be observed to occur.

Units and structure of body motion. Kinesics has been concerned with the exhaustive description and analysis of the American kinesic structure. Structural linguists have traditionally approached their data through the word and then, in one set of operations, engaged in morphological and phonological research, and, in another set, moved towards the isolation and description of lexemes and syntax. More recently, linguists have sought to analyse the longer sequences of discourse. Using an analogous model, kinesic studies have demonstrated that the 'gesture' is a *bound morph* (a stem form) and have gone on to analyse the position and activity of such forms. The tentative descriptions of kinemorphology prepared the ground for analysis of behaviour into the component *kines* and *kinemes*. As research proceeded, it became increasingly evident that the American kinesic pattern, at least, was not simply a sequence of these complex kinemorphs (kinemorphic stem plus suffixes). By conventions of junction, these word-like forms are combined into sentence-like sequences.

Clearly, kinesic forms at each ascending level of analysis resemble linguistic forms in their duality of patterning.[13] Just as syntactic sentences do not dangle isolated in nature, these extended, linked sequences of body motion behaviour, the *complex kinemorphic constructions*, do not exhaust the potentials of body activity in communication. These again are building blocks for still longer sequences of behaviour, evident in operation but which have thus far resisted analysis. Kinesic forms at each level of analysis (*kinelogical, kinemorphological* and *kinesyntactic*) have distinctive contrastive identity as significant forms and also operate as items of structure.

Over the past century, acoustic phoneticians have developed a sufficient theory and an increasingly complex and reliable technology for the description of the physiological behaviour that underlies the production of significant sounds utilized in human speech. It should not be surprising that some students confuse the activity of the apparatus for phonation with the linguistic process. At the present preliminary stage of kinesic research, it is even more difficult to keep the prekinesic activity of the body separate from the structured activity utilized in the kinesic code. Just as we are so impressed with the activity of the lips, the teeth, the tongue, the lungs, the larynx, the pharynx, etc., that we think of them as emitting speech, it is difficult not to be so preoccupied with musculature, bones, fatty tissue, the vascular system and skin that we think of these as emitting body motion language. Rather these must be regarded as sources of potentials for behaviour which are selectively regulated to form the kinesic code. The arm and hand of the telegrapher are of no direct consequence to the telegraphic code.

An example of kinesic communication. As long as the kinesic anthropologist can remain sufficiently disciplined so that he does not confuse the particular activity of a particular part of the body with the code that makes use of certain activities of that body part in certain situations, he can profitably examine the body as an instrument specifically adapted for interactive behaviour. Seemingly identical body movements supply the activity for quite different cue classes. To keep the example as simple as possible, movement of the eyebrows is the activity selected for discussion, and only the variables of context and duration are described. The specialized kinesic terminology and annotational conventions may prove confusing to the reader, but the examples chosen should be sufficiently familiar to soften the technicality of the illustration.

One of the more easily detectable *kines* (least perceptible units of body motion) is that of eyebrow lift and return (here transcribed as bb ∧ ∨). At times such movement is fleeting; I have been able to detect and record brow movement lasting but thousandths of a second. For instance, the brows may be raised in certain contexts and held for a short duration before returning to the zero or base position. Such positioning may operate as one of the allokines (again using the linguistic analogy, the allokines would be, as allomorphs are, members of a class of events that can be substituted for one another) of the junctural *kineme* (the least cue class) of ($/k//$). This bilateral eyebrow raise is quite comparable to, and may during phonation co-occur with, the linguistic single bar of terminally raised pitch, appropriate to the context of 'doubt' or 'question' or as a signal to repeat a message. If we ignore the duration of the action and attend only to the spatial movement of the brows, an identical movement of the brows may be seen in the circumvocal behaviour of speakers who select the brows for kinesic stress functions. Intensive experimentation on the relationship between spoken and moved American has demonstrated that there are four degrees of kinesic stress.[14] The brows form one of the positional allokines of the kinemes of stress. Other allokines are provided by the head, hand, foot, or body nodding, or the lid closure that accompanies speech.

Thus, the kine eyebrow raise (bb $\wedge$) may be allokinic with the kines of superior head nod (h $\wedge$) or hand nod ($/\wedge$), members of the class kineme of kinesic single bar ($/k//$) in one context position and an allokine of the form degrees of kinesic stress ($/$primary, secondary, unstressed or destressed$/$) in another. These two allokinic roles do not exhaust the cue potential of the brows. Furthᵉrmore, with the same muscular involvement, the (bb $\wedge$) may be an allokine of the kineme, the first degree of eyebrow raise ($/bb^1/$), which combines with other circumfacial kinemes to form a kinemorph.

I fully appreciate the reader's difficulty in picturing these abstractions. The point made here may be comprehended if the reader will conceive of a conversation in which an animated speaker is being attended to by an interested auditor. The eyebrows of the speaker rise and fall as he speaks (kinesic stress kinemes). From time to time, the speaker's eyes 'focus' upon the face of the auditor and he pauses in his speech and raises his brow ($/k//$). He may continue vocalization following the single head nod ($/hn/$) of the auditor. During one sequence of the conversation, the auditor may 'de-expressionalize' into the complex kinemorph of dead pan ($//O//$); the speaker, without signalling response, may continue vocalization until the auditor raises his brows ($/\text{o}b^1/$), while sustaining the dead pan ($//O//$), to form the kinemorph $\left(//\dfrac{bb^1}{O}//\right)$. At this point, the speaker hesitates in his speech flow, drops his head and lids $\left(//\begin{smallmatrix} h \vee \wedge \\ \text{oo} \vee \wedge \end{smallmatrix}//\right)$, and after several vocal false starts repeats part of his lexication. In the situations that we have observed, several conversation-alists returned in discourse correction to the topic under discussion at the onset of the auditor's dead pan ($//N \rightarrow O//$).

These three kinesic activities do not exhaust the cue potential of the eyebrows. Like the scalp, the eyebrows, while mobile in position in the young, gradually become relatively stationary in *base* placement (the point from which movement is initiated and the point of return following movement). As measured at the most superior aspect of the hirsute brow, there is a possible range of almost one-half inch for brow placement. While the diakinesic (comparable to language dialect) range is less marked in Americans, any observant traveller in England can mark the contrast between the high placement of the brows among people of certain regional and econ-omic groups (many Englishmen look to the American as though they were perpetually surprised) and the low brow placement in other areas and at different socio-economic levels (so-called beetle-browed). Such brow and scalp placement is learned behaviour and is, on the one hand, an aspect of unique identity, and thus part of signature behaviour, and, on the other, contributes to the common appearance of family, group and regional members. The latter represents signature behaviour at another level. From this example of certain eyebrow behaviours and from this view of communication it becomes clear that communicative units may vary in duration from milliseconds to years. It may be argued that individual appearances, such as diakinesic variation, are not to be classified as communicative behaviour. Such a position, focusing on short sequences, would also deny the communicative role of dialect and individual speaking style. However, any regular and systematically variable learned behaviour that redundantly contributes to the definition of an aspect of the code is in itself part of a larger code and must be understood if we are to comprehend the structure of the interactive process. As we have long realized intuitively, there is more that goes on in any conversation than is present in the immediate interaction. It is the researcher's duty to adapt his observations to the shapes of nature.

Future research

Kinesics has been preoccupied with the description and analysis of body positions and movements. It has been possible to isolate and test thirty-four kinemes in the American kinesic system. While such a prediction is risky, there may be no more than fifty base units in the system. However, as kinesic research proceeds to gain security from cross-cultural studies it is going to have to pay systematic attention to other body associated phenomena. Such matters as the oiliness, wetness and dryness of the skin, tension and laxity of the skin, and musculature, variable and shifting vascularity in the skin's surface, and shifts in the underlying fatty tissue are all going to have to be studied intensively and systematically. All of our present observations, and these have been extensive but crude and inconclusive, lead us to believe that these are coded in both long and short durational cue complexes. While at the moment these behaviours are assigned to paralanguage, a catch-all category for insufficiently analysed behaviour, there seems every reason to believe that they will be subject to isolation, analysis and communicative assignment. In this perspective particular attention must be paid to the work of Hall and Westcott. Using what may be an unnecessarily limiting dyadic model, Hall, in his conception of *proxemics*,[15] places emphasis on the human use of space arrangements as a coded system of transactional process. His work forces attention on all primary telecommunicative processes. Westcott,[16] in his discussion of *streptistics*, is attempting to order the various channels and their operative codes in structural relation to each other. These approaches, when taken together with the accumulating data from kinesic and linguistic anthropology, lay the groundwork for communication analysis.

Notes

1. C. DARWIN, *The Expression of the Emotions in Man and Animals* (1872), ed. Francis Darwin, University of Chicago Press, Chicago, Ill., 1965.

2. EDWARD A. SAPIR, 'Communication', *Encyclopedia of the Social Sciences*, vol. IV, Collier-Macmillan; Macmillan, New York and Free Press, Glencoe, 1931, pp. 78–80; 'Language', *Encyclopedia of the Social Sciences*, vol. IX, Collier-Macmillan; Macmillan, New York and Free Press, Glencoe, 1933, pp. 155–68.

3. D. EFRON, *Gesture and Environment*, King's Crown Press, Morningside Heights, N.Y., 1941.

4. WESTON LABARRE, 'The cultural basis of emotions and gestures', *Journal of Personality*, 16 (September 1947), 49–68.

5. RAY L. BIRDWHISTELL, *Introduction to Kinesics*, University of Louisville Press, Louisville, Ky, 1952.

6. LEONARD BLOOMFIELD, *Language* (1933), Holt, Rinehart, New York, 1951; EDWARD A. SAPIR, *Language: An Introduction to the Study of Speech*, Harcourt, Brace, New York, 1939; GEORGE L. TRAGER and HENRY L. SMITH Jr, *An Outline of English Structure* (1951), American Council of Learned Societies, Washington, D.C., 1963.

7. GORDON HEWES, 'World distribution of certain postural habits', *American Anthropologist*, 57 (n.s.), 2 (1955), 231–44.

8. ROBERT L. SAITZ and EDWARD J. CERVENKA, *Colombian and North American Gestures: A Contrastive Inventory*, Centro Colombo Americano, Bogotá, 1962.

9. ERVING GOFFMAN, *Behaviour in Public Places*, Macmillan, 1963; Free Press, Glencoe, 1963.

10. EDWARD T. HALL, *The Silent Language*, Fawcett Publications, Greenwich, Conn., 1959; Fawcett, New York, 1961.

11. JURGEN RUESCH and WELDON KEES, *Non-verbal Communication*, University of California Press, Berkeley, Calif., 1956.

12. ALBERT E. SCHEFLEN, *Stream and Structure of Communicational Behavior: Context Analysis of a Psychotherapy Session*, Behavioral Studies Monograph No. 1, Eastern Pennsylvania Psychiatric Institute, Philadelphia, Pa., 1965.

13. CHARLES F. HOCKETT, 'Logical considerations in the study of animal communication', *Animal Sounds and Communication*, Symposium on Animal Sounds and Communication, Indiana University, 1958, American Institute of Biological Sciences, Washington, D.C., 1960, pp. 392–430.

14. RAY L. BIRDWHISTELL, 'Communication without words', unpublished manuscript, 1965.

15. EDWARD T. HALL, 'A system for the notation of proxemic behavior', *American Anthropologist*, 65 (n.s.), 5 (1963), 1003–26.

16. ROGER W. WESTCOTT, 'Strepital communication: A study of non-vocal sound production among man and animals', unpublished manuscript, 1964.

Edward Hall:
'A system for the notation of proxemic behaviour' (excerpts)

From *American Anthropologist*, 65 (n.s.), 5 (1963), 1018, 1019.

One of the primary distinctions which semioticians make in their classification of sign systems is the distinction between arbitrary sign systems and motivated sign systems. In arbitrary systems, there is no 'natural' connection between the expressive signifier (e.g. the word 'apple') and the conceptual signified (e.g. the mental concept of what an apple is). That is, in arbitrary sign systems, there is nothing apple-like about the word 'apple', nothing big about the word 'big', etc. The American linguist Charles Hockett also made this distinction between arbitrary and non-arbitrary linguistic expressions. For Hockett, one of the prime characteristics of 'language' is that it is arbitrary.

Edward Hall in 'A system for the notation of proxemic behaviour' argues that proxemic behaviour (i.e. the spaces between people's bodies, etc.) is arbitrary and 'language-like'. I have criticized this conclusion of Hall's in my essay 'Social bodies' which appears in J. Benthall and T. Polhemus, eds., The Body as a Medium of Expression *(Allen Lane; Dutton, New York, 1975) and I refer the reader to that discussion. In brief, however, I should like to suggest that both verbal and non-verbal expression can be either arbitrary or non-arbitrary (motivated) and that social organization, structure and situations can serve as preconditions for either form of communication regardless of the media of expression. (See also Hall's* A Handbook for Proxemic Research, *Society for the Anthropology of Visual Communication, Washington, D.C., 1974.)*

Hockett[1] defines communication as any event that triggers another organism. While many other life forms communicate (as for example when a bee informs another where honey is, by means of an orientating series of dance steps), language is characteristically human. Hockett lists seven principal features of language: duality, productivity, arbitrariness, interchangeability, specialization and displacement, and cultural (not genetic) transmission.

Proxemic behaviour is obviously *not* language and will not do what language will do. Nevertheless a careful analysis demonstrates that proxemic communication as a culturally elaborated system incorporates more features named by Hockett than one might suppose. For example, language is both 'plerematic' and 'cenematic' – i.e. has both sets and isolates[2] or units that build up, or combine, to form a different kind of unit.

Proxemics lacks none of the seven features of language listed by Hockett. Its arbitrariness is not obvious at first, because proxemic behaviour tends to be experienced as iconic – e.g., a feeling of 'closeness' is often accompanied by physical closeness – yet it is the very arbitrariness of man's behaviour in space that throws him off when he tries to interpret the behaviour of others across cultural lines.

... proxemic behaviour parallels language, feature for feature. It is, however, much *less* specialized and more iconic. It tends to be treated as though certain features associated with language were lacking. The iconic features of proxemics are exaggerated in the minds of those who have not had extensive and deep cross-cultural experience.

Notes
1. C. HOCKETT, *A Course in Modern Linguistics*, Macmillan, New York, 1958.
2. HALL, *The Silent Language*, Fawcett Publications, Greenwich, Conn., 1959.

Mary Douglas:
'Do dogs laugh? A cross-cultural approach to body symbolism'

From *Journal of Psychosomatic Research*, 15 (1971), 387–90.

In two major works, Purity and Danger: An Analysis of Concepts of Pollution and Taboo *(Penguin Books, Harmondsworth, 1970) and* Natural Symbols, *Mary Douglas has set the stage for a sociological analysis of bodily symbolism. The roots of this work are in Mauss's 'The*

techniques of the body' and Hertz's 'The pre-eminence of the right hand'
(see my introduction to Part I and also Chapter 1), but more than simply
reminding us of the importance of these works, she has shown how 'The
Maussian programme' (as Gordon Hewes has called it) can be integrated
with the socio-linguistic theories of Basil Bernstein and modern communi-
cation theory.

   The reader is referred to Chapter 7 (pp. 137–53) of Purity and
Danger, *which deals with the symbolic aspects of bodily waste (urine,*
faeces, nail-clippings, etc.), the special problem of body boundary main-
tenance and the social influences upon each of these subjects. In Natural
Symbols *the subject of bodily symbolism is expanded and related to*
theories of communication and a central thesis emerges that 'the human
body is always treated as an image of society'. The reader will find
Chapter 5, 'The two bodies' (pp. 93–112), of particular relevance.

   Since writing Natural Symbols, *Professor Douglas has published a*
brief but precise collation of her work on body symbolism in 'Do dogs laugh?'
A cross-cultural approach to body symbolism'. In this essay she has
not merely summarized her previous work but has begun to refine her
notion of the role of the body as an image of the social system or social
situation. Now we begin to see that as a metaphor, or symbol, of society,
the body functions as an analog of the social system; reflecting and
responding to variations in the degree of control present in the social level
of experience.

The body, as a vehicle of communication, is misunderstood if it is
treated as a signal-box, a static framework emitting and receiving
strictly coded messages. The body communicates information for and
from the social system in which it is a part. It should be seen as
mediating the social situation in at least three ways. It is itself the
field in which a feedback interaction takes place. It is itself available
to be given as the proper tender for some of the exchanges which
constitute the social situation. And further it mediates the social
structure by itself becoming its image. Some of this I have discussed
in an earlier contribution to this journal,[1] and in *Purity and Danger*.[2]
To adapt the signal-box metaphor to show the full involvement of
the body in communication we should have to imagine a signal-box
which folds down and straightens up, shakes, dances, goes into a
frenzy or stiffens to the tune of the more precise messages its lights
and signal arms are transmitting. This paper is offered as a background to those others which treat of specialized signalling systems
such as the voice and the face. It is offered as a preface to Professor

Jenner's discussion of *endogenous* factors. I will suggest a parallel set of social factors *exogenous* to the biological organism, feedback pathways which control the rhythm of social interaction.

A young zoologist, who asked my advice about a study he was making of laughter in human and non-human species, complained that sociologists had given him very little help. Indeed it is very difficult for us to produce a theory or even a vague hypothesis on the subject. My own idea on the body's role in joke symbolism is not easily adapted to an experimental approach to laughter.[3] We know that some tribes are said to be dour and unlaughing. Others laugh easily. Pygmies lie on the ground and kick their legs in the air, panting and shaking in paroxysms of laughter.[4] Francis Huxley noted the same bodily abandonment to convulsions of gaiety in Haiti.[5] But we have so far found nothing to say about these differences that could help the zoologist. It is just as difficult for us to suppose that laughter in different tribes means the same thing, as to be sure that animals are laughing when they grin and splutter.

Bergson declared that laughter is the unique prerogative of humans.[6] However, we have it from a biologist that dogs laugh as they play. Lorenz in *Man Meets Dog* describes the case: '. . . an invitation to play always follows; here the slightly opened jaws which reveal the tongue, and the tilted angle of the mouth which stretches almost from ear to ear give a still stronger impression of laughing. This "laughing" is most often seen in dogs playing with an adored master and which become so excited that they soon start panting.'[7] He suggests that the same facial expression marks the beginning of erotic excitement.

Here is a description of the beloved master playing with his dog. Thomas Mann describes ways of rousing and stimulating his dog.

> Or we amuse ourselves, I by tapping him on the nose, and he, by snapping at my hand as though it were a fly. It makes us both laugh. Yes. Bashan has to laugh too; and as I laugh I marvel at the sight, to me the oddest and most touching thing in the world. It is moving to see how under my teasing his thin animal cheeks and the corners of his mouth will twitch, and over his dark animal mask will pass an expression like a human smile.[8]

The play produces in the dog 'a state of ecstasy, a sort of intoxication with his own identity so that he begins to whirl around on himself and send up loud exultant barks'. Both writers take the laugh to be essentially a facial expression, but both, being good observers, note the panting, the more generally visible excitement or ecstasy. I shall return to these two useful clues to the nature of laughter. First, it is a process which begins in a small way, observable on the face, and is capable of ending in involving the whole body. Second, it is normally a social response; private laughing is a special case. Here I should set out my assumptions about a systemic approach to the body as a channel of communication. The upshot will be to throw doubt on the attempt to isolate a complex such as laughter, or indeed facial expression, for comparative study.

I see the relation of the spoken word to the non-verbal communication as analogous to the relation between the written word and the physical materials and visible manner of its presentation. Californian sociologists are paying attention now to the unspoken part of any discourse, its reliance on shared, implicit assumptions.[9] In the same way, a written document communicates through a physical, metaphysical and social dimension. The typography, arrangement of footnotes, layout of margins and headings, acknowledgements, all witness to a set of implicit meanings about the realm of discourse it belongs in. Its physical embodiment indicates a social sphere to which it is directed. In the same way, the body comes into play to support the meanings of a spoken communication. Posture, voice, speed, articulation, tonality, all contribute to the meaning. The words alone mean very little. Verbal symbols depend on the speaker manipulating his whole environment to get the meaning across. We would have to make a special effort if we wished consider the meanings conveyed by the typography of a literary text in isolation from the verbal message. The whole trend of our education has been the other way. We now realize that we have unduly privileged the verbal channel and tended to suppose it could be effective in disembodied form. In the same way we should now make an effort to think of the body as a medium in its own right, distinct from the words issuing from the mouth. Speech has been over-emphasized as the privileged means of human communication, and the body neglected. It is time to rectify this neglect and to become aware of the body as the physical channel of meaning.

My first assumption is that normally the physical channel supports and agrees with the spoken one. The case in which the channels contradict one another is a special one, for conveying the special meanings of banter, irony, mistrust, etc. I have discussed this general concordance between channels of communication in *Natural Symbols*.[10] My second assumption follows: that conscious and unconscious bodily expressions need not be distinguished; since both exhibit the same tendency to reinforce speech, the degree of consciousness can be ignored. My third assumption is based on observation. The body is not always under perfect control. A screening process divests uncontrolled noises of meaning. The small hiccoughs, sneezes, heavy breathing and throat-clearings can and must be screened out as irrelevant noise, not to be treated as part of the bodily channel's message. There are limits of tolerance. Once the limit is passed, the discourse has to be stopped. A prolonged sneezing fit or other uncontrolled bodily movement forces the owner of the interrupting machine to withdraw if the noises cannot be framed with an apology. I would like to ask the zoologists whether animals screen off bodily interruptions or whether Bergson should have selected this capacity to ignore them, rather than laughter, as the distinctively human accomplishment.

The fourth assumption is that there is a cross-cultural, universal language of bodily interruptions. Instead of being ignored, they can be deliberately brought back artificially into the discourse to convey well-understood messages based on a hierarchy of bodily orifices. Back and lower orifices rank below frontal and upper. A development of Freudian symbolism to the social dimension fits the meanings in a quite straightforward way.[11] Fifth – here we come to the crux of the matter – laughter, though not controlled any more than any other upper/front eruptions such as coughing or breaking wind, is not screened off and ignored. Laughter is a unique bodily eruption which is always taken to be a communication. I suggest that this is because a laugh is a culmination of a series of bodily communications which have had to be interpreted in the usual way as part of the discourse. The finally erupting laugh cannot be screened off, because all the changes in bodily posture preceding it have been taken as part of the dialogue.

If this approach can be developed it will give a sociological perspective to those working on the study of facial signals. At this stage my provisional answer to the young zoologists asking for guidance in the sociology of laughter is this. Laughter is too complex a process; at the same time it is too narrowly defined for identification. It would be better to start by considering the exogenous social factors which govern the thresholds of tolerance of bodily relaxation and control. These thresholds are set socially. In some social situations it is proper to take cognizance fully of bodily eruptions as part of the symbolizing of familiarity and relaxation, in others the thresholds are lowered in response to the need to express finality and social distance.

If we ask of any form of communication the simple question: what is being communicated? the answer is: information from the social system. The exchanges which are being communicated constitute the social system. Let us assume a sensitive feedback between all the parties to the social exchange. The body is expressing both the social situation at a given moment, and also a particular contribution to that situation. Inevitably then, since the body is mediating the relevant social structure, it does the work of communicating by becoming, (a) an image of the total social situation as perceived, (b) the acceptable tender in the exchanges which constitute it. The possibilities of change and development arise in the first instance in the spontaneous bodily responses, precisely because they are treated as modifying messages by those who receive them. The uncontrolled frown or giggle can effectively rechannel all subsequent exchanges into a different set of pathways.

In its role as an image of society, the body's main scope is to express the relation of the individual to the group. This it does along the dimension from strong to weak control, according to whether the social demands are strong, weak, acceptable or not. From total relaxation to total self-control the body has a wide gamut for expressing this social variable.

What does it mean when one tribe laughs a lot and another tribe rarely? I would argue that it means that the level of social tension has set low or high thresholds for bodily control. In the first case, the full range of the body's power of expression is more readily available to respond fully to a small stimulus. If the general social control settings are slack, the thresholds of tolerance of bodily interruption will be set higher. Comparisons of laughter should take account of the load of social meaning which the body has to carry. Where we seek to compare laughter, we should compare also the pressure on the individual from the social structure. The two cases of the Pygmies and the Haitians cited above are instructive. The first, living in the equatorial Congo forest, sparse and freely mobile, are not under obvious social pressure. The second were admittedly part of a modern police state at a low level of economic development. The people whom Francis Huxley studied in Haiti were haphazard in their means of livelihood and their obligations to one another were tenuous and short-lived. Both peoples seemed to use the full bodily range of expression for grief and joy. In *Natural Symbols* I have said more about the significance of such variations in the strength and permanence of social relations for bodily expression.

Another aspect of social organization which is likely to be expressed in bodily symbolism is the length and complexity of messages. Social systems which vary on this point will have corresponding variations in the amount of pause that can be tolerated between verbal communications. An important experiment on hesitation phenomena was reported by Professor Bernstein.[12] The speech of middle-class and working-class boys was timed. It was found that cutting across measured differences of intelligence, the middle-class boys were more tolerant of long pauses in the discourse. Bernstein argued that the hesitation phenomenon reflected an expectation on their part that speech was subject to a complex and therefore slow process of programming. I would like to see this experiment repeated and developed as a valuable clue to the approach to non-verbal symbolic behaviour. I would also like to see something comparable devised for primates of like intelligence and different social organization. For example, when full studies are made of savannah chimpanzees, the comparison with forest chimpanzees along the lines indicated here would be interesting. Since their social organization would be likely to be more rigidly hierarchized in the savannah, we would predict more strictly defined and less variable responses, more control, longer pauses – less 'laughing'.

Notes

1. M. DOUGLAS, 'The relevance of tribal studies', *Journal of Psychosomatic Research*, 1, 12 (1968).

2. M. DOUGLAS, *Purity and Danger: An Analysis of Concepts of Pollution and Taboo*, Penguin Books, Harmondsworth, 1970.

3. M. DOUGLAS, 'The social control of cognition: Some factors in joke perception', *Man*, 3, 3 (1968), 361.

4. C. M. TURNBULL, *The Forest People*, Chatto & Windus, 1961.

5. F. HUXLEY, *The Invisibles*, Rupert Hart-Davis, 1966.

6. H. BERGSON, *Le Rire: essai sur la signification du comique*, Presses Universitaires de France, Paris, 1950; first published in *Revue de Paris*, 1899.

7. K. LORENZ, *Man Meets Dog*, Methuen, 1954.

8. T. MANN, 'A man and his dog', *Stories of a Lifetime*, Secker & Warburg, 1961.

9. H. GARFINKEL, *Studies in Ethnomethodology*, Prentice-Hall, Englewood Cliffs, N.J., 1967.

10. M. DOUGLAS, *Natural Symbols: Explorations in Cosmology*, Penguin Books, Harmondsworth, 1973.

11. C. R. HALLPIKE, 'Social hair', *Man*, 4 (n.s.), 2 (1969), 256.

12. B. BERNSTEIN, 'Linguistic codes, hesitation phenomena and intelligence', *Language and Speech*, 5, 1 (1962), 31; see also F. GOLDMAN-EISLER, 'On the variability of the speed of talking and on its relation to the length of utterances in conversation', *British Journal of Psychology*, 45 (1954), 94.

Epilogue

Horace Miner:
'*Body ritual among the Nacirema*'

From *American Anthropologist*, 58 (1956), 503–7.

The anthropologist has become so familiar with the diversity of ways in which different peoples behave in similar situations that he is not apt to be surprised by even the most exotic customs. In fact, if all of the logically possible combinations of behaviour have not been found somewhere in the world, he is apt to suspect that they must be present in some yet undescribed tribe. This point has, in fact, been expressed with respect to clan organization by Murdock.[1] In this light, the magical beliefs and practices of the Nacirema present such unusual aspects that it seems desirable to describe them as an example of the extremes to which human behaviour can go.

Professor Linton first brought the ritual of the Nacirema to the attention of anthropologists twenty years ago,[2] but the culture of this people is still very poorly understood. They are a North American group living in the territory between the Canadian Cree, the Yaqui and Tarahumare of Mexico, and the Carib and Arawak of the Antilles. Little is known of their origin, although tradition states that they came from the east. According to Nacirema mythology, their nation was originated by a culture hero, Notgnihsaw, who is otherwise known for two great feats of strength – the throwing of a piece of wampum across the river Pa-To-Mac and the chopping down of a cherry tree in which the Spirit of Truth resided.

Nacirema culture is characterized by a highly developed market economy which has evolved in a rich natural habitat. While much of the people's time is devoted to economic pursuits, a large part of the fruits of these labours and a considerable portion of the day are spent in ritual activity. The focus of this activity is the human body, the appearance and health of which loom as a dominant concern in the ethos of the people. While such a concern is certainly not unusual, its ceremonial aspects and associated philosophy are unique.

The fundamental belief underlying the whole system appears to be that the human body is ugly and that its natural tendency is to debility and disease. Incarcerated in such a body, man's only hope is to avert these characteristics through the use of the powerful influences of ritual and ceremony. Every household has one or more shrines devoted to this purpose. The more powerful individuals in the society have several shrines in their houses and, in fact, the opulence of a house is often referred to in terms of the number of such ritual centres it possesses. Most houses are of wattle and daub construction, but the shrine rooms of the more wealthy are walled with stone. Poorer families imitate the rich by applying pottery plaques to their shrine walls.

While each family has at least one such shrine, the rituals associated with it are not family ceremonies but are private and secret. The rites are normally only discussed with children, and then only during the period when they are being initiated into these mysteries. I was able, however, to establish sufficient *rapport* with the natives to examine these shrines and to have the rituals described to me.

The focal point of the shrine is a box or chest which is built into the wall. In this chest are kept the many charms and magical potions without which no native believes he could live. These preparations are secured from a variety of specialized practitioners. The most powerful of these are the medicine men, whose assistance must be rewarded with substantial gifts. However, the medicine men do not provide the curative potions for their clients, but decide what the ingredients should be and then write them down in an ancient and secret language. This writing is understood only by the medicine men and by the herbalists who, for another gift, provide the required charm.

The charm is not disposed of after it has served its purpose, but is placed in the charm-box of the household shrine. As these magical materials are specific for certain ills, and the real or imagined maladies of the people are many, the charm-box is usually full to overflowing. The magical packets are so numerous that people forget what their purposes were and fear to use them again. While the natives are very vague on this point, we can only assume that the idea in retaining all the old magical materials is that their presence in the charm-box, before which the body rituals are conducted, will in some way protect the worshipper.

Beneath the charm-box is a small font. Each day every member of the family, in succession, enters the shrine room, bows his head before the charm-box, mingles different sorts of holy water in the font, and proceeds with a brief rite of ablution. The holy waters are secured from the Water Temple of the community, where the priests conduct elaborate ceremonies to make the liquid ritually pure.

In the hierarchy of magical practitioners, and below the medicine men in prestige, are specialists whose designation is best translated 'holy-mouth-men'. The Nacirema have an almost pathological horror of and fascination with the mouth, the condition of which is believed to have a supernatural influence on all social relationships. Were it not for the rituals of the mouth, they believe that their teeth would fall out, their gums bleed, their jaws shrink, their friends desert them and their lovers reject them. They also believe that a strong relationship exists between oral and moral characteristics. For example, there is a ritual ablution of the mouth for children which is supposed to improve their moral fibre.

The daily body ritual performed by everyone includes a mouth-rite. Despite the fact that these people are so punctilious about care of the mouth, this rite involves a practice which strikes the uninitiated stranger as revolting. It was reported to me that the ritual consists of inserting a small bundle of hog hairs into the mouth, along with certain magical powders, and then moving the bundle in a highly formalized series of gestures.

In addition to the private mouth-rite, the people seek out a holy-mouth-man once or twice a year. These practitioners have an impressive set of paraphernalia, consisting of a variety of augers, awls, probes and prods. The use of these objects in the exorcism of the evils of the mouth involves almost unbelievable ritual torture of the client. The holy-mouth-man opens the client's mouth and, using the above mentioned tools, enlarges any holes which decay may have created in the teeth. Magical materials are put into these holes. If there are no naturally occurring holes in the teeth, large sections of one or more teeth are gouged out so that the supernatural substance can be applied. In the client's view, the purpose of these ministrations is to arrest decay and to draw friends. The extremely sacred and traditional character of the rite is evident in the fact that the natives return to the holy-mouth-men year after year, despite the fact that their teeth continue to decay.

It is to be hoped that, when a thorough study of the Nacirema is made, there will be careful inquiry into the personality structure of these people. One has but to watch the gleam in the eye of a holy-mouth-man, as he jabs an awl into an exposed nerve, to suspect that a certain amount of sadism is involved. If this can be established, a very interesting pattern emerges, for most of the population shows definite masochistic tendencies. It was to these that Professor Linton referred in discussing a distinctive part of the daily body ritual which is performed only by men. This part of the rite involves scraping and lacerating the surface of the face with a sharp instrument. Special women's rites are performed only four times during each lunar month, but what they lack in frequency is made up in barbarity. As part of this ceremony, women bake their heads in small ovens for about an hour. The theoretically interesting point is that what seems to be a preponderantly masochistic people have developed sadistic specialists.

The medicine men have an imposing temple, or *latipso*, in every community of any size. The more elaborate ceremonies required to treat very sick patients can only be performed at this temple. These ceremonies involve not only the thaumaturge but a permanent group of vestal maidens who move sedately about the temple chambers in distinctive costume and headdress.

The *latipso* ceremonies are so harsh that it is phenomenal that a fair proportion of the really sick natives who enter the temple ever recover. Small children whose indoctrination is still incomplete have been known to resist attempts to take them to the temple because 'that is where you go to die'. Despite this fact, sick adults are not only willing but eager to undergo the protracted ritual purification, if they can afford to do so. No matter how ill the supplicant or how grave the emergency, the guardians of many temples will not admit a client if he cannot give a rich gift to the custodian. Even after one has gained admission and survived the ceremonies, the guardians will not permit the neophyte to leave until he makes still another gift.

The supplicant entering the temple is first stripped of all his or her clothes. In everyday life the Nacirema avoids exposure of his body and its natural functions. Bathing and excretory acts are performed only in the secrecy of the household shrine, where they are ritualized as part of the body-rites. Psychological shock results from the fact that body secrecy is suddenly lost upon entry into the *latipso*. A man, whose own wife has never seen him in an excretory act, suddenly finds himself naked and assisted by a vestal maiden while he performs his natural functions into a sacred vessel. This sort of ceremonial treatment is necessitated by the fact that the excreta are used by a diviner to ascertain the course and nature of the client's sickness. Female clients, on the other hand, find their naked bodies are subjected to the scrutiny, manipulation and prodding of the medicine men.

Few supplicants in the temple are well enough to do anything but lie on their hard beds. The daily ceremonies, like the rites of the holy-mouth-men, involve discomfort and torture. With ritual precision, the vestals awaken their miserable charges each dawn and roll them about on their beds of pain while performing ablutions, in the formal movements of which the maidens are highly trained. At other times they insert magic wands in the supplicant's mouth or force him to eat substances which are supposed to be healing. From time to time the medicine men come to their clients and jab magically treated needles into their flesh. The fact that these temple ceremonies may not cure, and may even kill the neophyte, in no way decreases the people's faith in the medicine men.

There remains one other kind of practitioner, known as a 'listener'. This witch-doctor has the power to exorcise the devils that lodge in the heads of people who have been bewitched. The Nacirema believe that parents bewitch their own children. Mothers are particularly suspected of putting a curse on children while teaching them the secret body rituals. The counter-magic of the witch-doctor is unusual in its lack of ritual. The patient simply tells the 'listener' all his troubles and fears, beginning with the earliest difficulties he can remember. The memory displayed by the Nacirema in these exorcism sessions is truly remarkable. It is not uncommon for the patient to bemoan the rejection he felt upon being weaned as a babe, and a few individuals even see their troubles going back to the traumatic effects of their own birth.

In conclusion, mention must be made of certain practices which have their base in native aesthetics but which depend upon the pervasive aversion to the natural body and its functions. There are ritual fasts to make fat people thin and ceremonial feasts to make thin people fat. Still other rites are used to make women's breasts larger if they are small, and smaller if they are large. General dissatisfaction with breast shape is symbolized in the fact that the ideal form is virtually outside the range of human variation. A few women afflicted with almost inhuman hypermammary development are so idolized that they make a handsome living by simply going from village to village and permitting the natives to stare at them for a fee.

Reference has already been made to the fact that excretory functions are ritualized, routinized and relegated to secrecy. Natural reproductive functions are similarly distorted. Intercourse is taboo as a topic and scheduled as an act. Efforts are made to avoid pregnancy by the use of magical materials or by limiting intercourse to certain phases of the moon. Conception is actually very infrequent. When pregnant, women dress so as to hide their condition. Parturition takes place in secret, without friends or relatives to assist, and the majority of women do not nurse their infants.

Our review of the ritual life of the Nacirema has certainly shown them to be a magic-ridden people. It is hard to understand how they have managed to exist so long under the burdens which they have imposed upon themselves. But even such exotic customs as these take on real meaning when they are viewed with the insight provided by Malinowski when he wrote:

> Looking from far and above, from our high places of safety in the developed civilization, it is easy to see all the crudity and irrelevance of magic. But without its power and guidance early man could not have mastered his practical difficulties as he has done, nor could man have advanced to the higher stages of civilization.[3]

Notes

1. GEORGE P. MURDOCK, *Social Structure*, Macmillan, New York, 1949, p. 71.
2. RALPH LINTON, *The Study of Man*, Appleton-Century, New York, 1936, p. 326.
3. BRONISLAW MALINOWSKI, *Magic, Science and Religion*, Free Press, Glencoe, 1948, p. 70.

Further Readings

A. Firstly, the reader is referred to the bibliographies which appear above in conjunction with the various essays contained in this volume. In particular, the bibliographies attached to articles by Kluckhohn, Hewes, Firth, S. Fisher, Kristeva and Birdwhistell may serve as valuable starting-points for further research. Much of the present volume and my own research have been shaped by the bibliography of Birdwhistell's essay 'Kinesics' (see Chapter 9).

B. Other bibliographies which do not appear in this volume but which may be of value to students specializing in particular fields are found in the following sources:

BIRDWHISTELL, RAY L., 'Communication', *International Encyclopedia of the Social Sciences*, vol. III, Collier-Macmillan, 1972; Macmillan, New York and Free Press, Glencoe, 1968, pp. 24–9 (Non-verbal communication)
— *Kinesics and Context: Essays on Body-Motion Communication*, Allen Lane The Penguin Press, 1971 (Kinesics – body movement as communication)
HALL, EDWARD, 'A system for the notation of proxemic behaviour', *American Anthropologist*, 65(n.s.), 5 (1963) (Proxemics)
HINDE, ROBERT A., ed., *Non-Verbal Communication*, Cambridge University Press, London, 1972 (Non-verbal communication and ethology of body behaviour)
LOMAX, ALAN (with contributions by the Cantometrics staff and with the editorial assistance of Edwin E. Erickson), *Folk Song Style and Culture*, American Association for the Advancement of Science, Washington, D.C., publication No. 88, 1968 (Coreometrics – dance)
ROACH, MARY ELLEN, and JOANNE BUBOLZ EICHER, eds., *Dress, Adornment and the Social Order*, Wiley, New York, 1965, Chichester, 1970 (Clothing, adornment and society)
RUESCH, JURGEN, and WELDON KEES, *Non-Verbal Communication: Notes on the Visual Perception of Human Relations*, University of California Press, Berkeley and Los Angeles, 1956 (Non-verbal communication)

C. Specific individual works which have not been explored in this volume but may be of interest to the student are provided in the list below:

ARGYLE, MICHAEL, *Bodily Communication*, Methuen, 1975 (The most comprehensive review of the subject from the perspective of social psychology – valuable bibliographies)

ARGYLE, MICHAEL, ed., *Social Encounters: Readings in Social Interaction*, Penguin Books, Harmondsworth, 1973 (See especially the articles by Ekman and Friesen, and Watson and Graves)

ARGYLE, MICHAEL, and MARK COOK, *Gaze and Mutual Gaze*, Cambridge University Press, 1975 (Summary of experimental studies of eye behaviour)

BARBER, BERNARD, and LYLE S. LOBEL, ' "Fashion" in women's clothes and the American social system', *Social Forces*, 31, 2 (December 1952) (Social, cultural and political implications of fashion in U.S.)

BARNETT, S. A., 'The expression of the emotions' in S. A. Barnett, ed., *A Century of Darwin*, Heinemann, 1958 (Darwin and *The Expression of the Emotions in Man and Animals*)

BASTIAN, JARVIS R., 'Primate signalling systems and human languages', *Primate Behavior*, Holt, Rinehart & Winston, New York, 1965 (Evolution and verbal/non-verbal communication)

BELL, QUENTIN, *On Human Finery*, Hogarth Press, 1947 (Clothing and fashion)

BELO, JANE, *Trance in Bali*, Columbia University Press, New York, 1960, London, 1970 (Physical trance behaviour in Bali)

BENTHALL, JONATHAN, *The Body Electric: Patterns of Western Industrial Culture*, Thames & Hudson, 1976 (A call for a 'campaign for corporacy' to counteract our technological society and logocentric culture)

BIRDWHISTELL, RAY L., 'Communication', *International Encyclopedia of the Social Sciences*, vol. III, Collier-Macmillan, 1972; Macmillan, New York and Free Press, Glencoe, 1968, pp. 24–9 (Verbal and non-verbal communication)

BLACK, STEPHEN, *Mind and Body*, William Kimber, 1969 (Lays a framework for a more extensive understanding of psychosomatic phenomena)

BREWER, W. D., 'Patterns of gesture among the Levantine Arabs', *American Anthropologist*, 53 (1951), 232–7 (Gesture)

BROWN, NORMAN O., *Life against Death: The Psychoanalytic Meaning of History*, Routledge & Kegan Paul, 1959; Sphere, 1968 (See especially 'The Resurrection of the Body')

CHEIN, ISIDOR, *The Science of Behaviour and the Image of Man*, Tavistock, 1972 (See especially 'The Self and its Body')

CICOUREL, AARON V., *Cognitive Sociology*, Penguin Books, Harmondsworth, 1973 (Non-verbal communication, language and social interaction – particularly interesting material on deaf–dumb sign languages in final chapter)

CLARK, KENNETH, *The Nude: A Study of Ideal Art*, Penguin Books, Harmondsworth, 1970 (The social aspects of nude and naked bodies; the book that proves that naked bodies can be as boring as anything else)

CRAWLEY, A. E., *Dress, Drink and Drums: Further Studies of Savages and Sex*, ed. Theodore Besterman, Methuen, 1931 (Dress; the drink and drums material is only related in that they also start with the letter 'd'. Enjoyable reading but a movie would have been better.)

DARWIN, CHARLES, *The Descent of Man and Selection in Relation to Sex*, Murray, 1901 (Includes material on the subject of evolution and bodily expression)

DARWIN, FRANCIS, ed., *The Autobiography of Charles Darwin and Selected Letters*, Dover Publications, New York, 1958 (Includes material on the subject of Darwin and *The Expression of the Emotions in Man and Animals*)

DUNLAP, KNIGHT, 'The development and function of clothing', *Journal of General Psychology*, 1 (1928), 64–78 (Clothing)

EKMAN, PAUL, and WALLACE V. FRIESEN, *Unmasking the Face: A Guide to Recognizing Emotions from Facial Clues*, Prentice-Hall, Englewood Cliffs, 1975 (The most recent attempt by these authors to translate Darwin's work on the subject into a contemporary psychological framework)

FARIS, JAMES C., *Nuba Personal Art*, Duckworth, 1972 (Body art and language – fantastic photographs)

FAST, JULIUS, *Body Language*, Evans, New York, 1970; Pocket Books, New York, 1971 (The most popular introduction to non-verbal communication)

FISHER, SEYMOUR, *Body Consciousness*, Calder & Boyars, 1973 (More popular and enjoyable style than in Fisher's article in this volume)

FRANK, LAWRENCE K., 'Tactile communication' in M. McLuhan and E. Carpenter, eds., *Explorations in Communication: An Anthology*, Jonathan Cape, 1970, pp. 4–11 (Tactile communication)

GOFFMAN, ERVING, *Behaviour in Public Places*, Macmillan, 1963; Free Press, Glencoe, Ill., 1963 (Includes valuable sections on the role of body/non-verbal communication in social interaction)

— *Interaction Ritual: Essays on Face-to-Face Behaviour*, Allen Lane The Penguin Press, 1972; Penguin Books, Harmondsworth, 1972 (Includes material on role of body in social interaction)

— *The Presentation of Self in Everyday Life*, Allen Lane The Penguin Press, 1969; Penguin Books, Harmondsworth, 1971 (Physical appearance and non-verbal communication)

— *Relations in Public: Microstudies of the Public Order*, Penguin Books, Harmondsworth, 1972 (The most recent study of non-verbal interaction by this most perceptive author)

GOWING, LAWRENCE, 'Positioning in representation', *Studio International: Journal of Modern Art* (January 1972), 14–22 (Posture in art and medicine)

GRANT, EWAN C., 'Human facial expression', *Man* (n.s.), 4, 4 (1969), 525–36 (Facial expression – a not very impressive typology)

HALL, EDWARD T., 'The anthropology of manners', *Scientific American*, 192, 4 (April 1955), 84–90 (Introduction to proxemics and non-verbal communication)

— *The Silent Language*, Fawcett Publications, Greenwich, Conn., 1959 (Proxemics and verbal and non-verbal communication)

HALLIDAY, JAMES L., *Psychological Medicine: A Study of the Sick Society*, Heinemann, 1949 (A neglected classic, the implications of which have not yet been properly explored)

HARRISON, RANDALL P., *Beyond Words: An Introduction to Nonverbal Com-*

munication, Prentice-Hall, Englewood Cliffs, 1974 (An interesting and readable approach)

HESS, ECKHARD, 'Attitude and pupil size', *Scientific American*, 212, 6 (June 1965), 46–54 (An eye-opening study)

HILER, HILAIRE, *An Introduction to the Study of Costume: From Nudity to Raiment*, W. and G. Foyle, 1929 (Clothing; a classic but somewhat dated study)

HOEBEL, E. ADAMSON, 'Clothing and adornment', *Anthropology*, McGraw-Hill; New York, 1966, Maidenhead, 1972, pp. 277–86 (Textbook chapter which deals with clothing and adornment as an aspect of material culture – communicative, linguistic and symbolic implications are unfortunately ignored)

KÖNIG, RENÉ, *The Restless Image: A Sociology of Fashion*, George Allen & Unwin, 1973 (An attempt to move towards a much-needed sociology of fashion, but it spreads itself a bit thin on theory)

LABARRE, WESTON, *The Human Animal*, University of Chicago Press, Chicago, 1954 (Language – verbal and non-verbal)

— 'Paralinguistics, kinesics and cultural anthropology' in T. A. Sebeok, A. S. Hayes and M. C. Bateson, eds., *Approaches to Semiotics*, Mouton, The Hague, 1964 (Paralinguistics, kinesics, non-verbal communication)

LAVER, JAMES, *A Concise History of Costume*, Thames & Hudson, 1969 (Good reference work but the sociologist or anthropologist will have to supply his own background of social theory)

— *Modesty in Dress: An Inquiry into the Fundamentals of Fashion*, Heinemann, 1969 (Dress and undress)

LOMAX, ALAN (with contributions by the Cantometrics staff and with the editorial assistance of Edwin E. Erickson), *Folk Song Style and Culture*, American Association for the Advancement of Science, Washington, D.C., publication No. 88, 1968 (Includes material on coreometrics – dance; there are also some films which Lomax has put together which may be more helpful than the book for teaching purposes)

LOWEN, ALEXANDER, *The Betrayal of the Body*, Collier Macmillan, New York, 1969 (A psychiatrist's warning of the dangers of repression of the body in contemporary society)

LYONS, JOHN, 'Human language' in R. A. Hinde, ed., *Non-Verbal Communication*, Cambridge University Press, London, 1972, pp. 49–85 (Relationship of verbal and non-verbal communication)

MEAD, MARGARET, 'Vicissitudes of the study of the total communication process' in T. A. Sebeok, A. S. Hayes and M. C. Bateson, eds., *Approaches to Semiotics*, Mouton, The Hague, 1964, pp. 277–87 (Relationship of verbal and non-verbal communication)

MERLEAU-PONTY, M., *The Phenomenology of Perception*, Routledge & Kegan Paul, 1962 (Body imagery and phenomenology)

MONTAGU, ASHLEY, *Touching: The Human Significance of the Skin*, Columbia University Press, New York, 1971 (Important introduction to the subject of tactile communication, etc.)

MUNROW, A. D., *Physical Education: A Discussion of Principles*, G. Bell & Sons, 1972 (Intelligent study of the education of the body)

NEWSON, JOHN, and JOHN SHOTTER, 'How babies communicate', *New Society* (8 August 1974), pp. 345–7 (Non-verbal communication in infants – with implications for the study of communication in adults)

PEAR, T. H., *Personality, Appearance and Speech*, George Allen & Unwin, 1957 (Psychology, clothing and communication)

POLLENZ, PHILIPPA, 'Methods for the comparative study of the dance', *American Anthropologist*, vol. 51 (1949), pp. 428–35 (Ethnology of dance)

POOLE, ROGER, *Towards Deep Subjectivity*, Allen Lane The Penguin Press, 1972; Penguin Books, Harmondsworth, 1972 (Philosophical, semiotic and political implications of bodily expression)

RUESCH, JURGEN, and WELDON KEES, *Non-Verbal Communication: Notes on the Visual Perception of Human Relations*, University of California Press, Berkeley and Los Angeles, 1956 (Both text and photographs make this a valuable introduction to the study of non-verbal communication)

SAPIR, EDWARD A., 'Communication', *International Encyclopedia of the Social Sciences*, Vol. IV, Collier-Macmillan, 1972; Macmillan, New York and Free Press, Glencoe, 1931, pp. 78–80

— *Culture, Language and Personality: Selected Essays*, ed. David G. Mandelbaum, University of California Press, Berkeley and Los Angeles, 1966 (Language – including non-verbal)

— 'Fashion' in David G. Mandelbaum, ed., *Selected Writings of Edward Sapir*, University of California Press, Berkeley and Los Angeles, 1949; Cambridge University Press, London, 1949 (Fashion and dress)

— 'Language', *International Encyclopedia of the Social Sciences*, vol. IX, Collier-Macmillan, 1972; Macmillan, New York and Free Press, Glencoe, 1933, pp. 155–68 (Language – including non-verbal)

— *Language: An Introduction to the Study of Speech*, Harcourt, Brace, New York, 1939 (Language – including non-verbal)

SARTRE, JEAN-PAUL, *Being and Nothingness*, Methuen, 1969 (See especially 'The Other' and 'The Body')

SCHILDER, P., *The Image and Appearance of the Human Body*, International Universities Press, New York, 1950 (Body image and psychology)

SEBEOK, THOMAS A., 'Coding in the evolution of signalling behavior', *Behavioral Science*, 7, 4 (1962), 430–42 (Evolution and non-verbal communication)

SIMMEL, GEORG, 'Sociology of the senses: Visual interaction', in Robert E. Park and E. W. Burgess, eds., *Introduction to the Science of Sociology*, University of Chicago Press, 1921 (A pioneering work)

— 'Fashion', *American Journal of Sociology*, 62, 6 (1957), 541–58 (The social aspects of fashion and dress)

SQUIRE, GEOFFREY, *Dress, Art and Society 1560–1970*, Studio Vista, 1974 (Relates body/clothing styles to cultural changes in West European history 1560–1970)

STEVENS, RICHARD, 'Interpersonal communication', in *Communication*, Open University Press, Milton Keynes, 1975, pp. 7–74 (A clear and comprehensive introduction to the subject of non-verbal communication on pp. 39–52)

STRATHERN, ANDREW and MARILYN, *Self-Decoration in Mount Hagen*, Duckworth, 1971 (A valuable ethnographic study of body art in highland New Guinea – great photographs)

STRAUS, ERWIN W., 'The upright posture' in Maurice Natanson, ed., *Essays in Phenomenology*, Martinus Nijhoff, The Hague, 1966, pp. 164–92 (Phenomenology of posture)

TANNAHILL, REAY, *Flesh and Blood: A History of the Cannibal Complex*, Abacus, 1976 (Cannibalism, including social and ethical considerations)

VEBLEN, THORSTEIN, *The Theory of the Leisure Class*, Unwin Books, 1970 (Classic study of socio-economic implications of fashion)

WAX, MURRAY, 'Themes in cosmetics and grooming', *American Journal of Sociology*, 62 (1957), 588–93 (Social aspects of cosmetics in the West – reprinted in M. E. Roach and J. B. Eicher, eds., *Dress, Adornment and the Social Order*, Wiley, New York, 1965, Chichester, 1970)

YARDLEY, ALICE, 'Movement and learning', *Today's Education* (March–April 1974), 62–4 (The acquisition of (kinesic) body behaviour)

ZANER, RICHARD M., *The Problem of Embodiment: Some Contributions to a Phenomenology of the Body*, Martinus Nijhoff, The Hague, 1971 (Phenomenology, philosophy and the human body: not exactly light reading)

D. Although less 'academic', the following works may be of interest:

AMAYA, MARIO, *The Obsessive Image 1960–1968* (exhibition catalogue), Institute of Contemporary Arts, London, 1968 (The body in art)

BEATON, CECIL, *Fashion* (catalogue), Victoria and Albert Museum, HMSO, 1971 (Fashion as social history)

CAMUS, ALBERT, *The Plague*, Penguin Books, Harmondsworth, 1972 (The social aspects of physical illness)

DAHLBERG, EDWARD, *The Carnal Myth*, Calder & Boyars, 1970 (The body in Classical mythology)

GABOR, MARK, *The Pin-Up: A Modest History*, Pan Books, 1973 (The social aspects of the naked and the nude – definitely better pictures than in Kenneth Clark's book *The Nude*)

GREER, GERMAINE, *The Female Eunuch*, Paladin Books, 1971 (Introductory section on the politics of female bodies)

HARTLEY, L. P., *Facial Justice*, Penguin Books, Harmondsworth, 1966 (Science fiction novel about plastic surgery)

JONES, ALLEN, *Allen Jones Figures*, Galerie Mikro, Edizioni O, Milan, 1969 (A pleasantly non-verbal look at some disturbing/enjoyable contemporary body images)

JONES, BARBARA, *Design for Death*, André Deutsch, 1967 (The social aspects of the dead body)

LARRAIN, GILLES, *Idols*, Links, London, New York, 1973 (Non-verbally illustrates that 'beauty' is a socially – rather than a 'naturally' – defined concept)

LAVER, JAMES, 'Fashion, art and beauty', *Metropolitan Museum of Art Bulletin*, 25, 3 (November 1967) (Discussions with fashion designers, etc., about whether fashion is an art form – nice illustrations)

PERUTZ, KATHRIN, *Beyond the Looking Glass: Life in the Beauty Culture*, Penguin Books, Harmondsworth, 1972 (Cosmetics, dress and body 'deformation' in the modern West)

QUANT, MARY, *Quant by Quant*, Pan Books, 1967 (Autobiography by the famous designer which deals, in part, with the social roots and significance of fashion design)

RUDOFSKY, BERNARD, *The Unfashionable Human Body*, Hart-Davis, 1972 (Delightful illustrations and anecdotes, but only tacked-on theory)

SAINT-LAURENT, CECIL, *The History of Ladies' Underwear*, Michael Joseph, 1968 (The definitive study)

TOMKINS, WILLIAM, *Indian Sign Language*, Dover Publications, New York, 1969 (Indian sign language made simple – learn how to communicate silently at parties and make friends with American Indians – there is also a great picture of Chief Flying Hawk with his arm around the author which says a lot about the cross-cultural variations of the social aspects of the body and its clothing and adornment)

WAUGH, EVELYN, *The Loved One*, Penguin Books, Harmondsworth, 1971 (Social aspects of the dead body)

E. Finally I should like to present Trevor Millum's bibliography of non-verbal communication which first appeared in *Working Papers in Cultural Studies* (Centre for Contemporary Cultural Studies, University of Birmingham, 1971, pp. 132–7) and which appears here with some significant additions which Trevor Millum has been good enough to contribute.

Compiled by Trevor Millum:
A bibliography of non-verbal communication

Ostensibly, the term 'non-verbal communication' includes all communication which is not in the form of words, spoken or written. Once having realized how immense an area this constitutes one is all the more surprised that it should have been considered something of an 'extra', a residual category of communication, for so long at least in the field of cultural studies. There has been a widespread and largely unexamined assumption that all important communication is conveyed through the medium of words. However as more work becomes available it becomes increasingly apparent that an enormous amount of information – in the widest sense – is conveyed by other means and, moreover, that this communication is often of greater intensity and significance than the (often accompanying) explicit, verbal communication.

It is not the purpose here, however, to raise the status of one aspect of communication at the expense of others or to pursue imperialistic aims on behalf of some hitherto neglected areas. It is enough to state that, in any study of human beings and their situations, from laboratory experiments through to participant observation, an awareness of merely verbal communication overlooks crucial aspects of behaviour. Crucial are aspects which are sometimes more deeply revealing because unintentional, unthought-out, uncodified in a way which makes them altogether different from written or spoken language. Any study of the mass media must likewise take account of these non-verbal aspects of communication.

It may be useful to understand non-verbal expressions as falling loosely into two categories: the animate and the inanimate, or perhaps transient and permanent – or even actions and artifacts. On the one hand facial expressions, gestures, touch, extra-verbal communication, and so on, and on the other, photographs, drawings, objects. Film can be placed in the latter category only on the basis of the fact that it can be stopped and examined at any point; it clearly has a transitional place in this dichotomy. Similarly, fashion and appearance are both animate and inanimate; the dress is a static object, but the wearer is human, and the way the dress is worn will affect its meaning.

Apart from their lack of explicit structure, one of the main difficulties in analysing such expressions as facial movements and gestures is their transience, which in itself inhibits the attempt to organize, classify and perhaps to uncover structures and relationships in order to discover meaning. This is to some extent overcome by the use of cameras, mirrors and laboratory equipment, but the disadvantages of these are obvious. Another technique is that of developing a system of detailed notation, as in the approach of kinesics. A further problem applies to many actions and artifacts – that of multi-dimensionality and simultaneity – even a painting, still, and framed before us, presents us with all of itself at once, and prescribes no order in which we are to understand it. The conscious mind, so trained in the way of verbal thinking (whether it works naturally in a linear fashion is an ongoing argument), adjusts with difficulty to images of a completely different dimension. There is then a whole area of discussion on the problem of how we 'see' things at all – on visual perception and the process of symbolization. The titles included in the following bibliography confront these and other problems and go some way towards resolving them. The list is by no means complete (and indeed, further suggestions would be welcomed), but it attempts to bring together some of the disparate pieces of work which are relevant to the field.

There are some areas which are neglected in this booklet, for example, music and other non-verbal sounds; tactility is barely touched upon, and the stress is admittedly on the various aspects of visual communication. The bibliography proceeds in general in accordance with the division suggested above – moving from action through to artifacts. It is divided into such sub-sections as seem useful in order that the student may avoid the necessity of obtaining and reading material not strictly relevant to his particular concern. The material is organized as follows:

1. Animate non-verbal communication
2. Kinesics
3. Facial expression and body movements, jointly considered
4. Facial expression
5. Gaze
6. Body movements, posture and gesture
7. Non-verbal aspects of speech
8. Tactile communication
9. Spatial relationships
10. Appearance and fashion
11. Film
12. Pictures
13. Philosophical and psychological problems
14. Miscellaneous

1. ANIMATE NON-VERBAL COMMUNICATION

The following are mainly experimental and theoretical works concerned with the whole area of animate, non-verbal communication which proceed from strictly scientific methodological premises, but not all of which should be taken as upholding a behaviourist position. This applies to most of the works in the sections up to and including (9). Of these Argyle's *Social Interaction* and Ekman's and Friesen's 'Repertoire of non-verbal behaviour' are two of the central texts. Some of the items here and in subsequent sections might prove difficult to obtain: the main points of many of them are, fortunately, resumed in Argyle's works.

ARGYLE, M., *The Psychology of Interpersonal Behaviour*, Penguin Books, Harmondsworth, 1967
— *Social Interaction*, Methuen, 1969
BURNS, T., 'Non-verbal communication', *Discovery*, 25, 10 (1969)
EKMAN, P., and W. FRIESEN, 'The repertoire of non-verbal behaviour', *Semiotica*, 1, 1 (1969)
— 'Non-verbal behaviour in psychotherapy research', *Research on Psychotherapy*, 3 (1967)
LAVER, J., and S. HUTCHESON, eds., *Communication in Face-to-Face Interaction*, Penguin Books, Harmondsworth, 1972
MEHRABIAN, A., and S. FERRIS, 'Inference of attitudes from non-verbal communication', *Journal of Consulting Psychology*, 31 (1967)
ROSENFELD, H., 'Non-verbal reciprocation of approval', *Journal of Experimental Social Psychology*, 3 (1967)
RUESCH, J., and W. KEES, *Non-verbal Communication*, University of California Press, Berkeley, Calif., 1956
— 'Non-verbal language and therapy', *Psychiatry* (November 1955)

2. KINESICS

Kinesics is the study of the visual aspects of non-verbal, interpersonal communication. Of the texts on the subject, Birdwhistell's *Introduction to Kinesics* is the most useful.

BIRDWHISTELL, R., *Introduction to Kinesics*, University of Louisville, Louisville, Ky, 1953
— 'Kinesics', *International Encyclopedia of the Social Sciences*, vol. VIII, Collier-Macmillan, 1972; Macmillan, New York and Free Press, Glencoe, 1968 [see Chapter 9 in this volume]
— 'Kinesics and communication' in M. McLuhan and E. Carpenter, eds., *Explorations in Communication*, Beacon Press, Boston, 1960; Jonathan Cape, 1970
— *Kinesics and Context*, Allen Lane The Penguin Press, 1971
HAYES, A., 'Paralinguistics and kinesics: Pedagogical perspectives', *Approaches to Semiotics*, Mouton, The Hague, 1964
LaBARRE, W., 'Paralinguistics, kinesics and cultural anthropology', *Approaches to Semiotics*, Mouton, The Hague, 1964

3. FACIAL EXPRESSION AND BODY MOVEMENTS

Feldman's book is something of a classic, but is based in parts more upon assertion than upon evidence. The restrictions of the following texts, i.e. 3–9, are that where they are based on precise scientific procedure they tend to be less useful when applied generally (for example, to non-laboratory situations) and that where they proceed less rigorously the findings are often of questionable validity.

FELDMAN, S., *Mannerisms of Speech and Gesture in Everyday Life*, International Universities Press, New York, 1935

GAGE, N., 'Judging interests from expressive behaviour', *Psychological Monographs: General and Applied*, 66, 18 (1952)

HANKAVARA, S., 'The psychology of expression', *British Journal of Psychology* (1961), Monograph Supplement 32

ROSENFELD, H., 'Instrumental affiliative functions of facial and gestural expressions', *Journal of Personality and Social Psychology*, 4 (1966)

4. FACIAL EXPRESSION

COLEMAN, J., 'Facial expressions of emotions', *Psychological Monographs*, 63, 296 (1949)

EXLINE, R., 'Explorations in the process of person perception: Visual interaction in relation to competition, sex and need for affiliation', *Journal of Personality*, 31 (1963)

GOLDBERG, KIESLER and COLLINS, 'Visual behaviour and face-to-face distance during interaction', *Sociometry* (March 1969)

GUILDFORD, J., 'An experiment in learning to read facial expressions', *Journal of Abnormal and Social Psychology*, 24 (1929)

LANDIS, C., 'Studies of emotional reactions – general behaviour and facial expressions', *Journal of Comparative Psychology*, 4 (1924)

OSGOOD, C., 'Dimensionality of the semantic space for communication via facial expressions', *Scandinavian Journal of Psychology*, 7 (1966)

SHAPIRO, J. G., 'Responsivity to facial and linguistic cues' (bibliography), *Journal of Communication*, 18, 1 (March 1968)

SPITZ and WOLF, 'The smiling response', *Gen. Psychol. Monthly*, 34

VINE, I., 'Communication by facial–visual signals' in J. H. Crook, ed., *Social Behaviour in Animals and Men*, Academic Press, 1969

5. GAZE

ARGYLE, M., and D. DEAN, 'Eye contact, distance and affiliation', *Sociometry*, 28 (1965)

KENDON, A., 'Some functions of gaze direction in social interaction', *Acta Psychologica*, 26, 1 (1967)

RIEMER, M. D., 'The averted gaze', *Psychiatric Quarterly*, 23 (1949)

— 'Abnormalities of the gaze: A classification', *Psychiatric Quarterly*, 29 (1955)

6. BODY MOVEMENTS, POSTURE AND GESTURE

CRITCHLEY, M., *The Language of Gesture*, Arnold, 1939

DITTMANN, A. T., 'The relationship between body movements and moods in interviews', *Journal of Consulting Psychology*, 26 (1962)

EFRON, D., *Gesture, Race and Culture*, Mouton, The Hague, 1972

EKMAN, P., and W. FRIESEN, 'Head and body cues in the judgement of emotion: A reformulation', *Perceptual and Motor Skills Research Exchange*, 24 (1967)

HEWES, G. N., 'The anthropology of posture', *Scientific American*, 196 (1957)

LABARRE, W., 'The cultural basis of emotions and gestures', *Journal of Personality*, 16 (September 1947), 49–68 [see Chapter 1 in this volume]

LAMB, W., *Posture and Gesture*, Duckworth, 1965

MACHOTKA, P., 'Body movement as communication', *Dialogues: Behavioural Science Research*, 2 (1965)

MEHRABIAN, A., and FERRIS, 'Inference of attitudes from non-verbal communication in two channels', *Journal of Consulting Psychology*, 31 (1967)

MEHRABIAN, A., 'The inference of attitudes from the posture, orientation and distance of a communication', *Journal of Consulting Psychology*, 32 (1968)

MELLY, G., 'Gesture goes classless', *New Society*, 176 (1965)

SCHEFLEN, A. E., 'Significance of posture in communications systems', *Psychiatry* (1964)

7. NON-VERBAL ASPECTS OF SPEECH

The following are texts concerned with the meaning of 'ums and ers', the rate of speaking, pauses in speech and so on.

BOOMER, and A. T. DITTMANN, 'Speech rate, filled pause and body movement in interviews', *Journal of Nervous and Mental Disease*, 139 (1964)

COOK, M., 'Anxiety, speech disturbance and speech rate', *British Journal of Social and Clinical Psychology*, 8 (1969)

KASL and MAHL, 'The relationship of disturbances and hesitations in spontaneous speech to anxiety', *Journal of Personality and Social Psychology*, 1 (1965)

KRAMER, E., 'Judgement of personal characteristics and emotions from non-verbal properties of speech', *Psychological Bulletin*, 60 (1963)

KRIS, E., 'Laughter as an expressive process', *Psychoanalytical Explorations in Art*, Allen & Unwin, 1953

STARKWEATHER, J., 'Content-free speech as a source of information about the speaker' in A. G. Smith, ed., *Communication and Culture*, Holt, Rinehart & Winston, New York, 1966

8. TACTILE COMMUNICATION

It may be that there are some important works overlooked here, but it seems that the field of tactile communication is as yet only very slightly explored. Much of the available work, moreover, appears to be concerned with the taboos involved with touch and the body rather than with the way touching communicates meaning.

FRANK, L., 'Tactile communication', *Genetic Psychology Monographs*, 56 (1957)
— 'Tactile communication' in A. G. Smith, ed., *Communication and Culture*, Holt, Rinehart & Winston, New York, 1966
GIBSON, J., 'Observations on active touch', *Psychological Review*, 69, 6 (1962)
JOURARD, S. M., *The Transparent Self*, Van Nostrand, Rineholt, Princeton, N.J., 1972
ROSENBLITH, W. A., *Sensory Communication*, Massachusetts Institute of Technology Press and Wiley, New York, 1961

9. SPATIAL RELATIONSHIPS

Space, proximity and distance and the way they are used have been termed (by E. T. Hall) 'the silent language'. His two books, in which the approach is more cultural or anthropological than psychological, constitute a wide-ranging and stimulating introduction to the area.

BALINT, M., 'Friendly expanses – horrid empty spaces', *International Journal of Psycho-Analysis* (1959)
HALL, E. T., 'The anthropology of manners', *Scientific American*, 192, 4 (1955), 84–90
— *The Silent Language*, Fawcett Publications, Greenwich, Conn., 1959
— 'A system for the notation of proxemic behavior', *American Anthropologist*, 65 (n.s.), 5 (1963)
— *The Hidden Dimension*, Doubleday, Garden City, New York, 1966
LITTLE, K., 'Personal space', *Journal of Experimental Social Psychology*, 1 (1965)
SOMMER, R., 'Studies in personal space', *Sociometry*, 22 (1959)
— 'Leadership and group geography', *Sociometry*, 24 (1961)
— 'The distance for comfortable communication', *Sociometry*, 25 (1962)
— 'Further studies of small group ecology', *Sociometry*, 28 (1965)

10. APPEARANCE AND FASHION

The way we dress and groom ourselves is a further form of communication – often one of which we are well aware. The most systematic approach to this aspect of self-presentation is the work of Barthes, unfortunately not available in English. Stone's essay is a useful introduction to this area.

BARBER and LOBEL, 'Fashion in women's clothes and the American social system', *Social Forces*, 31, 2 (1952)

BARTHES, R., *Système de la mode*, Seuil, Paris, 1967. See also Barthes's *Elements of Semiology*, Jonathan Cape, 1967 [see Chapter 8 in this volume]

FLUGEL, S., *The Psychology of Clothes*, Woolf/Institute of Psychoanalysis, 1930

SAPIR, E., 'Fashion', *Encyclopedia of the Social Sciences*, vol. VI, Collier-Macmillan, 1972; Macmillan, New York and Free Press, Glencoe, 1931

STONE, G. P., 'Appearance and the self' in E. Rose, ed., *Human Behaviour and Social Processes*, Routledge & Kegan Paul, 1962

Texts concerned with hair:

BERG, C., *The Unconscious Significance of Hair*, Allen & Unwin, 1951

BROWN, W., 'Why "hair" has become a four-letter word', *Avant-Garde* (May 1970)

MILLUM, T., 'Long hair: Taboo in England', *Journal of Popular Culture*, 4 (1970)

11. FILM

The analysis of film of course includes attention to the verbal component, but most of the works below concentrate on the more powerful conveyor of meaning in film: the visual component. Wollen's book is probably the best introductory text.

ALLOWAY, L., 'Iconography of the movies', *Movie*, 7 (February 1963)

BAZIN, A., *What Is Cinema?* (essays selected and translated by H. Gray), Cambridge University Press, 1967

ECO, U., 'Articulations of the cinematic code', *Cinemantics*, 1 (January 1970)

— 'Towards a semiotic inquiry into the television message', *Working Papers in Cultural Studies*, 3 (1972)

EISENSTEIN, S., *The Film Sense*, Harcourt, Brace, New York, 1942; Faber & Faber, 1969

KRACAUER, S., *The Theory of Film*, Oxford University Press, Oxford, 1965

METZ, C., *Language and Cinema*, Mouton, The Hague, 1974

SPOTTISWOODE, R., *A Grammar of the Film*, Faber & Faber, 1935

WEST, F., 'Semiology and the cinema', *Sociology and Semiology, Working Papers on the Cinema*, British Film Institute, 1969

WOLLEN, P., *Signs and Meaning in the Cinema*, Secker & Warburg, 1969

— 'Cinema and semiology', *Sociology and Semiology, Working Papers on the Cinema*, British Film Institute, 1969

12. PICTURES

In view of the number of years that pictures of various sorts have been studied, it is surprising that so little systematic work exists. Gombrich's books are interesting theoretical texts – in the main taking painting as the subject – and the works by Kepes and Arnheim form a bridge between the section and the one following. Panofsky and Barthes have the most precise and systematic approaches, though Panofsky tends to concentrate on fine art. For a summary of these approaches and an example of the close study of visual communication in pictures, see T. Millum, *Images of Woman*.

ARNHEIM, R., *Art and Visual Perception*, Faber & Faber, 1956

— *Towards a Psychology of Art*, Faber & Faber, 1967

BAKER, S., *Visual Perception*, McGraw-Hill, New York, 1961

BARTHES, R., 'Rhétorique de l'image', *Communications*, 4 (1964); (translation in *Working Papers in Cultural Studies*, 1 (1971))

BERGER, J., *Ways of Seeing*, Penguin Books, Harmondsworth, 1972

BONSIEPE, G., 'Persuasive communication – towards a visual rhetoric', *Uppercase*, 5 (1961)

GAUTHIER, G., *Initiation à la sémiologie de l'image*, La Revue du Cinéma, Paris, 1974

GOMBRICH, E., *Art and Illusion*, Pantheon Books, New York, 1960; Phaidon Press, 1962

— *Meditations on a Hobby-Horse*, Pantheon Books, New York, 1963; Phaidon Press, 1963

HALL, S., 'The determinations of news photographs', *Working Papers in Cultural Studies*, 3 (1972)

KEPES, G., *The Language of Vision*, Paul Theobald, Chicago, Ill., 1964

— *Sign, Image and Symbol*, Studio Vista, 1966

MARMORI, G., *Senso e Anagramma*, Feltrinelli, Milan, 1968

MILLUM, T., *Images of Woman: Visual Communication in Advertising*, Chatto & Windus, 1975

PANOFSKY, E., *Studies in Iconology*, Harper Torchbooks, New York, 1939

— *Meaning in the Visual Arts*, Penguin Books, Harmondsworth, 1970

13. PHILOSOPHICAL AND PSYCHOLOGICAL PROBLEMS

The anthology edited by Hogg or the books of Gregory are the best introductions to the area of the psychology of visual perception. The reader is also referred back to the works of Arnheim (see above). The function of symbolism and other problems associated with perception (especially visual perception) are probably best tackled through the writing of Langer, whose work is closely related to that of Cassirer.

CASSIRER, E., *Language and Myth*, Harper, New York, 1946
— *The Philosophy of Symbolic Forms*, 3 vols., Yale University Press, New Haven, Conn., 1953–7
GIBSON, J. J., *The Perception of the Visual World*, Harvard University Press, Cambridge, Mass., 1950
GREGORY, R. L., *Eye and Brain*, Weidenfeld & Nicolson, 1966
— *The Intelligent Eye*, Weidenfeld & Nicolson, 1970
HOGG, J., ed., *Psychology and the Visual Arts*, Penguin Books, Harmondsworth, 1969
LANGER, S., *Philosophy in a New Key*, Harvard University Press, Cambridge, Mass., 1957
— *Problems of Art*, Routledge & Kegan Paul, 1957
MALE, P., *For those with Eyes to See*, Screen Education (13), 1975
WERNER, H., 'On physiognomic perception' in G. Kepes, ed., *The New Landscape in Art and Science*, Paul Theobald, Chicago, Ill., 1956
WHITE, L. A., 'The symbol: The origin and basis of human behavior' in *The Science of Culture*, Farrar, Straus & Cudahy, 1949
WHITEHEAD, A. N., *Symbolism: Its Meaning and Effect*, Cambridge University Press, Cambridge, 1928

14. MISCELLANEOUS

This section includes works on dance and drama, ethography and some more general works, together with some less academic approaches to the subject.

BENTLEY, E., ed., *The Theory of the Modern Stage*, Penguin Books, Harmondsworth, 1968
BERNE, E., *Games People Play*, Deutsch, 1966; Penguin Books, Harmondsworth, 1967, 1968
BRINSON, P., *The Choreographic Art*, Black, 1963
BRUN, T., *The International Dictionary of Sign Language*, Wolfe, London, 1969
CARNEGIE, D., *How to Win Friends and Influence People*, Simon & Schuster, New York, 1936; World's Work, Tadworth, 1953

DARWIN, C. R., *The Expression of the Emotions in Man and Animals* (1872), republished in 1965, ed. Francis Darwin, University of Chicago Press, Phoenix Books, Chicago, Ill., and London

GOFFMAN, E., *Asylums*, Anchor, New York, 1961; Penguin Books, Harmondsworth, 1970

— *Behaviour in Public Places*, Macmillan, 1963; Free Press, Glencoe, Ill., 1963

— 'Embarrassment and social organization', *American Journal of Sociology*, 62 (1956)

HEDIGER, H., *Studies of the Psychology and Behaviour of Captive Animals in Zoos and Circuses*, Butterworth Scientific Publications, 1955

HUMPHREYS, D., *On the Art of Making Dances*, Grove Press, New York, 1959

KOWZAN, I., 'The sign in the theatre', *Diogenes*

LABAN, R., *Principles of Dance and Movement Notation*, MacDonald & Evans, 1956

LORENZ, K., *King Solomon's Ring*, Cromwell, New York, 1952; Methuen, 1952

McLUHAN, M., and E. CARPENTER, eds., *Explorations in Communication: An Anthology*, Beacon Press, Boston, 1960; Jonathan Cape, 1970

MOORE, S., *An Actor's Training: The Stanislavsky Method*, Gollancz, 1960

MORRIS, D., *The Naked Ape*, Jonathan Cape, 1967

POTTER, S., *One-Upmanship*, Hart-Davis, 1952

PRESTON-DUNLOP, V., *An Introduction to Kinetography Laban*, MacDonald & Evans, 1966

Index

Page numbers printed in italics indicate illustrations

121, 124; place of myths and
transformation stories, 116, 123, 127–
8; idealized standards, 116;
depersonalization in neurotics and
schizophrenics, 116, 119; areas of
research, 118, 121, 122; human-figure
drawing, 118–19; perceived body size,
119–20; projective techniques, 120,
123; self-revelation in
conceptualization, 121; importance in
self-identity formulation, 122–3; and
the study of culture, 123, 129n.3;
variations as reflected in folk tales,
123–9; and external and internal
sources of danger, 124, 125
body painting, 28, 149; *164, 167*
Bogatyrev, Petr, 257–9, 263n.3
Borneo, 52, 55
Boumédienne, Pres. Houai, 197
Brewer, W. D., 222
burial customs, Tikopia, 92–3
Burma, 61–2

Canary islands, 60
cartoons, 59–60
caste status, 108n.16
ceremonial, 107n.3
Ceylon, 52, 61, 62
Chaplin, Charlie, 61
chest ornamentation, *172*
childbearing, ritual proceedings, 99
childbirth, Nuer customs, 186–7
child-rearing, 48; and posture, 92–3
children, initiating new behaviour
patterns, 48; parental role in
developing potential, 48–9; role of
constitutional and temperamental
endowment, 49; earliest sense of
identity, 117; cranial deformation, *155,
157*; development of language from
mimism, 276
Chinese, use of protruding tongue, 57;
and kissing, 57–8; ideographically
written language, 58–9; tonemic
character, 60; variation in phonetic
pronunciations, 60; *natya* dancing
semantics, 61; gait distinguished from
Singhalese, 62; stylized acting, 63;
expressions for awkwardness, 67n.15;
'saving face' metaphor, 101; practice of
'kowtow', 105, 108n.23; foot-binding,
162; imitation of their dress, 213, 217;
costume as sign object, 259; division in
handwriting characters, 269
Christian theology, Garden of Eden,

205–6, 207, 216–17; and nakedness,
206, 207; Original Sin, 206–7, 216;
capitulation to lust, 206; sin and
servitude, 207; and flesh as sacred, 207;
martyrdom, 208–10; concept of
'private parts', 216–17; symbolism in
rite of communion, 259
Cicero, and gesture, 227
clothing, 126, 140; and respect, 57; and
posture, 82, 83; and body imagery,
116, 125; and status and power, 126,
139, 185, 188; related to the human
body, 149, 180; arguments on their
origin, 180–82, 188, 192n.4; covering
the pudenda, 181, 189, 190, 191;
interrelationship with language, 221,
248; written about, photographed and
worn, 250–51; Haute Couture, 251
communication, 48; non-verbal and
verbal 'channels', 220–21, 285–6;
socially conditioned assumptions, 265;
digital coding, 257; importance of
body behaviour, 274, 285; three
categories of signs, 276; continuous
interactive process, 285–6; isolation
and description of sensory channels,
286; *see also* kinesics
constitutional types, 65–6
costume, variation in function, 259–60,
262; as status signs, 260, 262; married/
unmarried women, 260; an indication
of environment, 262
courtesy, 94, 103
cranial modification, 28, *155, 156, 157*
Crawley, A. E., and loin girdles, *183*
Critchley, Macdonald, 221, 222
crying, 55, 99, 110; *see also* weeping
Cuba, 213, 216

dance, 28, 63; use of gesture, *44*;
initiation of Balinese children, 46–7,
46, 47; attempts at international
notation, 61; *natya*, 61, 63;
kinaesthetic language, 61, 63, 65; Nuer
female dresses, 183, 188; access to
trance and spiritual elevation, 210, 217
Darwin, Charles, and biological
inheritance of bodily expression, 9,
31–2, 34, 35, 51, 69, 75, 220–21;
opponents, 27, 36, 110, 263; and
universality of bodily expression, 73–
7, 81, 109–10; bodily structure/mental
disposition correlation, 78–9; doctrine
of evolution, 79; *The Expression of the
Emotions in Man and Animals*, 9, 73,